"Schaede truly understands Japanese business strategy and culture. With deep insights and keen analysis, she offers an update on how Japanese companies are evolving to compete in the new global economy, and she shows how they carefully harmonize social stability with economic success."
—Kyota Omori, Chairman, Mitsubishi Research Institute

"A gem! Schaede links corporate culture to incentives and outcomes, and shows how Japanese firms have kept the tight corporate culture that makes things right, but add elements of the loose culture that makes the right things. She gives concrete examples of Japanese firms that got it right and how they did it."
—Robert Alan Feldman, Professor, Tokyo University of Science

"Japan's economy and its evolving business systems matter, and this insightful evaluation explains how and why. A definite read."
—Hugh T. Patrick, Chairman, Center on Japanese Economy and Business, Columbia Business School

"Ulrike Schaede's new book combines an invaluable primer on Japanese business culture with a striking analysis of Japan's little-understood strategy for producing enduring economic strength based on manufacturing excellence and constant, managed change. I came away with renewed admiration for the country's political and corporate leadership, and Japan's ability to forge a successful economic future despite the many daunting challenges one often hears about."
  —Ambassador Ira Shapiro, former U.S. Trade Negotiator with Japan, and former Chairman of the National Association of Japan-America Societies

"Japan still matters. Corporates have reinvented themselves and seized important niches in high-tech supply chains, ensuring Japan remains a critical global business leader. So argues Ulrike Schaede in her important new book, *The Business Reinvention of Japan*. Her painstakingly curated argument helps dispel perceptions of a permanently stagnating Japanese economy and demonstrates Japan's important economic balancing role against China. Must-reading for scholars and policymakers alike."
  —Roy Kamphausen, President, The National Bureau of Asian Research

"Dr. Schaede provides a deeply researched and powerfully argued analysis of Japan's 'reinvention' in the face of a rising China. Her thesis is that Japan's 'aggregate niche strategy' offers important lessons for the West by balancing the pursuit of corporate profits with social stability, economic equality, and social responsibility and sustainability. A must-read for those who seek a 'third path' between the unbridled capitalism of America and the state-led capitalist socialism of China."
  —Glen S. Fukushima, Senior Fellow, Center for American Progress, and Former President, American Chamber of Commerce in Japan

"This authoritative and sophisticated account of how Japanese companies have quietly reformulated how they compete in the global economy is a timely reminder of why we need to pay attention to Japan. Japanese companies and their technologies remain, and will continue to remain, critically relevant in our fast-changing world."
  —Alberto Moel, VP of Strategy and Partnerships, VEO Robotics

"For more than a generation, the outside world has been ready to write off Japan's economy as yesterday's story, in contrast to the tomorrows being created elsewhere, especially in China. Ulrike Schaede clearly and convincingly lays out how out-of-touch that judgment is—and how much more impressive the creativity, flexibility, and re-invention of the Japanese business system look when examined up close. The crispness and concision of the book make it a pleasure to read, and its originality will make it useful for anyone who wants to understand the next stage in global business."
  —James Fallows, *The Atlantic*

THE BUSINESS REINVENTION OF JAPAN

INESS

REINVENTION

OF JAPAN

HOW TO MAKE SENSE

OF THE NEW JAPAN

AND WHY IT MATTERS

ULRIKE SCHAEDE

STANFORD BUSINESS BOOKS
AN IMPRINT OF STANFORD UNIVERSITY PRESS
STANFORD, CALIFORNIA

Stanford University Press
Stanford, California

Special discounts for bulk quantities of Stanford Business Books are available to corporations, professional associations, and other organizations. For details and discount information, contact the special sales department of Stanford University Press. Tel: (650) 725-0820, Fax: (650) 725-3457

Printed in the United States of America on acid-free, archival-quality paper

Library of Congress Cataloging-in-Publication Data
Names: Schaede, Ulrike, 1962– author.
Title: The business reinvention of Japan : how to make sense of the new
    Japan and why it matters / Ulrike Schaede.
Description: Stanford, California : Stanford Business Books, an imprint of
    Stanford University Press, 2020. | Includes bibliographical references
    and index.
Identifiers: LCCN 2020004513 (print) | LCCN 2020004514 (ebook) | ISBN
    9781503612259 (cloth) | ISBN 9781503612365 (ebook)
Subjects: LCSH: Corporate reorganizations—Japan. | Industrial
    management—Japan. | Corporate culture—Japan. | Industrial
    relations—Japan. | Japan—Economic conditions—1989–
Classification: LCC HD2907 .S33 2020 (print) | LCC HD2907 (ebook) | DDC
    338.70952—dc23
LC record available at https://lccn.loc.gov/2020004513
LC ebook record available at https://lccn.loc.gov/2020004514

Cover design: Christian Fuenfhausen

CONTENTS

PREFACE

In 1982, U.S. presidential candidate Walter Mondale asked, "What do we want our kids to do? Sweep up around Japanese computers?"[1] At the time, Americans feared a rising Japan, which had recovered from the ruins of World War II and looked set to challenge American economic hegemony. Two decades later, Japan's economic bubble had burst, wiping out US$10 trillion in value from its stock and real estate markets. Japan then entered what pundits would later call the Lost Decade—so named for the country's anemic growth, deflation, bad debt, and poor corporate performance.

The new millennium brought little relief. From 2000 to 2007, nominal GDP fell from $4.9 to $4.5 trillion, and Japan-watchers began referring to the period as the Second Lost Decade.[2] After the 2008 global financial crisis, just as things began to turn around, the country suffered one of its worst disasters in history with the 2011 Tohoku earthquake and tsunami. And just the year before, China had surpassed Japan as the world's second largest economy.[3] As China continued to rise, Japan continued to struggle with deflation. Today, while China is a frequent topic of conversation for many international businesspeople, economists, and political scientists, few are talking about Japan.

Yet look closer, and it becomes clear that Japan still matters. Japan is the third largest economy in the world. It also ranks third, behind the United States and China, in terms of manufacturing output and number of Global Fortune 500 companies—even though it has a much smaller population, and its workforce of 65 million is roughly the size of China's three largest cities. What is more, Japanese companies have adjusted to the rise of China and the emergence of global supply chains by reinventing their strategies, operations, and financial markets. In this book, I argue that there are three key reasons why Japan is once again important. First, as a result of their reinvention, Japanese companies now anchor global supply chains by dominating world markets in a large number of critical input components and materials, meaning global manufacturing has become dependent on Japanese inputs. This has increased Japan's economic power, in particular within Asia. Second, Japan's business reinvention is creating new, lucrative markets for financial and consumer products within Japan. And third, Japan continues to uphold its alternative model of balanced capitalism in an economic system that moderates inequality and values social stability while pursuing economic success. This may prove informative in the ongoing discussion in the United States of the social responsibility of the corporation.

Despite years of sluggish growth and bad press, and in the face of two supposedly lost decades, Japan is a highly developed, stable democracy with high levels of productivity and low levels of corruption and crime. This story—how the headlines can be deceiving—is also part of the closer look. Japan never threatened the United States, as Mondale and many Americans in the 1980s feared. But, unlike the United States, Japan has universal healthcare, one of the highest life expectancies in the world, and a top tier primary and secondary education system. It is the safest of any large industrialized country, with just 0.28 homicides per 100,000 inhabitants in 2016 (18 times lower than the U.S. rate). Japanese cities are famously clean and in great repair; it is rare to find a piece of trash or graffiti in Tokyo, a mega-metropolis of over 14 million. There are an estimated 13,000 homeless people in *all of Japan*, which is fewer than in New York City.[4] The country is also a center of culture, technology, and innovation. In the early 2000s, as the Lost Decade dragged into the Lost Score, a British Member of Parliament visited Tokyo, and upon seeing the bustling activity and bright lights of Ginza, he said: "If this is what recession looks like, I want one."[5]

How has Japan managed to maintain stability in the face of economic stagnation and business reorganization? My core argument is as follows: In response to the rise of China and the new competitive dynamic in Northeast Asia, Japanese companies have reinvented their business operations and built deep-technology competencies in critical components, inputs, and materials, while maintaining core strengths in manufacturing and systems engineering. While many of these products are small niches, in the aggregate they result in a sizable business portfolio that anchors Asian supply chains. This reinvention is managed within Japan's tight business culture setting—a framework introduced later in this book. As a result, change is proceeding in ways and at speeds very different from what an American observer would expect, which makes it easy to misinterpret or miss entirely. And this means that Japan's business system continues to function differently from the U.S. system. Even with globalization and financial market pressures, Japanese companies still operate within an alternative, more balanced model of capitalism, one that is characterized by social stability and slow change.

Japan's new approach to global competition is what I call an *aggregate niche strategy*. For the managers of large Japanese companies, this translates into two separate assignments as they lead the reinvention:

1. *Strategic repositioning*: Choose a set of core businesses and focus on upgrading those, and carve out or sell off non-core units and subsidiaries. At the same time, explore and invest in future businesses to compete in the digital economy.

2. *Organizational renewal*: Build new internal processes and a new corporate culture that foster the coexistence of mature and new businesses and are conducive to creativity and deep-technology innovations.

The New Japan company has vacated lower value-added markets, such as basic electronics, and moved upstream into high-technology materials, components, and production machineries. While these inputs do not carry a "Japan Inside" label, there is a fairly high probability that you are using products containing critical parts from Japan on a daily basis. No matter the brand, Japan is inside your car, TV, headphones, computer, smartphone, watch, kitchen gadgets, router, printer, scanner, camera, and perhaps even your electric toothbrush. From Tesla's car batteries, Hewlett-Packard's printers, and Boeing's airplane fuselage materials, to any Apple product, Japanese technology is fundamental.

As Japan's corporate leaders are managing this transformation, they are guided by the behavioral norms of Japanese business, which shape expectations of appropriate behavior and set the proper pace of change. Because business norms are socially created, not innate, they can be changed. The management essence of Japan's business reinvention is to nudge employees to embrace a new, shared understanding of what constitutes appropriate workplace behavior, in order to compete globally. The ways in which Japan's senior managers are rolling out this change process is also part of this story.

You may wonder who or what "Japan" is in this description: who or what is the mastermind behind this business reinvention? The answer is that there is no central actor. Rather, the results are an integration of the discourse between reformists and guardians from a cross-section of business, government, and society. They disagree on most matters, yet they all share a set of common values and norms. As you will see later in this book, these norms prescribe that whatever path Japanese managers take, changes have to be made in ways that are, or at least are presented as, considerate of all interests and polite and respectful to all parts of society. This balancing act has allowed significant corporate reorganization while preserving social stability.

Japan's business reinvention carries important implications for the United States and Asia. As Americans search for new ways to balance corporate profits with social prosperity, Japan's process of change can be informative. The outcomes of the reinvention are also significant because Japan is an economic powerhouse and Japanese companies are deeply embedded in the U.S. economy—as suppliers, producers, and employers. What is more, Japanese companies are positioning to compete in the digital economy—with its 5G-based internet of things (IoT), artificial intelligence, and cloud-based, data-driven information sharing and connectivity—in ways that differ markedly from the U.S. and Chinese approaches, and that may afford them a long-term advantage in digital manufacturing. Quietly, some Japanese companies—such as SoftBank, Toyota, and Recruit—have extended their business models into the new economy, in ways that may come as a surprise.

Some readers will be skeptical of the positive tone of this book. They may say that I am overstating the amount of change that is actually happening, and point to Japanese firms, small and large, that are hopelessly mired in unproductive approaches to business. They may point out that I have not discussed the budget deficit, debt levels, the aging society, regional poverty, or the root causes of low economic growth. It's fine if Japan builds the critical sensors and robots, they might say, but the money is in big data and artificial intelligence, and Japan will simply not be an economic factor if it cannot play in the cloud.

I disagree and look forward to this discourse. While we cannot be sure what the future will be bring, as of the time of this writing in 2019, my initial responses will be along the following lines.

This book puts a spotlight on the changes in Japanese companies and their business strategies. It highlights important new developments in cutting-edge markets that are relevant to global business, and shows how these approaches aim to maintain stability first and growth second. I challenge the naysayers by pointing out that they have probably not taken a deep and unbiased look at Japan for a long time. But if you step back and ask, "What is Japan trying to accomplish with these gradual reforms?" you will realize that Japan is making choices and tradeoffs that are different from those of most Western economies. And as much as everybody in Japan enjoys higher economic growth rates, there are other considerations—first and foremost social stability—that are even more important than growth. The danger is that by dismissing Japan for its alleged stagnation, you will miss out on something rather exciting that is happening in Japan right now. And by the way, who says that Japanese companies cannot play in the cloud? Although the spotlight of the digital transformation is currently on the United States and China, we should not dismiss what is quietly happening in other parts of the world. Ignore Japan at your own peril.

Acknowledgments

Over the past three decades, I have lived and worked in Japan for a total of more than nine years—as a student, a professor, and a resident scholar at Hitotsubashi University, the Bank of Japan, the Ministry of Finance, the Ministry of Economy, Trade and Industry, and the Development Bank of Japan. The people at these institutions allowed me to become part of their daily life and work, and shared their thoughts and insights in many lunch and dinner conversations. Through these observations, I developed a sense of the different office dynamics and workplace rules in Japan. I have had many, repeated, and long conversations with CEOs, board members, managers, young employees, entrepreneurs, small shop owners, mothers and fathers, students, government officials, consultants, bankers, IT hackers, language teachers, steelworkers, private equity investors, and hedge fund managers. This experience is the primary source of information on which this book is built.

Over the past three decades, I have also had the enormous privilege to learn from a group of wonderful colleagues and friends. For intellectual stimulus and deep insights, I thank, in particular, Christina Ahmadjian, Reiko Akiike, Michael Alfant, Koji Asada, David Brady, Lei Cao, Andreas Dannenberg, Robert Eberhart, Hiroshi Fujiwara, Brad Glosserman, Ryozo Hayashi, Takeo Hoshi, Masanori Kato, Mika Kiyomoto, Jesper Koll, Patricia MacLachlan, Curtis Milhaupt, Alberto Moel, Yasunori Nakagami, Toshihiko Omote, Eriko Oiwake, Sōzaburō Okamatsu, Yuri Okina, Kyota Omori, Erich Pauer, Takeshi Saito, Masakazu Sekiguchi, Masaaki Shirakawa, Kaori Takato, Yūichirō Takenami, Saki Tomita, Kazuhiko Toyama, Masakazu Toyoda, and Louise Young. There are many others who have shaped my thinking about Japan's business reinvention who preferred not to be mentioned here; I respect their wishes and express my gratitude. I am grateful to the Hoover Institution at Stanford University, the Japan Society for the Promotion of Science, and the Center on Global Transformation at the University of California San Diego, School of Global Policy & Strategy (GPS) for research support.

At GPS, I have benefited from terrific colleagues and students—especially in my class "Business and Management in Japan," which I have taught for 25 years, meaning that I have learned from more than 600 students about ongoing change in Japan. It is a privilege to teach and conduct research in such a highly stimulating environment. Regular events and visitors at the Japan Forum of Innovation and Technology (JFIT) at GPS have brought a continuous flow of new perspectives. I thank my colleagues Peter Cowhey, Peter Gourevitch, Gordon Hanson, Stephan Haggard, Barry Naughton, and Krislert Samphantharak, and the entire faculty, for being great intellectual sounding boards, as well as Kate Leonard, Richard Forsyth, and the many supporters of JFIT for ensuring that UC San Diego maintains a vibrant Japan research program.

This book would be less without the outstanding research assistance of Grayson Sakos and his constructive suggestions, as well as his direct contributions to Chapter 5. Benjamin Irvine brought challenging questions, penmanship guidance, and new ideas as the first reader. Ryōsuke Fujioka planted important seeds and greatly informed Chapter 9, and Jonathan Shalfi and Matthew Matsuyama provided research assistance on various data projects leading to this book. I also thank Naoki Ando, Robert Hill, Takashi Kiyoizumi, Shūichi Ōi, Takahiko Osako, Yoshito Sakakibara, Carsten Schaede, and Ken Shigeta for explanations and insights for various chapters. A shout-out also to all my former students in Tokyo, including Gary Bremerman, Samuel Gordon, Takashi Kobanawa, Takashi Kono, Danyal Qazi, and the entire GPS alumni group in Kasumigaseki.

My first readers have greatly helped to improve this manuscript. I am indebted to Christina Ahmadjian, Annalisa Barrett, Amy Borovoy, Gerald Curtis, Amir Fahrai, Tracy Gopal, Stephan Haggard, Ryoko Imai, Timothy Kane, William Lazonick, XiaoXiao Liu, Patricia Maclachlan, Alberto Moel, Charles O'Reilly III, Hugh Patrick, David Richards, and Yoshito Sakakibara for commenting on early versions of this book. Their demanding yet encouraging feedback and great suggestions were instrumental in pushing the project forward. I am grateful to Steve Catalano and Sunna Juhn at Stanford University Press for pushing this project at a fast clip, Tim Roberts and Elspeth MacHattie for excellent copyediting, and two anonymous reviewers for helpful advice on the book's main message.

I thank Pat and Jennifer Johnson who took me to a Hanshin Tiger game, Jeffrey Pfeffer who suggested listening to Ricky Nelson, and Charles O'Reilly III who has changed the way I look at people.

THE BUSINESS REINVENTION OF JAPAN

INTRODUCTION

The Reinvention

In the late 1980s, Japan was on everyone's mind. The successes of the *kaisha*—the Japanese company—with its very different management practices, and their astounding capture of global consumer markets, challenged many U.S. industries and triggered a trade war. Brands like Sony, Panasonic, Hitachi, Toshiba, and Sanyo were prominent in U.S. homes, followed by Toyota, Nissan, Honda, and Mazda on the roads. Then, as the global trade order changed, Japan fell into a 20-year-long slump, with sluggish economic growth and an ongoing struggle with deflation and debt. Japanese electronics have largely disappeared from our radar, and what little news we read about Japan tends to be negative, usually peppered with adjectives like lost, low, or lagging.

Yet, while we were not looking, Japanese business has launched a great process of reinvention, and the results are beginning to show. As of 2020, Japan is the third-largest economy in the world. Japanese companies anchor Asian supply chains with advanced materials and components and are key players in cutting-edge technologies for the digital transformation, occupying dominant global market shares in hundreds of critical global input products. For example, Japanese companies provide one third of the world's semiconductor manufacturing equipment, and more than half of that industry's most critical materials. Japan has long recorded the lowest unemployment rate in the industrialized world, and recently labor and total factor productivity have been rising in ways that would make many parts of the U.S. envious. Profitability is back, and Japanese companies have accumulated large amounts of cash that are fueling strategic global acquisitions and investments in Southeast Asia, the United States, and Europe.[1] According to a 2018 Morgan Stanley report, Japan's ongoing reinvention is also reflected in "the most interesting and underrecognized turnaround story in global equity markets."[2]

Driving this reinvention is the emergence of a new business strategy to compete through deep-technology leadership in a series of small yet critically important materials and components segments. Over time this has gelled into what I call an *aggregate niche strategy*. This strategy requires change in two domains: (1) a strategic repositioning into a series of critical technology niches, achieved by building new competencies at the technology frontier; and (2) internal management and organizational change, to structure new processes that foster breakthrough innovation. Strategic repositioning means redefining the businesses that the company will compete in, and management renewal means building a new mindset for global competition. Success in these domains depends upon a company's ability to shift its traditional corporate culture, which has long prioritized certainty, predictability, and due process, toward a new mindset that fosters risk-taking, innovating, and achieving speed and agility in fast-changing global markets. This reinvention has begun to transform Japan's workforce, work processes, and employment patterns—so much so that the outcome has been deemed the "end of the *kaisha*," the prototypical Japanese company of the 1980s.[3]

Importantly, this reinvention is not so much about replacing old with new as it is about, ideally, creating a type of New Japan corporation that can augment the competencies built in the past with new capabilities that afford competitive advantage in the digital economy. The traditional strength of making things well, consistently, and reliably with continuous improvement (*kaizen*) is still key to Japan's reinvention. In sharp contrast to companies in the United States and China that are betting on dominating the cloud with data mining and artificial intelligence (AI) applications, Japanese companies are positioning to compete in digital manufacturing. Already, Japanese companies, together with Germany's, are leading the world in the hardware needed for the digital transformation, and they operate at the frontier of the advanced systems solutions and edge computing that will shape the future of digital manufacturing. From there, some companies will then attempt to build out into the cloud. The future of the digital economy is far from written, and Japan will undoubtedly be an important part of that story.

Meanwhile, great attention is being paid to reducing externalities for society and minimizing the disruption associated with this reinvention. From the outside, the slow pace of change in Japan can be frustrating, mistaken for stagnation or even confused with incompetence. But upon closer examination, it is clear that this slow pace is by design: being *slow* is the price Japan is paying for stability. The orderly transition to the new system cushions the blow to society and doesn't allow the few to win at the expense of the many. This is why employment reform has taken almost 20 years—long enough to allow an entire generation to adjust. Similarly, as large companies had to downsize and move production abroad to create global supply chain networks, government loan programs were extended to small-firm suppliers to curtail bankruptcies and job losses.[4] While these "welfare in disguise" policies can obscure some of the country's corporate successes, they are widely preferred to the slash-and-burn approach that has come to characterize the United States. Japan's reinvention is showing that corporate reorganization and adjustment need not be messy or destructive.

Since the destruction of World War II, Japan has gone from failure to success to failure and now quietly back to reemergent success. Its return to global relevance has flown under the radar of many U.S. business observers but represents a new path already becoming widely admired by other Asian countries. In 2020, Japanese companies anchor global supply chains, and their reinvention is invigorating Japan's domestic markets as more and more new global competitors are emerging from Japan. How Japan has reinvented quietly without upheaval—and what business lessons it holds for other countries—is the focus of this book.

The Aggregate Niche Strategy

Lately, when Americans hear "Asia," they tend to think "China," which is understandable given that country's sheer size and geopolitical importance. China's emergence has also had a profound impact on how Japan competes. With a population of 1.4 billion and a workforce of 776 million, China dwarfs Japan by a factor of 11, and its rise to become the factory of the world has greatly threatened Japan's business strategies of exporting high-quality electric and precision machinery and consumer products. The globalization of supply chains and the cost differentials within Asia have created new competition and collaboration among South Korea, Taiwan, China, and Japan. To succeed in this new Northeast Asian dynamic, Japanese companies have to adapt by exiting the export markets for commoditized products, and instead becoming agile competitors that can win at the technology frontier.

The industrial structure that made Japan the world's third largest economy was based on massive industrial installations, like those built by Hitachi, Nippon Steel, Bridgestone, and Mitsubishi Heavy Industries, as well as the just-in-time manufacturing networks of companies such as Toyota, Nissan, Panasonic, and Sony. Today, still more than 21% of Japan's GDP is generated in manufacturing, with the pillars of electric machinery, transportation equipment, IT and electronic devices, as well as steel and chemicals. As each of these industries has been challenged by new competitors in East Asia, over the past 20 years Japanese companies have upgraded the technology levels of their existing markets—by moving, for example, into specialty steel and chemicals, luxury cars, or very high-level home stereos. This is why many Japanese companies remain global leaders in their industries, including Bridgestone in tires, AGC in glass, Toyota in cars, Uniqlo in clothes, Panasonic in car batteries, and Sony in games. And even now, as they are positioned at the technology frontiers, they continue to draw on their deep-rooted competencies in high-quality manufacturing.

But in addition, to escape the Asian competition, these companies have begun to augment the existing industrial structure by building a new, deep-technology layer on top of this industrial base, in particular in product categories where they own or can build core competencies that Chinese companies, in particular, either do not have yet or do not want. These industry segments involve high-tech, very difficult-to-imitate and difficult-to-make manufacturing products, such as advanced materials based on specialty chemicals, and they are often in small niches. For potential Asian competitors, these niches are either unreachable or not worth the effort, as they are complicated and unlikely to scale.

Thus, Japan's new strategy to compete with China is to dominate through an aggregate niche strategy: an approach in which Japan competes against, and coexists with, its giant neighbor as an agile, technically sophisticated leader in a set of advanced products and industries critical to the global supply chain. There is a huge range in the size of these product markets, but most are fairly small and concentrated—amounting, on average, to roughly $2 billion in annual sales each.[5] Across several hundred product categories, this sums up to a stately number that contributes to Japan's economy, trade, and global technology impact in important ways. The companies that make these products also range from large to small, and include well-known multinational enterprises as well as companies that few industry outsiders have heard of, even though they are large, listed companies in Japan. Moreover, these advanced materials and components are manufactured by Japanese companies around the world, so that the aggregate niche strategy is also an expression of Japan's growing global manufacturing network. These products are sold into many different industries and sectors, and because they are critical inputs, they are characterized by strong, fairly predictable global demand and high profit margins. By continuously enhancing these essential future technologies, Japanese companies stand to occupy central positions in the Asian supply chains even as the world moves beyond the iPhone and into the digital economy.

However, Japan's industrial architecture was not initially set up for the pursuit of this aggregate niche strategy, geared as it was toward large-scale efficiencies in mass production, not small-batch deep-technology innovation. Building out the new niches is requiring two separate yet related domains of change for Japan's large manufacturing firms: a strategic approach to repositioning, and new internal processes to gear the organization toward innovative capabilities.

STRATEGIC REPOSITIONING

To stay ahead as the technology leader in difficult-to-make and difficult-to-imitate materials and components, Japanese companies need both incremental and breakthrough innovations, as well as high-class manufacturing techniques. To operate at the technology frontier, they need to be fast and smart. This means that the vast, highly diversified conglomerates that enabled Japan's postwar economic miracle have outlived their purpose and need to be disassembled. Companies need to refocus, by choosing a set of concrete core competencies for forward-looking competition, and then focusing all resources on those businesses while exiting all others. Non-core businesses need to be spun off, simple processes have to be outsourced to cheaper locations, and difficult processes must be focused in Japan. Meanwhile, a global network of supply chains needs to be maintained, and internal corporate cultures, people, and processes have to be realigned toward leadership at the technology frontier.

A first wave of refocusing began in Japan at the turn of the present century, when companies began to shed businesses far removed from their cores. I analyzed this strategy shift in my 2008 book *Choose and Focus*, in which I forecast that it might take a decade for very large conglomerates to accomplish this restructuring.[6] Despite the 2008 global financial crisis and the Tohoku earthquake of 2011, the first wave of refocusing has proceeded, as many large firms have closed down or sold off many nonprofitable and non-core subsidiaries and business units.

In this current next step—the reinvention—Japan's competitive companies are redefining their main competitive thrust, as they identify the new business segments in which they want to compete, and the requisite innovative capabilities they need to build. This has invited a second wave of choose-and-focus, one that entails a true strategic pivot. Large firms, ranging from Hitachi, NEC, NTT, Komatsu, Honda, and Toyota to most of the companies that bear the names of the former large business groups such as Mitsubishi, Mitsui, Sumitomo, and Fuji, are now selling off some of their crown jewels—their former core businesses—in order to shift their entire organizations into a new core and a new corporate identity to compete in the digital economy.

ORGANIZATIONAL RENEWAL

But strategic refocusing alone is not enough; new management processes are also needed. To compete powerfully at the technology frontier—from flying cars and clever robots to smart cities and connectivity grids—companies need to build new systems of innovation and reorient their R&D processes from incremental to breakthrough innovation. This necessitates something completely new for many large Japanese companies: a corporate culture of creativity and curiosity, and a break-it-fix-it experimental approach to innovation. Moreover, to address the rapidly shrinking and changing labor force, firms also have to reinvent workflow and workspaces, and accommodate new demands for work-life balance. To do so, companies must redesign promotion and training processes so that men, women, and foreign employees alike can fulfill personal career aspirations, pursue more individualized career tracks, and advance to important positions in management. All of these aspects require a change in the business mindset, and a reinvention of how companies operate and compete.

Importantly, to result in true competitive advantage, these new cultures and workflows need to coexist and create synergies with the company's traditional strengths in incremental innovation and high-powered manufacturing at exceedingly high levels of quality. Thus, companies must learn to simultaneously exploit and enhance existing capabilities, while continuously exploring new businesses and technologies; that is, they must become ambidextrous.[7] However, even though ambidexterity—the dual strategy of running maturing and future businesses simultaneously under one roof—has become a new business catchphrase in Japan, it poses tremendous difficulties for many firms: making these changes to their organizations is a tremendous effort, and many companies are struggling with the realities of these challenges. Not all of them are addressing the necessities of the new global competition, and those who don't will fall behind and disappear. In 2016, the takeover of the Sharp Corporation, the erstwhile global leader in LCD panel technologies, by Taiwan's Foxconn, was a clear signal that the previous mechanisms of domestic protectionism were no longer a reliable shield. Among the companies that try to change, many are struggling with exiting business segments that many employees perceive as their legacy. Not all of Japan's companies will be successful in restructuring, all efforts notwithstanding. Yet, as we will see in the following chapters, the reinvention is happening in more places than not, and it is positioning Japan in new ways to compete in the digital transformation.

The Great Transition During the Lost Decades

After the defeat in World War II, Japan embarked on a 30-year period of rapid economic growth, not unlike China's rise over the past two decades. Japan's fast growth of the 1950s to the 1980s greatly benefited from the security alliance forged between the United States and Japan in 1952. Japan had little debt and low military expenditures, and faced few regional competitors. The trade regime at the time allowed for export promotion and infant industry protection policies. Japan soon emerged as Asia's leader and built a capitalist model that became the envy, and fear, of the United States in the 1980s, and the growth model for the rest of Asia. However, except for the security umbrella, this all changed in the 1990s.

Japan's goal during the postwar system was to catch up to the West, namely the United States, in terms of affluence, technology, innovation, and power. The government's industrial policies encouraged companies to embark on a highly leveraged growth path based on a system of high value-added manufacturing for exports. Japan's increasingly diversified conglomerates became leaders in the high-quality mass production of machinery and consumer products. Made-in-Japan cars and electronics were sold around the world, through Japanese sales offices abroad run by Japanese executives following the same rules as the home offices, like a tight ship with well-oiled machinery. This staggering success culminated in the bubble economy of the late 1980s, when asset prices rose to exorbitant levels due to huge real estate and financial speculation based on a belief that Japan would become "number one."

When the bubble burst in 1991, it wiped out the equivalent of at least three years of GDP (or more than $10 trillion) in stocks and real estate alone.[8] The Nikkei index fell from a high of 39,000 in 1989 to 16,000 in 1992, and below 8,000 in 2003. While it has now recovered, into the low 20,000s in 2019, to this day this colossal collapse has left many Japanese with a deep suspicion of stock price as a measure of corporate value or managerial performance. The collapse also brought a severe banking crisis that lasted until 2003. The bubble's burst plunged the nation into an economic abyss and ushered in two decades of slow, painful readjustment that foreign observers labeled "lost." Japan's average annual GDP growth rate was 0.8% in the 1990s, and 1.4% between 2000 and 2007, before the 2008 global financial crisis depressed world trade and turned it negative again.[9] As we will see in Chapter 3, indicators of social distress skyrocketed, by Japanese standards, in categories ranging from homelessness to suicides. But as much as it is true that the 1990s and early 2000s were a long and difficult two decades for Japan, from a business perspective they were also a period for overcoming adversity, adjusting to a sea change in the rules of global competition, and the reinvention of the business system.

Beginning at the turn of the century, deregulation and the rewriting of most of Japan's domestic business laws combined with the emergence of competitors in South Korea and Taiwan, the globalization of supply chains, and finally the rise of China to annihilate Japan's postwar business model of exporting well-made consumer goods. As Japanese electronics companies lost their consumers to Apple and Samsung, they eventually realized the need for true renewal and reorganization. Other industries followed suit. While many companies were slow to respond to these changes, gradually but certainly companies began the difficult process of readjusting their strategic approaches. The early 2000s saw a modest economic recovery in the "Koizumi Boom," named for Prime Minister Junichirō Koizumi, who led the reform effort. Carefully staged, annual revisions of corporate law allowed the large conglomerates to embark on the long road of refocusing and turning their sprawling organizations into nimble competitors for the 21st century. Cumulatively, these legal changes were so fundamental that they constituted a strategic inflection and invited the first wave of choose-and-focus.[10] Alas, the Koizumi Boom ended when the world economy was thrown into turmoil by the 2008 global financial crisis. Then, just as Japan was recovering, the 2011 Tohoku earthquake and tsunami and the Fukushima nuclear disaster delivered another major blow.

In 2012, Prime Minister Shinzō Abe's first reform program—dubbed

Abenomics—called for another decade of reform. Companies were to be reorganized, the employment system was to become more flexible and inclusive, and innovation and R&D would make Japan a key player in the digital transformation.[11] Borrowing from Japanese folk wisdom and archery, the policy plan consisted of "three arrows," a term suggesting that these policies in combination would be strong and irreversible, just as it is impossible to break three arrows all at once. The three-pronged policy agenda consisted of macroeconomic measures, fiscal stimulus, and structural reforms. But perhaps the most important impact of the Abenomics program was symbolic, as it gave the government's imprimatur to the business reformers, by celebrating New Japan companies and coaxing all into embracing change and renewal that would trigger a business revival.

In the mid-2010s, the reform movement caught a strong tailwind through the confluence of three factors that created new urgency. The first was the 2020 Tokyo Olympics, which brought a construction boom as well as a convenient deadline for all kinds of reforms, in the name of being ready when the world was focused on Japan. A second boost for change came through excess global liquidity, including in Japan itself, at a time of growing global uncertainty. In the financial markets, investments in the BRICs (Brazil, Russia, India, and China) had failed to deliver expected returns, and zero or negative interest rates had led to a worldwide search for returns on investment. Politically, Europe was going through its own financial and political turmoil, topped by Britain's expected exit from the European Union (EU) in 2019, while the United States under the Trump administration was internally split and seemed highly volatile. In comparison, Japan looked like a safe haven, with a stable government, newfound economic strength, and asset markets to invest in.

Third, and perhaps most importantly, the digital transformation was presenting a new goalpost for corporate renewal and target for the aggregate niche strategy. The transition to 5G and digital manufacturing, edge computing, the shared economy, ubiquitous connectivity, machine learning, big data, the arrival of autonomous vehicles, and smart cities all present huge opportunities that play directly to Japan's existing strengths. All this has offered a new direction, a compelling compass, and the rallying cry for corporate reinvention.

Managing Change in a Tight Culture

The backdrop to the business reinvention is Japan's social culture overall, and its business culture in particular. These bring obstacles and offer opportunities for change management that are very different from those a CEO in the United States or continental Europe may face. A deeper insight into the preferences and expectations as well as the hesitations and objections of Japanese society, employees, and senior management can help us to better understand the processes through which Japan's reinvention is being rolled out, and how to assess their success.

Our understanding of this backdrop is informed by *tight-loose theory*.[12] As will be presented in more detail in Chapter 2, this framework points to persistent cross-country differences in the strength of social norms of behavior, and tolerance toward behavior that violates these norms. Tight cultures, such as Japan's, are characterized by strong norms for what constitutes the "right" behavior, as well as strong mechanisms for ostracizing deviants. In contrast, loose cultures, such as that in the United States, have a much wider definition of what is acceptable and do not sanction noncompliance to nearly the same degree.

In the field of social psychology, culture is thought of as a set of socially constructed norms that prescribe codes of behavior and are shared by society overall, or a subset thereof. There are country cultures, corporate cultures, and other in-group cultures. These norms have three dimensions: the *content*, which defines what constitutes the "right" behavior; the *consensus*, which is the degree to which people agree about the content; and the *intensity*, which is the extent to which people are willing to admire adherence or sanction a violation.[13] The tight-loose framework employs the latter two dimensions, namely how strongly people agree on a set of norms and how intensely they feel about violations, and shows that these tend to be baked into a society (see more on why and how in Chapter 2). In contrast, the content—that is, the prescribed behaviors—is neither innate nor carved in stone but rather created by leaders and developed over time. This means that it can be changed and, in the case of corporate culture, managed and guided by senior leaders. When we think about managing strategic change and organizational renewal, we refer to adjusting the content of the behavioral code of the company. However, such a change has to be introduced in light of the other two dimensions, and those determine the level of ease or resistance to culture change in an organization.

The content of Japan's business norms can be described by three core behavioral propositions: (1) to be polite and considerate; (2) to behave appropriately; and (3) to not cause trouble, that is, to not make decisions that are disruptive. Deviation from what is seen as polite, appropriate, and normal, in society at large or within a particular company, will cause confusion or uncertainty and may result in sanctions that could derail one's career, in ways that are very different from those in the United States. Being late for a meeting, having colored hair or visible tattoos, or announcing a sudden decision without prior deliberation might be part of the daily office routine in California. But in Japan such actions are considered unacceptable and tend to result in a sense of awkwardness or rejection so severe that they are generally avoided.

The tight-loose culture concept—the shared consensus about what is the right conduct—helps us appreciate why Japanese managers behave as they do. It also sheds light on the speed, content, and progress of change management. If we assess Japan's business reinvention through the tight culture lens, we get a much more granular view of the depth of ongoing change. Because so much emphasis is placed on procedure, etiquette, and consideration of all interests, Japan's reformers have to operate differently from what we might expect in the United States. Being noisy, pushy, or brazen will rarely yield success in Japan. Rather, reformers—including CEOs, politicians, and bureaucrats—have to maneuver delicately, lest their actions trigger resentment and rejection. Tight culture also explains the actual measures that Japan's senior leaders adopt to execute change management. Because CEOs cannot change the tight country culture, they have to work within it. It may sound like an oxymoron, but in Japan, change toward more flexibility and creativity needs to be introduced in highly regimented, methodical ways. We will see how companies are creating structured programs and organized events—from design thinking workshops to guided innovation tourism—to encourage employees to embrace less formulaic work approaches.

A tight culture also has distinct advantages for managing change. The most important is that once a decision has been made and everybody is on board, change can happen swiftly. The preparation may seem to take forever, but the execution can be expeditious. Tight cultures also lend themselves to *soft law* approaches to regulation, where nudging and shaming are the main levers. As we will see in more detail in later chapters, *nudging* refers to creating a choice architecture such that people's own biases lead them to pick the desired option, while *shaming* refers to highlighting noncompliance to affect those biases over time. These are particularly effective in tight cultures, where people are even more concerned about *social proof*, our tendency to mimic the behavior of those around us. We will see how nudging and shaming have played an important role in rolling out Japan's regulatory reforms, ranging from corporate governance reforms and a new focus on corporate profitability to the Womenomics reform initiative to increase the number and impact of women in business, politics, and society.

Affluence, Equality, and the Social Role of Companies

One characteristic of tight-culture countries is a widely shared risk aversion and a societal preference for stability and predictability. This further explains the slow pace at which Japan responded after the 1980s bubble economy burst, and why many companies were so deliberate in adjusting to the changing competitive pressures in Asia since the 1990s. Although many see this slow pace of change as costly for companies and the economy overall, it is serving the nation well.

Despite two decades of crisis and a consequential business transformation, today Japan is both one of the wealthiest and one of the most egalitarian countries in the world. Figure 1.1. shows that, in 2017, there were an estimated 3.16 million "high net worth individuals" (HNWI) in Japan, second only to the United States with 5.3 million, and far ahead of Germany and China.[14] Expressed as a percentage of the population, 2.5% of Japanese were wealthy at that level, as compared to 1.6% in both the United States and Germany, and 0.09% in China. Partially, this reflects Japan's long and steady economic growth, hard work, and propensity to save, but it is also due to the country's recent strong economic performance.

Yet even with these high HNWI numbers, Japan's inequality measures remain comparatively low. Figure 1.2 shows the proportion of total income earned by the top 1% of income earners in Japan and the United States. Clearly, the rapid increase in inequality in the U.S. since the 1990s contrasts with a much more moderate uptick in Japan. Moreover, this statistic does not take into account the comparative decline in the quality of American infrastructure. Unlike in the United States, trains, roads, and airports in Japan are world class. As economist William Lazonick argues, the United States has allowed itself to become a country of "profits without prosperity."[15] Also noteworthy from Figure 1.2 is that Japan saw a huge correction after the bursting of its bubble economy in the early 1990s, meaning the richest paid the highest price. There was much less correction in the U.S. after the 2008 global financial crisis.

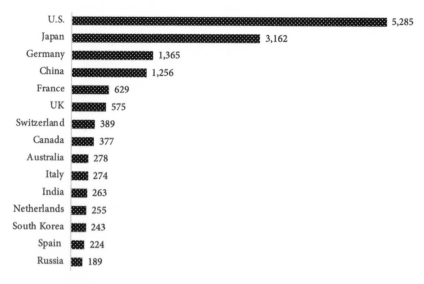

Figure 1.1. World Ranking of High Net Worth Individuals (HNWI), 2017, defined as having investable asssets over $10 million, in thousands of people. Constructed with data from Capgemini (2018).

Nevertheless, the perception of increased inequality in Japan since around 2004 led to the catchphrase *kakusa shakai* (unequal society) and a search for ways to stem this ratio from notching up further. Some have suggested that the increase is partially caused by the rapidly aging society, because income inequality tends to be higher among the elderly.[16] Others are pointing to increases in executive pay (see Chapter 6). One aspect to watch with Japan's reinvention, then, is whether, with the new pressures toward higher performance, more foreign shareholders, and active corporate governance, Japanese industry will succumb to the lure of being driven by financial metrics such as the stock price, at the expense of their social responsibilities, as has become common in the U.S. and elsewhere.

So far, one of the most remarkable things about Japan over the past two decades is how resilient the country's societal underpinnings have proven to be in the face of deep, prolonged crisis and corporate reorganization. The bursting of the bubble economy in 1991 was, by some measures, three times more severe than the Great Depression in the United States.[17] But remarkably, Japan saw no social or political unrest, no rise of aggressive populism, no large outbreaks of poverty or crime, and comparatively limited increases in inequality. This is because, when faced with social crisis, Japan as a nation has prioritized stability over economic growth, slow adjustment over stock price indicators, and prosperity for many over profit for a few. It has persisted, even in the face of constant, public criticism by

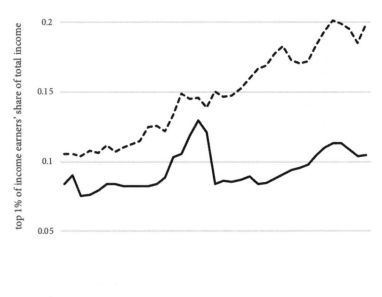

Figure 1.2. Trends in Income Inequality in the US and Japan, 1973–2010.
Source: Constructed with data from World Inequality Lab.

U.S. pundits ranging from former Federal Reserve chairman Ben Bernanke and Nobel prize winner Paul Krugman to a host of journalists, many of whom have since withdrawn their advice and offered apologies.[18] At the turn of the century, a time of severe crisis for Japan, societal cohesion and political stability took precedence over GDP growth. Japan's reemergence in the world economy illuminates a new perspective on how to think about the tradeoffs between economic performance and the larger social welfare, and on how to reorganize business and the economy in ways that are less volatile and less damaging than in the United States.

It is hard to imagine the United States growing at 1% a year for two decades. This scenario is almost impossible because, unlike Japan, the U.S. prioritizes growth—even above societal cohesion, the environment, public safety, and notions of social justice. This emphasis on growth at all costs and personal gain resonates with individualism and the American dream. It contributes to the country's attractiveness, but also to its drawbacks.[19] In Japan's mindset, economic growth was an important goal when the economy had to rebuild after World War II and the goal was to catch up with the West, but now that this has been accomplished, Japan's goals are to be an innovative leader and stable country, and the tradeoffs it is willing to make are very different from the U.S. choices.

The United States used to have so-called organization men, who—similar to Japan's "salarymen"—worked their entire careers for one company, in office and manufacturing jobs. However, in the U.S., the transition to high labor mobility in the new economy was associated with what William Lazonick has called the "financialization" of the economy.[20] This was in no small part brought about by the birth of venture capital funds that invested in young companies in the hope of making a quick, lucrative exit through a stock listing. These new companies also offered stock options to poach young talent from secure positions at large established firms. In the process, innovative enterprise became associated with the stock market, and a company's stock price became critical for attracting finance and labor. Eventually, the new hypermobility of people and money undermined collective and cumulative innovation processes, as speed to market became the mantra. Companies like Intel, Microsoft, and Apple benefited greatly from this process, but lured by social trends and large compensation packages, their executives became obsessed with boosting stock prices. It became common for companies to use their earnings to buy back shares in order to increase the stock price, instead of investing in innovation and long-term value creation.

Thus, in the United States in recent years, the large company has morphed from being a part of the community and a stable employer to being what many consider merely a legal entity, incorporated in Delaware, tasked with optimizing profit, and sometimes in the headlines for laying people off due to missed earning targets. The "organization man" has turned into a "transaction man," whose every action is expressed by a monetary value, and societal cohesion has been undermined by a turn toward viewing everything as an investment.[21]

In contrast, Japan's large companies remain much more than profit maximizers. To this day, the company—the *kaisha*—is considered to be social entity, with clearly defined social responsibilities. It is respected for its contributions to the long-term growth and stability of the country, and seen as a place that shapes employee identity, offers opportunity, builds community, and contributes to progress. The *kaisha* innovates, trains, creates, and grows, and also builds tradition.[22] The respect society has for the large corporations brings with it an obligation for senior management to abide by the trust bestowed upon them—meaning first and foremost that they do the utmost to avoid laying off people.

When Japanese CEOs want to pivot their corporations toward a new strategy, they face anxieties and often huge resistance. Society expects companies to move slowly, in order to allow employees to adjust. When a corporate decision disadvantages people, management often tries to find ways to cushion the blow. When a subsidiary or business unit has to be phased out, it is usually done through "graceful attrition," that is, in a slow process over many years that saves everyone's face and livelihood. While this is expensive for the companies, deviating from these societal expectations would carry immense reputation costs.

Perhaps due to the disastrous experience of the bubble economy, many in Japan still feel ambiguous about stock price as a measure of anything, and are concerned about placing too much value on the stock market. As we will see in Chapter 7, the ongoing choose-and-focus reorganization by large companies is increasingly done with the help of private equity funds, partially in order to avoid stock market pressures for the spun-out business units and subsidiaries. However, unlike the U.S. Wall Street approaches, Japan's private equity deals are set up in ways that aim to deter short-term-oriented financial engineering that may be detrimental to the company. Likewise, corporate governance reforms are meant to invite a certain market discipline to help managers move forward, but they also include measures specifically intended to repel any deleterious influence from self-interested rent-seekers. Japanese CEOs are still cautious not to be guided in critical decisions by the stock price, nor are they paid much in stock options. Corporate cash holdings—criticized so vehemently by Wall Street analysts—are seen in Japan as the best option to safeguard hard-earned money in an era of global low interest rates and political turbulence. Whether this can be continued in an era of global finance remains to be seen. But by describing Japan's ongoing business reinvention, this book is also about how Japan continues to represent a different kind of capitalism that aims to be good for all.

Japan's Business Reinvention: The Structure of this Book

The book is organized around five large themes:

background and history: the tight-culture framework and Japan's postwar business and employment system (Chapters 2 and 3);

the *aggregate niche strategy and Japan's new global impact* (Chapters 4 and 5);

corporate governance reforms and the rise of *private equity* for corporate refocusing and pivoting (Chapters 6 and 7);

inside the firm, *change management* and new *employment* structures (Chapters 8 and 9); and

a glimpse into the future of Japan's competitiveness (Chapter 10).

Chapter 2 introduces tight-loose theory and Japan's business norms. Japan's tight culture translates into strong preferences for safety, certainty, predictability, and due process, all of which affect the speed and nature of managing the reinvention. The chapter introduces examples of everyday and office situations to highlight how these preferences shape business routines. Managing change in a tight culture means carefully structuring processes through which people are nudged toward a new definition of appropriate and normal behavior at the workplace.

Chapter 3 looks back on the main components and the social contract underlying Japan's business system from the 1950s to the 2000s. Even during the go-go years of rapid economic growth, which propelled the country into the top ranks of global trade in manufactured goods, Japan deployed an array of insurance mechanisms to provide stability and predictability, especially through lifetime employment. Large companies had a social responsibility to provide stability, and in return, employees surrendered their rights over career paths and work hours. The postwar success story ended with the delirious bubble economy of the late 1980s and its subsequent bust. The 1990s and early 2000s were two long and difficult decades that brought tremendous hardship. Still, the country eventually managed to return to previous levels of prosperity with limited social displacement and its social fabric still intact.

Chapter 4 then turns to the aggregate niche strategy. Japanese companies have responded to globalization and the rise of China by moving into high-technology, high value-added technology niches in critical input materials and components. This has translated into a trade imbalance in Northeast Asia in favor of Japan: whereas trade between Japan and China is roughly balanced, South Korea and Taiwan have a trade deficit with Japan (due to imports of materials, components, and machinery), and China has a trade deficit with South Korea and Taiwan (importing the parts for end product assembly). Following a first wave of choose-and-focus reorganization in the early 2000s, in the 2010s the necessity to pivot to compete in the new economy is beginning to redefine the core identities of Japan's largest companies. Since the late 1990s, the Koizumi and Abenomics policy programs have enabled and encouraged this corporate rebuilding, and have afforded the reformers the government's imprimatur. The two "lost decades" were in fact a period of deep-seated corporate transformation.

Chapter 5 draws attention to the growing impact that Japan has on global business, in particular in its relations with the United States, South Korea, China, and Southeast Asia. Japan has become one of the most important economic partners for many Asian countries, playing multiple roles as trading partner, investor, financier, and cultural beacon. For many young Asians, Japan is increasingly the place to look up to, as evidenced in rising sales of cosmetics, fashion, and games. This has important implications for Japan's competitiveness in the digital economy, as the Southeast Asia beachhead will give Japanese companies deep access to data, places, people, and businesses. Japanese companies have also become avid global acquirers of large companies, from UK pharmaceutical manufacturers and newspapers to Silicon Valley startup companies, Oregon insurance companies, Kentucky bourbon distillers, and Colorado craft beer brewers. These merger and acquisition (M&A) activities are helping Japanese companies buttress and expand some of their footholds in the aggregate niches on a global scale.

Next, Chapters 6 and 7 look at the changes in financial markets and corporate governance that have enabled repositioning for the aggregate niche strategy. Chapter 6 analyzes how the rise of foreign and institutional shareholders, and reforms toward transparency and shareholder rights, have changed Japan's processes of corporate governance. Corporate decisions are now influenced by new voices and made in new ways. In terms of board structure, disclosure, and managerial rights and responsibilities, Japan's system has become similar to OECD practices. All of Japan's largest companies now have outside board members, and proactive shareholder participation at annual meetings has increased markedly. Yet, Japan's system continues to be based on a different logic from the U.S., as it begins with the assumption that managers and shareholders share the same goal, namely, to create long-term value. Toward this goal, Japan's new governance system includes mechanisms to deter deleterious investors, including a new stewardship code that empowers large institutional investors. Executive pay, too, is characterized by societal constraints on egregious overpay of CEOs, and in spite of recent increases, CEO pay continues to be significantly lower than in other countries.

Chapter 7 sheds light on the role of Japan's fast-growing private equity (PE) market and domestic mergers and acquisitions in the unwinding of Japan's highly diversified conglomerates. As the latter put big business units up for sale, they need a liquid market with big buyers. While PE funds are often seen as ruthless profiteers, in Japan they are emerging as important players and partners for large companies. The insight is that Japan's business norms are enforcing a system where PE investors have to earn their right to get a deal by delivering long-term value creation and employment at the portfolio firm. Any PE firm that violates this privilege is unlikely to get another deal. Regardless of its long-term successes, this system offers insights into alternative ways of protecting markets from self-interested financial engineering, and underscores the powers of nudging and ostracism as regulatory tools even in private market exchanges.

Chapters 8 and 9 turn the focus onto the second domain of Japan's business reinvention, internal management change. Japanese companies have long enjoyed core competencies in advanced manufacturing, based on the meticulous execution of world-class operational processes. This relied on a culture of hard work, knowledge sharing, and organizational learning. While this is a great fit with Japan's tight-culture preferences, by itself it no longer suffices for the new aggregated niche strategy. New processes and corporate cultures that foster deep-technology innovation have to be added onto the existing competencies. Perhaps ironically, loosening up ossified structures and rigid processes in a tight-culture setting requires organized, structured processes. Chapter 8 introduces the new management alignments that are being built, and offers examples of the processes companies are using to effect culture change.

Chapter 9 addresses the challenges facing lifetime employment. The triple threat of a structural labor shortage, changing workstyle expectations, and global cost pressures are putting substantial strain on the system, even as all sides—companies, employees, and the government—are eager to preserve its many benefits. The 2019 Abenomics' workstyle reforms have introduced limits on overtime, new rules on diversity and inclusion, and a new dual-jobs system that allows one person to work for two companies simultaneously. Many companies have adopted this system as a pressure valve, to facilitate mid-career job switching and to attract and retain scarce talent. The system also allows entrepreneurial employees to take a sabbatical to explore a new business, with the insurance of a return option. The system's biggest impact may be in the creation of a new type of innovation ecosystem that offers entrepreneurial opportunities with a stability mechanism.

The main topic of this book is an analysis of Japan's manufacturing industries, which account for 21% of Japan's GDP and continue to form the main pillar of industrial activity. Moreover, the digital economy is about to disrupt the economics of these industries in important ways. Digital manufacturing processes will make economies of scale less relevant, and will also greatly change shopfloor labor relations. The business model of manufacturing firms is also about to change, as manufacturers are switching from selling products at a one-time price, to offering complete product solutions based on subscription models. The question, then, is whether Japan can reinvent its core competence of *monozukuri*—the art of manu-facturing—to compete in the digital economy. Chapter 10 looks into the future, and explores how business reinvention may enable Japanese companies to compete. As U.S. companies compete with China in AI and the cloud, companies in Japan are methodically enhancing their shopfloor strengths in production machinery, robots, sensors, and advanced system solutions. Companies such as Recruit and Monet, a joint venture between SoftBank, Toyota, Honda, and Hino Motors, are already deep into MaaS global data collection. The future is anybody's data gold mine.

This book illustrates how Japanese business has evolved over the past two de-cades into a new competitive force. Dominance in a series of niches, that in the aggregate translate into a powerful business profile, makes Japan the anchor of many global supply chains. The country has recovered from the bubble economy and subsequent disasters, and domestic markets are vibrant. There is a new sense of purpose as companies are finally making the hard strategy choices to be in posi-tion to compete in the digital economy. Japan is a rich, clean, safe, and egalitarian democracy. It has figured out how to pursue profits *and* uphold civic benefits.

The result is a New Japan that is much more important for the global economy than meets the eye, a rich market for international investors, and an alternative example of how to think about corporate renewal. Japan matters because it repre-sents a unique kind of capitalism; it is a very attractive entry point and bridge to Asia for Western business; within Asia, it anchors regional trade and is a source of aspiration for millennials; for world trade, it is a critical provider of relevant input technologies and a central player in global supply chains; and for the U.S. economy, Japan's wealth and its corporate renewal and reinvention are opening up new and important business opportunities.

2

THE SETTING

Corporate Renewal in a Tight Business Culture

When I first traveled through Japan in the 1980s, I noticed many construction sites, all flying white banners with a green cross and the characters for *anzen dai-ichi*, or "safety first." The longer I stayed in Japan, the more I was convinced that this must be the national motto: everybody was constantly so deeply concerned with safety! Only later did I learn the logo was designed in 1919 by Japan's Industrial Safety and Health Organization to promote a "safe workplace and safe city without disasters, accidents, crimes," and to "protect the vulnerable such as workers, women, children, and pedestrians."[1] The deep concern endures. In 2017, I passed a construction site in Tokyo boasting, "Safety is not just a priority but a CORE VALUE."[2]

Also in 2017, I happened upon an office building in the Tokyo Station area with a sign that listed no fewer than 12 admonitions, ranging from the fairly standard "No smoking" and "No demonstrations" to "No disturbing others" and "No spoiling the appearance of the area."[3] While there are admonitions all over Tokyo to be quiet and cautious, this seemed excessive. Why was it necessary to have so many prohibitions of behaviors that most Japanese city dwellers were not doing anyway? And what explains this great concern with public order, and not inconveniencing others?

Even in foreign pastimes adopted in Japan, Japanese behaviors can initially be hard to understand from a U.S. perspective. In the American sport of baseball—which Japan has wholeheartedly embraced—the coach can take a time-out to discuss strategy with the pitcher and the catcher. This short meeting on the pitcher's mound is typically about how to throw the ball, given the particular moment in the game. It does not affect the other members of the team, so in the U.S. this is a brief conversation among three people. In a Japanese game, these time-outs occur much more often, and each time the fans must wait for the entire team, including the outfielders, to run to the mound to be part of the deliberation and then return to their positions. This takes quite some time and effort and, for the American observer, seems rather unnecessary: if the rest of the team does not need to be involved, why do all of them have to attend the meeting? Why have so many meetings? And, why do the outfielders run so fast during a time-out?

This vignette encapsulates an important aspect of Japanese culture, in which meetings follow a very particular process and upholding the proper etiquette of this process is essential. Because all players are part of the team and need to constantly improve, it would be wrong and inconsiderate for the coach to talk to only two of them, so everybody must be included. Yet the outfielders don't want to cause an inconvenience—to the coach, the team, and the fans—by holding up the game more than necessary, so they run. During the conversation, it is important to ensure that all agree. People speak in order of hierarchy, with the outfielders mostly nodding in agreement. In the end, everyone agrees with the coach.

This process is a mirror image of Japanese office life. People have strongly shared views as to what constitutes the right behavior regarding meetings. Failing to call a meeting to assure shared understanding, not including all team members, or speaking at the wrong time may cause awkwardness and uncertainty. The need for all to attend is also one reason why office workers tend to take vacations on the same days, and why vacation reforms are so difficult to implement. While some of these processes may be followed for a good reason, others seem curious to the Western eye.

To understand the challenges that Japanese senior managers face as they try to manage the business reinvention, we need to appreciate the social setting in which this corporate renewal is taking place. This chapter introduces tight-loose theory as a framework to guide the analysis of the specific management methods needed for Japan's business reinvention. Looking at Japanese business through the tight-loose lens also helps us understand why it has taken a generation for companies to modify lifetime employment, why large conglomerates cannot more easily sell off subsidiaries, and why women cannot or will not lean in more strongly to push for faster progress toward workplace equality. These behaviors are due not to inability or lack of initiative but to the norms that guide the processes of change and by which reformers will be perceived and judged.

This chapter begins with a brief review of culture in international business and then introduces tight-loose theory. Next, it develops a Japan-specific application of the tight-loose framework by introducing the content of Japanese business norms, and what these norms mean for managing the reinvention.

Culture in Japanese Business Research

Our understanding of the role of culture in management and organizational change is informed by research in the field of social psychology, where culture is defined as the set of socially constructed values and norms that guide behavior. Values are shared beliefs about the underlying principles of the community, and norms are expectations about appropriate attitudes and behaviors. At the country level, it has been shown that there are persistent differences across countries in both values (principles) and norms (behaviors), and these differences are important to heed in international business. At the corporate level, values and norms are important because they must be managed to align with the company's corporate strategy and the critical tasks the company wants to accomplish.

Management research in the United States has been in no small part informed by Japan's economic successes in the 1980s, and in particular the country's human resources (HR) approaches that were vastly different from those in the United States at the time.[4] The first insight derived from this work is that Japanese firms establish, maintain, and honor long-term relations based on a particular set of shared values. These values include respect, loyalty, and commitment to a trading partner, as well as reciprocity in obligations. Respect is expressed in a keen awareness of hierarchy and rank, and the particular rights and responsibilities associated with each rank. Lower ranks are often associated with sentiments of servitude, whereas promotions to higher ranks bring with them a responsibility to care and manage with benevolence. This give-and-take also underlies most business transactions and entails an intricate set of mutual obligations. Trust is built and loyalty cemented through reciprocal and escalating commitments over time that tie both sides closer and closer together. Breaking a promise, leaving a trading partner in the lurch, or not balancing favors is considered dishonorable. Being put to shame causes a loss of face, which is abhorred; in fact, one of the worst attributes one can attach to another person in Japan is "shameless" (*haji-shirazu*). While all this may read like the script of a medieval samurai movie, it still describes most Japanese business situations to this day.

For companies, this means that trade relations are long-term, including those with trusted suppliers. Historically, many Japanese companies have not had marketing departments because most domestic sales channels were stable and international marketing was outsourced to trading companies. Instead, companies maintain a sizable budget for gifts for their long-standing clients, including customary seasonal gifts and contributions to important client events, such as an expensive flower bouquet for a supplier's new branch opening. Managing a business relationship requires regular contacts, even if only for a short greeting, but rarely involves a lawyer. And deals are often made in a restaurant over a long dinner, and celebrated with bows and toasts. Such informal, relationship-based deal making works due to the power of reputation: trading partners that fail to uphold their end of a deal are instantly *non grata*, and once a reputation is ruined, it is usually unrepairable.

In the 1980s, some of the work examining these practices was extended into superficial hypotheses about how Japan works. Initially, the research on shame and loyalty in Japanese culture had been carefully done.[5] However, when America became infatuated with Japan's economic successes, this morphed into strained applications of culture to explain Japan. These were often simplistic or overdrawn, such as the *Nihonjin-ron* (theories on being Japanese) which claimed that Japan's national and cultural identity was "uniquely unique." These approaches were characterized by the cognoscenti as cultural determinism, and triggered significant backlash against the conceptualization of culture in Japan studies. In the heyday of Japan research in the early 1990s, culture and shame as explanatory variables were set aside, and replaced with theories of rational choice.

However, over the past three decades, the social sciences have made great strides in identifying more clearly the underlying mechanisms that drive human behavior, and explaining the elements of human nature and social settings that determine how people act.[6] Leaning on the original insights of social psychology, research in organization theory, behavioral economics, and political science has brought new currency to the study of behavioral differences, and the norms or institutions that shape behavior. For example, new approaches in public policy regulation have embraced concepts of nudging and shaming.[7] Nudging means offering a choice architecture and using positive reinforcement and indirect suggestions as ways to subtly influence behavior and decision making, such that people voluntarily choose the desired outcome. As a regulatory tool, this has been shown to work well in situations ranging from influencing healthier choices at school lunches to opting into pension savings plans.[8] The mechanism invoked in this process is the human desire to fit in: people make the "good" choice in order not to look weird or be embarrassed. The power of this approach lies in its voluntary nature, because the choice aspect means that less monitoring and sanctioning is required than for formal rules and regulations. Nudging is becoming an important policy approach in many parts of the world, and it is also an important instrument of Japan's Abenomics programs today.

The Tight-Loose Framework: Cross-Country Differences in Business Culture

In international management, researchers have tried for decades to understand cross-country cultural differences in order to inform global entry strategies, HR practices, and the management of cross-cultural mergers and acquisitions.[9] Here, too, Japan has been an important case study of a system offering an alternative to U.S. practices. The most prominent framework for understanding cultural differences has long been Hofstede's *dimensions of culture*, a tool based on research conducted with 116,000 IBM employees in 40 countries in the 1960s.[10] Hofstede developed four measurement scales, related to power, risk aversion, collectivism, and assertiveness. Japan and the United States were seen to be very different on all four. However, even though these dimensions triggered substantial follow-up research and allowed key insights into country-level differences, they lacked the granularity needed to understand what is happening within organizations. In 2011, Michele Gelfand introduced a new approach called tight-loose theory.[11] This framework builds on these previous attempts yet offers a more intuitive and also quantifiable approach to the study of cross-cultural management.

Culture is the set of norms that guide behavior, namely, the socially created standards that shape our expectations and assessments of what is right and wrong. Norms have three dimensions: content, consensus, and intensity.[12] *Content* is the actual behavior that is prescribed. *Consensus* is the degree to which people agree that the norms are important, and *intensity* is the extent to which deviance is tolerated. Two social settings might have the same degrees of consensus and intensity, yet be guided by completely different content as to what is the "right" behavior. For example, your outfit and behavior at a rock concert would be very different from your clothes and actions at a Sunday gospel choir, even though you may feel equally strongly about these two sets of behavioral rules.

The tight-loose framework employs the latter two of these dimensions, *consensus* and *intensity*, to position country cultures on a spectrum from tight to loose. The core proposition is that countries (or regions, companies, schools, families, and so on) differ significantly in consensus and intensity. Tight cultures have strict prescriptions on the "right" way to do things, and out-of-line behavior easily creates unease, awkwardness, and even confusion. In contrast, loose cultures are generally much more easygoing about variance and unpredictability. What is considered spontaneous fun in a loose culture might be perceived as confusing chaos in a tight culture.

The empirical research that informs these insights was conducted through survey work with 6,823 respondents in 33 countries, who were asked to assess whether certain public behaviors were appropriate in a variety of everyday life situations, including eating in an elevator; talking in the library; cursing at the workplace; laughing out loud in the classroom; flirting at a funeral; singing on a city sidewalk; and using headphones in a restaurant.[13] The level of within-country agreement on the "right" behavior was then assessed, as was the level of variance in respondents' answers.

Figure 2.1. shows the distribution along the tight-loose spectrum of a select group of countries from Gelfand's study. Japan is located at the tight end of the spectrum, whereas the United States is on the loose end. Among the large industrialized democracies in the world, Japan is among the tightest, and the U.S. the loosest. Note, again, that this ranking does not refer to content. Thus, daily life in two tight cultures—such as Japan and India—could be vastly different: they are both tight, but the content of their behavioral codes often appears to be almost opposite.

Of course, within a given country, individual people will differ in where they fall on the tight-loose spectrum. Individuals are innately more tight or loose, depending on upbringing, geography, generational attitudes, social class, and occupation, as well as personality traits such as how cautious and controlled or adventurous and impulsive they are, and how much social order and structure they prefer. This individual diversity is the engine for progress and change, and it is essential for an appreciation of Japan's ongoing business reinvention,

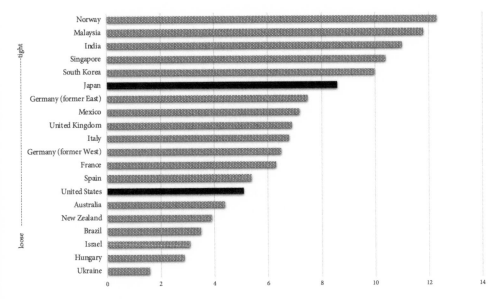

Figure 2.1. Tightness Scores for Select Countries. Source: Constructed with data from Gelfand et al. (2011).

because it explains differences across firms and leaders and, within companies, between reformers and resisters.

A prime source of the tight-loose framework's utility is that it is not normative. This book is not about whether Japan is better or worse than any other country. It is about why Japan is reinventing itself in the way it is, why its business reinvention is being done slowly, and what the behavioral patterns mean for corporate leaders as they manage the reinvention.

The Triggers and Mechanisms of a Tight Culture

Norms have pragmatic underpinnings: they exist and persist because they serve an important purpose. Our survival as a species depends on our adherence to social order: research has shown that groups that cooperate can survive, thrive, and spread.[14] We have evolved as we did thanks to our ability to conform to a given social setting. Our understanding of what it means to conform is often tacit, acquired early on, refined throughout life, and constantly reinforced in daily social situations.

THREATS AND DISASTERS

Countries and regions differ in how much social order they need, depending on their exposure to external threats and resource constraints. Places that face recurring threats of natural disasters (e.g., earthquakes, droughts, famines) or territorial threats (wars, diseases) are more likely to build safety precautions and societal mechanisms of solidarity that coordinate self-help, avoid chaos, and increase the chances of survival in time of crisis. Over time, these mechanisms get coded into a set of acceptable behaviors in everyday life.

Japan—with about 1,500 earthquakes per year—offers many examples of how such deeply ingrained solidarity behavior can be beneficial. In the days following the Tohoku earthquake and subsequent disasters of March 11, 2011, the response and social behavior of the Japanese people exemplified the benefits of a tight culture in the face of crisis. On that Friday afternoon, people in Tokyo were thrown around in their office buildings and homes, the subways stopped, and news began to trickle in of the horrors at the epicenter 150 miles north, in Tohoku. Even as everything shook, nobody screamed (at least not in my whereabouts, in a department store and later in the streets of Tokyo walking home for ten miles). Because the subway stopped, people just quietly began to walk home. Some slept in the subway stations, while others asked to be picked up by car. This caused a crazy traffic jam that stopped all buses; yet, riders simply stood in line at the bus stop in orderly fashion, and nobody jumped the queue. There was no looting, no stealing (including in the subway stations), no wailing or other noisy expressions of suffering. At this moment of great national threat, citizens adopted their second-nature behaviors and tightly adhered to the norms of being quiet and not being a nuisance to others.

PLANS AND RULES

Gelfand's research shows that tight cultures are much more structured, methodical, and formulaic than loose ones. They tend to have clear hierarchies, tight lines of command, and exact protocols. In Japanese companies, this is reflected in the dominant role of the Planning Department, which is in charge of the strategic direction of the firm. In most companies, its main assignment is to produce annual and midterm strategy plans which then become benchmarks for performance. As a result of this orientation toward midterm plans, managers are not trained so much in how to become leaders with a vision and intuition for strategic opportunity as they are in how to run business units and manage budgets so as to hit the key performance indicators outlined in those plans. Skill assessments for leadership positions often anchor on the ability to announce and methodically execute such plans. As we will see in later chapters, this translates into excellence in manufacturing but also introduces a certain rigidity and a focus on narrow goals.

Tight cultures are also often marked by strict laws and severe punishment for violations. Moreover, to avoid slack and uphold second-nature behavior even in normal times, tight cultures tend to have many signs displaying admonitions and warnings of danger, as well as many surveillance mechanisms and installations, as can be observed throughout Japan. In general, it has been shown that "watched people are nice people."[15] Take, for example, research on public bathroom behavior showing that many more people wash their hands when others are around than when they think they are unobserved. Japanese companies, too, are set up to enable a lot of watching and monitoring, and this is the bailiwick of the other powerful department in large firms, Human Resources. This department is in charge of selecting new hires and running the initial socialization and training programs to ensure there is no ambiguity about the behavioral norms at the company. Human Resources is also in charge of the company's "business rules," a code of conduct that covers important matters such as pay, promotions, and pensions, and the possibly even more important minutiae of behavioral restrictions, including the dress code and, in some places, even allowable footwear. In addition to the rules, the standard office layout in Japanese companies is an open floor plan with desks arranged such that the boss can easily observe the entire unit. This makes it easy for employees to satisfy the basic job requirements, such as working long hours, being focused on the assignment, and showing appropriate dedication and behavior. We will see in Chapters 8 and 9 that many companies are now trying to change performance evaluations from assessing process and behavior to measuring outcomes, yet they often encounter tendencies among employees to adhere to the deeply ingrained practices.

THE SOCIAL RADAR

The enforcement of behavioral norms occurs through individuals' perception of how the environment perceives them. Reflecting our fundamental human need to belong, when we sense that our actions are evaluated, we pay attention and adjust. The stronger the sense of what is "right," and the tougher the sanctions for deviating, the more sensitive our social radar becomes and the better we get at complying. Individuals differ in how keen their self- and situational awareness is, but on average, people who live in a tight culture develop a more sensitive social radar and better ways to calibrate it. This is because violations are so much more consequential in tight cultures, where individuals are met with many different mechanisms for shunning and shaming.

None of this is in any way associated with the degree of homogeneity in a society—which was one of the misleading *Nihonjin-ron* claims in asserting Japan's unique identity. A sensitive social radar is not innate but acquired, as any loose-culture person who has come to live in Japan can attest. Many visitors to Japan begin to adjust their behaviors almost instantaneously: as they try to fit in, they lower their voices in the subway car, queue properly, and try not to litter, all in order to not stand out as a strange *gaijin* (foreigner). Gelfand reports a study from the Netherlands showing that people are less likely to litter when they are in a clean place, but do not think much of dropping something when streets are already dirty. This can be observed in Japan, too. Similarly, when Japanese travel abroad they may be much looser than they are at home. This social proof, our tendency to draw cues from our surroundings and mimic others' behavior, applies globally.

A sensitive radar and keen desire to fit in are typically associated with a strong preference for predictability, structure, schedules, and routines. In Japan, we see this in low levels of surprise or spontaneity, exact punctuality, and a sense of comfort in having a reservation—be that on a train, for work appointments, or preplanned group travel with highly detailed, hour-by-hour sightseeing schedules. Trains running like clockwork are important and satisfying to travelers, and one would be hard-pressed to find a clock in Tokyo that is not running precisely on time. Predetermined timetables are also a common feature of Japanese reforms, announced far in advance and with no surprises. Office meetings are planned meticulously, and a change in plan is often disconcerting to people. For companies, this has great advantages for tasks that require exact execution, attention to detail, and conscientiousness about quality and timing of delivery—such as in the Toyota Production System.

Japan's office language has a special adjective for being dense and behaving inappropriately: "KY" (short for *kūki o yomenai*). Literally, this means "unable to read the air," and it is a true deficiency when doing business in Japan. Rather than responding to social cues, people who are KY follow their own beliefs and desires across situations, as a loose-culture person might; for example, they may speak at the wrong time or say the wrong thing. For Japan's business reinvention, this poses a challenge when the appropriate office behavior is so narrowly defined that reformers and change agents are considered KY. In this setting, managing change also includes the task of calibrating people's social radar toward a broader acceptance of diversity in behavior.

Content: The Three Norms of Japanese Business

Tight-loose theory concerns itself only with the consensus and intensity of norms. To utilize this framework for the analysis of Japan's business reinvention, we need to add the specific *content* that characterizes the Japanese workplace. In defining this content, I rely on concepts from business ethics theories,[16] combined with information from conversations with many Japanese businesspeople and from my own observations and experience while living and working in Japan for over nine years. I posit that there are three categories of behavioral norms that guide Japanese business, and they are accompanied by a rule of "2 out of 3," which allows for important variance as well as wiggle room when pushing reforms. The three categories are human-to-human interaction, public appearance and conduct, and the choice of one's actions.

BE POLITE AND CONSIDERATE

Being polite and considerate means to care about others and do one's utmost to uphold human dignity in all business situations. This includes behaving such that everyone can save face and avoid embarrassment. It also means being thoughtful, paying attention to what the other side might need or feel, and being forthcoming with help. There is a certain self-reinforcing element in this behavior, as not being seen as kind would be embarrassing.

Language reflects these connotations, and there are many Japanese terms for this behavior, especially *reigi* (the demeanor of politeness) and *yasashii* (being gentle, mild, tender—a very positive word I have seen used to describe everything from a person to cream cheese). Grammar plays an important role as well, as the Japanese language knows many different, complicated constructions to express various levels of politeness, hierarchy and relative rank, and respect. Body language, too, tends to be quite prescribed, such as bowing at the exact angle commensurate with the status of the counterparty. This allows subtle means of signaling power relations, as well as putting people in their place without even saying a word. Body language habits often become so connected to speaking that many people in Japan—including foreigners who have lived there for an extended period of time—bow even when speaking on the phone.

Politeness is an important aspect in business relations, as well as in Japan's fabled service culture, where it is called *omotenashi*. This term refers to the ability to anticipate a customer's need and offer a solution before it is even articulated. It is visible not only in everyday situations such as shopping, but also in business-to-business relations: suppliers often take it upon themselves to predict the customer's order so as to be ready at short notice. It would also be considered impolite and uncivilized to break a promise or fail to meet an implicit obligation for reciprocity. As we will see in Chapters 6 and 7, this politeness is setting different standards from what is seen on Wall Street for Japan's new system of corporate governance, how private equity deals are arranged, and even how U.S. activist investors behave in Japan.

An important proviso to this norm is Japan's long-standing, fine-grained differentiation between *honne* (the real intention) and *tatemae* (the façade, public stance, or pretext). While honesty is important, preserving everybody's dignity and avoiding shame is valued even more highly. In win-lose business situations, being kind often requires acting. For example, at the conclusion of a competitive negotiation or business deal, instead of gloating and fist-pumping one often sees deferential compliments and expressions of gratitude to the loser, and even a reframing of the event as a "win-win." Western businesspeople (and star athletes) have also been trained to do this, but Japanese executives have truly mastered the art of pretense and polite self-deprecation.

Be Appropriate

The second norm refers to public appearance, and how to be suitable and situationally correct in each set of circumstances. Standing out and drawing attention to oneself, or displaying brash or irreverent public behavior, are strong offenses. This norm includes being obedient (a term also used in school grades, especially for girls), unassuming, and respectful of status, hierarchies, and age. Many Japanese words describe propriety, such as *otonashii* (modest, quiet, well-behaved), or *chanto shita* (orderly). The language describing violations of this norm ranges from the somewhat curious to the expressive. The word *hen* (odd) is used for somebody who deviates too far from the mean; such as a foreigner unwittingly pouring soy sauce over rice (which is not done). In contrast, the colloquial *kawatteru* (literally, changed) is a derogatory term and signals a lack of judgment or sophistication, denoting somebody who is unacceptable and needs to be shunned becuase they are clearly unusual, peculiar, crazy, or eccentric.

What constitutes acceptable and appropriate outward appearance is taught early in life and cemented in school. There is a preference for uniforms, which reduce the probability of unwittingly dressing in the wrong way. Most middle and high schools in Japan have uniforms, complete with school-issued bags (compared to about 20% in the United States and zero in Germany). Beginning in middle school, there are prescriptions regarding hair style and makeup, and inspections can be nitpicky. Tattoos and any hair color other than black are not allowed. Japanese kids with naturally brownish hair may even be admonished to dye it black so that they fit in better. And pupils are under great pressure to follow the right way of speaking, eating, and writing (e.g., with the right hand, and writing characters strictly within the box). As we will see later, when companies began to introduce "leisure days," which meant a relaxation of the dress code on certain days of the week, many HR departments held special orientation sessions to prescribe the appropriate outfit for those days.

In addition to outward appearance, public conduct also needs to be appropriate. Good behavior implies maintaining personal space and not crowding other people, unless it cannot be avoided, such as in busy subways. And even there, people usually attempt to take up as little space as possible and to stand or read so as to not encroach on others. Another example is noise pollution. Admonitions are ubiquitous. In public transportation, you are constantly reminded to turn off your phone or lower the volume on your headset, "lest you annoy your neighbors." Your phone should be in "manner mode" (*manna-mōdo*), and good manners means quiet. Loud is considered vulgar and rude, and raising one's voice in a business meeting is highly unlikely to lead to success. "Noisy" (*urusai*) also has the figurative meaning of being bothersome due to being shrill or getting on others' nerves. It is the Japanese label for activist investors, reformers who move too fast, and even the *yakuza* (mafia). Noisy can be used to describe fashion, color-sense, and architecture. Subtlety is an expression of tight culture, and it has become a prime marker of Japan's impact on global food, fashion, art, and minimalism in design.

DON'T CAUSE TROUBLE

The third category of business norms refers to the actions one chooses and disturbances one causes. The norm is to always "go with the flow," to not stand out, to keep one's head down and wait one's turn, and most importantly, to not rock the boat. Actions and choices that bother others are seen as a *meiwaku* (nuisance, inconvenience). The prescription for not causing a *meiwaku* is to consider the consequences of one's choices and actions for others, to be respectful of their needs, and to honor the system as it is. Sanctions are typically delivered with strong words, and in a language known for having no real word for "no," there are a surprising number of phrases to express disagreement or disgust with another person's behavior that is out of bounds. And, one of the most frequent apologies one hears in the Japanese workplace is, "sorry for the inconvenience."

As we have seen, people in tight cultures tend to have a low tolerance for ambiguity: not knowing what is right may result in accidentally causing a *meiwaku*. The fear of causing an inconvenience makes people cautious and focused on preventing mistakes. This can translate into high levels of risk aversion, and a strong preference for *anzen dai-ichi* (safety first) options. In companies, it may result in decisions not to make a bold investment, and in resistance to change. For individuals, it creates obstacles to unorthodox career moves such as quitting a company and becoming an entrepreneur. For professional women, it is a key reason why they cannot just "lean in" more strongly to bring about workplace change.

To see how easy it is to inadvertently cause a *meiwaku*, consider this explanation by an employee of a Japanese company in the United States: "Our Japanese colleagues often complain that we take too many vacation days, even though they have nearly triple the number of national holidays as we do. What they really mean is that we take holidays on our own, individual terms, rather than choosing to travel on the national holidays like everyone in Japan does. Taking two weeks off to go to Europe is seen as so much *meiwaku* to colleagues who have to fill in. It's inconsiderate and causes only trouble."

Thus, the necessity to be normal limits choices. Making a choice that others do not like or know how to accommodate risks causing a *meiwaku*. One epitome of such limitations is the daily ritual surrounding work lunches, including when to eat lunch (always at noon, to avoid a scheduling *meiwaku*), where to sit, and what food to order (whatever the oldest person chooses). There are some practical reasons for this, including that if everybody has the same order, the food will all arrive at the same time. But that this routine can be ridiculous is obvious to many within Japan as well. Movie buffs may recall a hilarious scene in Juzo Itami's movie *Tanpopo*, a parody of Japan's choice limitations and the strength of its social norms, where a group of office workers, all dressed the same but of different ages, have a business lunch in a French restaurant. The oldest person gets to order first and chooses "curry rice" (a very basic Japanese dish), and grudgingly, everybody else orders the same thing, until it comes to the youngest employee. He ignores all pressures and upstages his superiors by ordering an à la carte gourmet dish, displaying his vast culinary knowledge in French. The mix of horror and envy in the facial expressions of his superiors is priceless.

How to Push for Change in a Tight Culture: "2 out of 3"

Given these restrictive patterns, how can change be effected and reorganization launched? Reformers run the risk of being seen as KY or noisy, and rejected for causing a *meiwaku*. Thus, managing corporate renewal and change necessitates subtle maneuvering. Of course, not all people in tight cultures are equally constrained, and individual variation creates friction that reformers can employ for forward movement. What is more, according to my own observations of Japanese business situations, it may not be necessary to fulfill all three norms at all times; it is usually sufficient to comply with two. For example, very polite people may get away with looking a little bit "weird," as long as they are otherwise conformist. Conversely, considerate and highly appropriate people may be allowed to push the envelope toward reform.

This observation confirms research in psychology on likability, showing that a person with a tiny flaw is more likable than somebody who is perfect. In various interviews with employees of large Japanese manufacturing firms and government ministries, I have found a growing frustration with tightness and the slow pace of reform. This frustration is expressed in a certain admiration for those who lean toward rebellion, as long as that leaning is presented appropriately and in considerate ways. As the number of reformers grows, they become less unusual, and as we will see in Chapter 4, the thrust of Abenomics is to make business reform the "new normal." Still, change in Japan will always be slow, because it has to be carefully orchestrated, at least in appearance, and implemented in line with social expectations of being polite, appropriate, and not too disruptive.

Managing Organizational Renewal
and Innovation in a Tight Culture

Japan's tight culture is not a positive or negative, but a reality. Japan's tight behavioral norms are a mechanism needed in times of crisis, such as a major earthquake, and they translate into a widely shared preference for safety-first, risk-averse, methodical and sometimes formulaic processes. In the calculation of many Japanese, the benefits to Japanese society from a tight culture outweigh the costs of slow progress. Polite is more important than efficient, and appropriate and normal are more important than disruptive or trail-blazing.

Any change management in this setting requires an approach that matches these preferences, as otherwise it will be rejected. As large Japanese firms are trying to implement the aggregate niche strategy and move their companies toward breakthrough innovation at the technology frontier, some looser mechanisms are needed that allow for making risky technology bets and building more peripheral vision for innovation. A first insight from the tight culture framework is that, perhaps paradoxically, moving people to embrace more diversity, curiosity, and risk-taking experimentation requires a highly structured, methodical approach—because that is the dominant perception of how change is done "right."

Another takeaway is that managing culture change means modifying the definition of what constitutes appropriate, normal behavior. The tight culture—high consensus on a set of widely shared behavioral rules—cannot be changed, but the content of the "right" thing to do can be adjusted. This requires careful nudging and a slow phase-in, and again, this can be done through a highly structured series of seminars, workshops, and retreats. These structured events take enormous time. But once employees have embraced the new vision, they are likely to charge ahead at full speed, because their keen social radar is likely to accelerate the rollout of the new behavioral norms.

Research on the management of culture has identified five primary tools to bring about culture change.[17] The first is to supply *direction*: consistent, unambiguous signaling from top management of what constitutes the "new normal" behavior in the organization. The second is to get *buy-in* from employees; they need to be heavily involved in the formulation of this new normal. A third tactic is to make change attractive, by showcasing vivid *examples* of the new culture. A fourth tool is to deepen the buy-in by offering frequent *social approval*, such as through rewards and public celebrations for those who have adopted change;

implicitly, such events also exclude and shame those who resist. The fifth element is to carefully manage all this within larger *HR system changes* that support the new culture, such as employee selection, training, and promotion. When leaders employ these five levers simultaneously, culture can be managed and changed.

Some of Japan's largest companies are now employing these levers to bring about the reinvention. As we will see in more detail in Chapter 8, AGC—previously known as Asahi Glass—is one such example. In 2015, a culture change was launched with clear statements about the need to change the company from a glass company to a materials company. The senior management team laid out what behaviors were needed (the new culture) and began a series of more than a hundred meetings with employees at all levels of the company to hear their hesitations and explain how and why change was needed. Leadership was consistent in signaling what the new culture looks like, and promoted and celebrated employees who reflected the new culture. Finally, the human resource systems (including hiring and training) were adjusted to emphasize the new culture. Using these five levers, AGC was transformed into a 21st-century global company.[18]

If this change process is done right, a tight culture may actually facilitate the rollout. In looser cultures, herding the entire workforce in a new direction may be more difficult. Resistance is likely to manifest itself differently as well. In a loose setting, one might expect direct and open debates or even protests. In contrast, perhaps the biggest challenge in managing culture change in Japan is to figure out where pockets of resistance remain. The norms of politeness and not being noisy mean that opponents to a change regime often stay silent and express their objections in quiet boycotts within their divisions. Research has shown that resistance among mid-level and general managers is a frequent obstacle to Japan's reinvention.[19]

Japan's values of loyalty, commitment, and obligation offer an additional lever that can be pulled. For example, change can be motivated by showing how the new direction will ensure the company's longevity, or even how it perpetuates the spirit of the company founder—a rallying cry one hears quite often. And employees' concern about saving face and avoiding awkward situations makes nudging and shaming ideal managerial tools to guide the organization onto a new path. While for some U.S. managers this may sound difficult, the Japanese managers are of course very familiar with these sentiments and often share their employees' expectations and concerns. The most successful reformers in Japan are those who know how to pull these culture levers, at the right speed and embedded in the necessary processes.

The Dark Side of Japan's
Tight Business Culture

Both tight and loose cultures are good at some things, and bad at others. Within Japan, there are many who are growing impatient with the slow pace of change, the limits to expressions of individuality, and the *anzen dai-ichi* leanings that often block progress. Others attach great value to the stability, predictability, and clear direction that the tight-culture norms produce. Ingrained perceptions of what constitutes proper behavior often translate into tremendous social resistance to companies that want to innovate, or entrepreneurs who want to blaze a new trail. There are three obstacles in particular that often cause reform efforts to stall: the stickiness of traditional customs, the obsession with process over outcomes, and inefficiency.

THE YARIKATA

Every organization has its own "way of doing things," its *yarikata*. In Japan's tight culture, that *yarikata* can be as strong as religion, and arguably, it has enabled Japanese companies to excel in manufacturing and *monozukuri*, or the "art of making things." Once established as the one and only way to do something, the *yarikata* becomes a powerful tool in assembly lines, construction, and even incremental innovation. The *yarikata* supersedes individual variation and represents the spirit and rules of work. Note that the *yarikata* and its focus on technical brilliance is also a guiding principle in Japanese arts, where the first stage of accomplishment is to be able to replicate a certain master perfectly—be it with a kabuki facial expression, a tea ceremony turn of the cup, an ikebana twist, a calligraphy stroke, or a karate stance.

Yarikata is also my preferred translation for "corporate culture," as it describes the norms and values that guide a company's operations and behaviors. In that sense, leading a corporate culture change means adjusting the way of doing things within the organization. In particular, the congruence model— explained further in Chapter 8—posits that the tighter the alignment between strategy, organization, and culture, the more successful the company. And the more successful the company, the more likely it is to grow a bureaucracy and develop a deeply entrenched inertia and excessive adherence to the "way we do things around here." This can lead to corporate decline if the company becomes unable to adjust to technological change or market disruptions.[20]

Japanese companies have long been known for their strong culture. And while corporate culture can be changed, in the words of many seasoned Japan-based consultants, doing so in large companies is akin to changing the course of a cargo ship. Managing culture change requires strong leadership, but tradition-ally, Japanese executives did not even perceive managing change as one of their roles. Moreover, companies are usually very proud of their culture and often use past successes or tradition as reasons why they cannot implement change. Thus, the *yarikata* is yet another contributor to the slow pace of change in Japan, and because it is deeply ingrained, it is often a formidable barrier to reform.

PROCESS ORIENTATION AND RISK AVERSION

Although soccer has become one of Japan's most popular team sports, the men's national team has yet to advance far in international tournaments. It often ap-pears as though the players are so focused on process and perfect technique in passing the ball in midfield that they forget to get the ball over the opponent's goal line. Similarly, Japanese companies often appear to be obsessed with pro-tocol and process to a degree that interferes with getting things done.

Process orientation—at the expense of focusing on the results—is a double-edged sword. On the one hand, it creates camaraderie and signals that the workplace is kind, caring, and inclusive. It is also driven by the (sometimes unrealistic) expectation that going through the same process many times, as if in piano practice, nurtures knowledge and leadership skills. But it can also result in a lack of decisive decision making when the focus on the process supersedes the goal. Thus, where a loose-culture person would find frequent and endless business meetings inefficient, a tight-culture person might see an important and egalitarian process that allows all parties to learn through repetition. Recently, in a realization of the value of time and importance of accomplishing goals, many Japanese organizations and ministries have embraced the concept of using key performance indicators as new tools to guide their work tasks. This is helping to counteract the downsides of process orientation in Japan's busi-ness reinvention.

Relatedly, the norms of being kind and normal are also manifest in Japanese companies in a common preference to avoid confrontation and withhold personal opinions. It can be difficult to identify what a person really thinks or wants, and as a result there is often little variance in the ideas proposed. Together with tendencies to move in lockstep, to be careful not to make a mistake, and to exercise high levels of personal self-control, this results in slow and deliberate decision making that can be detrimental when the competitive environment is changing quickly.

Waste and Exclusion

A third detrimental aspect of Japan's tight business culture is that the emphasis on predictable processes, safety, and careful deliberation often results in what an observer from a loose culture might consider waste. This ranges from a waste of paper (everything is printed out) and time (long meetings) to a waste of talent (by putting all employees through the same rotations). Opportunity costs include slow decision making, missing out on a business deal, and quashing entrepreneurial spirit and innovation. A person leaning toward the loose end of the culture spectrum—including many within Japan—may find this waste exasperating. But for a tight-leaning person, the very definition of waste is different, and the strong preferences for not leaving anybody behind or making a mistake often override efficiency concerns. In business, this can mean forgone investment possibilities, although sometimes there are benefits to being slow. For example, the 2008 global financial crisis did not directly affect Japan's financial system because the Ministry of Finance, in a move of safety-first regulation, had not yet allowed Japan's banks to engage in the market for collateralized debt obligations, the instruments at the core of the financial disaster.

The norms of consideration and kindness could also be viewed as a source of waste, and this is reflected in Japan's employment system and human resource practices. As we will see in Chapter 3, the Japanese company has historically also functioned as a social entity and anchor. In companies large and small, to this day, people will not be dismissed just because there is an economic rationale. This often results in overemployment, including in the executive suite, when retired managers from a company, its affiliates, or the government are kept on the payroll as expensive advisors without real assignments. On the shopfloor, overemployment and leniency for unproductive workers can reduce both profit and morale. While this sense of loyalty to employees and obligation to care for their livelihood is an important contributor to social stability, it is placing large companies under increased pressure as they try to answer calls to increase performance metrics.

The most glaring instance of wasting talent has long been the effective exclusion of women from advanced career paths. As we will see in more detail in Chapter 9, this has various root causes, one of which is traditional corporate expectations of long work hours and obligatory late-night drinking sessions.

Until the 2019 labor reforms, it was quite common for white-collar employees in Japan to work later than 9 p.m., and the traditional family setting was structured around this schedule, with the stay-at-home wife having full responsibility for all household decisions. Women who chose to have children were pushed out of the workforce, and those who stayed often had to forgo a family for their career. This is beginning to change, but the workplace reality often still remains that there are deeply ingrained assumptions about gender roles in the workplace, and these often lead to a waste of talent.

REPRESSION AND RELEASE VALVES

Readers living in a loose culture may wonder whether people living in tight cultures are repressed. There are some indications that this is indeed a challenge, such as the *hikikomori* phenomenon in Japan. People with this psychological condition seek extreme isolation. Japan's comparatively high degrees of censorship, ostracism, and bullying (*ijime*) can be viewed not just as mechanisms to enforce compliance with behavioral norms but as an expression of stress. Bullying, in particular, has been a long-standing challenge at Japanese schools, and can be surprisingly brutal, given the otherwise kind and considerate behavior in Japan. Returnee children (*kikoku shijo*), who have attended school abroad for a few years due to a parent's work assignment, are a particularly easy target for bullying because they have often acquired different abilities and behaviors. This can be so severe that in some families the father takes on the two-year foreign rotation alone, while the mother stays in Japan with the children. In poorly managed firms, this bullying may continue in the workplace and is said to be a common cause of demotivation and depression among mid-career employees.[21]

Both tight and loose cultures have pressure valves that offer reprieve from either the constraints or the chaos. For loose cultures, these take the form of highly structured, organized, and synchronized activities that people seek out to voluntarily fall into a conscribed role. One example is the popularity in the United States of structured Japanese sports such as karate, and highly synchronized yoga classes, or team road biking, complete with uniform high-fashion outfits and accessories.

Conversely, in tight cultures, the pressure valves are opportunities to escape the rigidities of the norms. In Japan, anything goes when people get together after work for drinks, and even more so during the second drink (*nijikai*) or a karaoke session. Many workplace dynamics are handled when people are drunk, because that is the time when they may say publicly what they want or think. While there is a tacit agreement that such directness will not be reprimanded, these inputs often shape business decisions or office work patterns. Of course, happy hour office talk is not special to Japan, but it is arguably more important there because the possibilities for frank discussion are otherwise so limited. As the general manager of a large company told me, his daytime office was for dealing with suppliers, customers, and administrative matters, and the beer restaurant was for managing the staff. The new inclusion of women in the managerial tracks and a changing preference among young male employees has necessitated new mentoring mechanisms in the office, and greatly reduced the beer outings. But to this day, restaurants continue to be the place where many office problems are solved and deals are struck.

Overall, Japan's business reinvention requires that CEOs and their senior management teams assume stronger roles and guide a top-down process toward building a new type of organization with a new corporate culture. This is happening against the backdrop of Japan's tight culture, which requires top managers to take steps that may look slow and timid to those outside. But in reality, these are often highly structured, careful approaches to nudge employees into accepting new workplace dynamics and a new definition of the norms that guide their organizations and shape their self-identity. The results of these changes are now becoming apparent in many companies, as employees' tone, demeanor, and appearance have begun to change.

3

THE BACKGROUND

Japan's Economic Rise—
Stability Through Lifetime Employment

In April 2019, Keidanren—the Japan Business Federation, Japan's conservative business and employer lobby representing all large companies—announced the phasing out of one of the most peculiar aspects of Japan's human resource management system: the *shūkatsu*.[1] The *shūkatsu* is the annual job-hunting process that determines where university graduates will pursue their lifetime careers as *salarymen*. Since the 1990s, the system had become increasingly synchronized and standardized, to the point where it had wiped out any signs of individuality among job applicants, and had lost its ability to effectively match employees with employers. The end of this important institution symbolizes a sea change in Japanese employment relations and challenges the underlying logic of Japan's postwar employment patterns.

Under the *shūkatsu* system, the entire job application for university graduates was scripted by Keidanren, and executed primarily by Recruit, Japan's leading HR company. Over time, it had become more ossified than perhaps lifetime employment itself. Foreshadowing the core features of lifetime employment—lockstep promotion for the first decade, no individualized career choices, and pay by company size instead of job category—students interviewed in the spring, at the end of their third year in college, and received job offers in October. This made any study in their fourth year unnecessary, and it also left little room for people looking for jobs at other times of the year. For HR departments, it was efficient to hire only once a year, and to conduct a unified company initiation and training program for the newbies, which paved the way for lockstep job rotations, evaluations, and promotions. HR managers picked their new staff based mostly on pedigree and university rank, and the purpose of the job interview was to assess candidates' future potential and personality fit with the company culture, not their individual knowledge or skill. For students wanting to enter a large company, the sole purpose of the *shūkatsu* interview was to receive a job offer. Salaries, job assignments, and even locations were typically not negotiable, because in exchange for their lifetime job, employees gave up their say on most of those decisions. So, the best strategy for getting a job was to check off all the boxes for Japan's business norms: be polite, appropriate, and completely normal. This push toward sameness got worse during the recession of the 1990s and early 2000s, when many companies reduced hiring. Also, in its handbook at that time, Recruit began to advertise a particular outfit for the *shūkatsu*—black suit, blue tie, certain hairstyle—together with advice on how to answer the interview questions. This had resulted in a bizarre annual event when long lines of well-educated 21-year-olds queued up in interview venues, all dressed in the same way, and prepared to give the same answers to the same questions.

The year 2020 will be the last occasion for this hyper-unified process. While the system had long been under pressure, the onset of the structural labor shortage and the rise of mid-career job changers in the late 2010s eventually meant it had run its course. Early cracks were caused by foreign firms not bound by Keidanren's script who were able to pick up the best talent, sometimes even offering pay commensurate with skill levels. Then new high-tech firms also began to jump the queue, as synchronized hiring was useless for their search for highly skilled specialists. Eventually, the system was nearly fully undermined by the individualization of young people's job aspirations and—as we will see later—a major modification of the logic of lifetime employment itself. And with that, Japan has begun to tinker with a major pillar of stability in society: employment.

By the time all is said and done, the transition to a new era of human resource management will have taken a generation. The reforms are beginning to affect the widely shared understanding of the social responsibility of the Japanese company. The *kaisha*, the company that anchored postwar Japan's rise to economic riches, was and in many ways continues to be much more than a firm. It is a social entity, a place where people grow up, learn, exert effort, show dedication, and seek protection—it has been referred to as a family.[2] The long-term employment structures reinforce societal preferences for stability and reciprocity and extend into the supplier system and families. Employment has long been the anchor of Japan's social contract, and since the 1990s, it has been the main reason for the slow and guarded speed at which Japan has adapted to the changing global competitive environment. As of 2020, Japan is building a new employment system that attempts to maintain the stability, predictability, and dedicated lifetime work of the old system while responding to demands for more diversity, individualized career paths and skill formation, and new types of labor mobility.

This chapter reviews Japan's postwar business system, and then outlines the old system as a baseline for the discussion of reform and change. During the go-go years of post–World War II recovery, companies answered the government's call for rapid growth but also established several insurance mechanisms. They formed business groups and associated with a main bank, and they built vast conglomerates to ensure survival and be able to uphold their long-term employment obligations over the business cycles. The chapter then describes the typical life and career of the salaryman, Japan's version of the erstwhile U.S. organization man, and the role of non-regular workers and small firms in the system. It ends with a brief summary of the bubble economy of the late 1980s and the subsequent collapse and crisis that caused huge economic losses and threw Japan into two decades of stagnation, low growth, and social distress. It is perhaps due to these tremendous losses and the social distress caused by the post-bubble collapse that Japan has so far eschewed the hypermobility of labor and money and the centrality of the stock price to corporate strategy that has come to characterize the U.S. economy.

The Go-Go Years of Postwar Economic Growth

Japan's post-WWII economic story, in a nutshell, is this. To emerge from the rubble after World War II and catch up technologically with the West, Japan crafted a business model built on export promotion and infant industry protection. The government proactively picked export industries, and supported corporate champions in each of these industries, to expedite growth and avoid wasteful duplication. It established import barriers to protect domestic industries from foreign competition, and strict financial regulation that limited access to the stock and bond markets to only the largest firms. These constraints channeled corporate finance through the banking system, and interest rates were regulated to keep the cost of borrowing low. This invited high financial leverage and put the banks at the center of private sector investment.[3] The phenomenal successes of Japan's fast growth period owed much to hard work and ingenuity, but they were also fortuitous, as the country faced few regional competitors at the time, had little government debt, was Asia's anointed leader, and operated under a U.S. security guarantee. This approach worked: Japan became Asia's most advanced economy and built a relatively egalitarian, democratic society where few are left behind.

INDUSTRIAL POLICY

In the 1950s, Japan was a producer mainly of silk cloth and mechanical metal toys, and until the early 1970s, the label "Made in Japan" carried the connotation of cheap and low-tech. The policies and corporate strategies enacted to escape this reputation centered on encouraging fast learning and upgrading the industrial and technology base. This was done through industrial policy, predominately in the hands of the economics ministry, now called the Ministry of Economy, Trade and Industry, or METI. In the 1960s, the winning industries that METI picked were steel, shipbuilding, chemicals and processing (e.g., refineries, rubber, ceramics, pharmaceuticals), and heavy electric machinery (turbines, generators, power plants). Then the OPEC oil cartels of 1973 and 1979 brought about the so-called oil shocks: between 1972 and 1981, oil prices skyrocketed from $3.40 to $31.80 a barrel.[4] This rattled Japan's energy-intensive heavy industries to the core, and METI swiftly launched a new policy program to add less polluting and less energy-intensive high-technology sectors to Japan's industrial base. The ministry picked automobiles, electronics, and precision machinery, which continue to be among Japan's banner industries today.

The goal of Japan's postwar business model was to create a virtuous cycle of growth that fostered continuous upgrading, as outlined in Figure 3.1. Because Japan has very limited natural resources of its own, the cycle began with the import of energy and input materials. These were used to create value-added manufacturing exports, which earned the foreign reserves needed to purchase or license Western technologies (in addition to occasionally just copying them). Initially, there was a lot of trial and error, and plenty of catching up to do in terms of design and manufacturing quality. But with each round, there was rapid organizational learning and quality improvement, and companies developed new mass-manufacturing processes and innovation capabilities that were

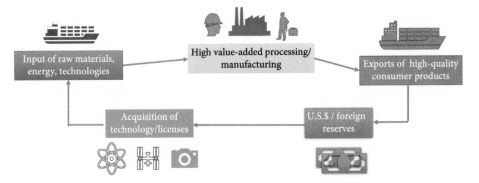

Figure 3.1. Flowchart of Japan's Postwar Business Model.

then extended into the next round of ever more complicated, higher value-added technology adoption.

One example of the successes of this growth model is Japan's specialty chemicals industry, which has built out and maintained its global competitive advantage to this day. To tell but one story, in 1964, Toray, a company that had begun as a rayon yarn manufacturer, invested heavily in carbon fiber to learn the required complex manufacturing processes. This was done merely on a hunch that one day the material would be important, even though there was no use case at the time. Even though expensive, it was seen as an investment in the future. And indeed, it gave Toray's engineers a head start on building the experience and knowledge to make this material in large batches with high quality and low variance. Today, carbon fiber is in everything from golf equipment and bicycles to cars and airplane fuselages, and Japan is its leading producer. Based on 50 years of experience in making carbon fiber at consistently high quality, for decades now Toray, Teijin, Mitsubishi Chemical, and Kureha have owned over half of the global market for this product.

Over time, this reiterative learning and upgrading process resulted in a core competence in manufacturing—or *monozukuri*, the "art of making things"—based on the ability to produce very complicated, high-quality products with high yields and low variance. This focus was a good match with some of Japan's tight-culture inclinations, such as the affinity for due process and the *yarikata* (the way of doing things) as well as low tolerance for deviance. Employees could be easily trained to do tasks exactly how they were supposed to be done.

The most famous illustration of this constant upgrading and built-in quality and improvement approach is the Toyota Production System, which was developed in the early 1960s and has since been adopted globally for automotive manufacturing. It was born out of necessity, as Toyota was a small company at the time, with limited resources and no room for waste; outsourcing most parts was a necessity. The company's genius was to build and carefully manage a stable hierarchy of suppliers, and then build the flow of production around a highly synchronized system of just-in-time delivery, built-in quality controls, and continuous improvement and learning.[5]

THE TRADE SURPLUS

Figure 3.2 shows the results of Japan's postwar efforts. The 1950s and 1960s were labeled the "period of rapid growth," as Japan recorded an average annual GDP growth rate of 10%, similar to China's rate 40 years later. The growth rate halved after the oil shocks, to an average of 5%, and then fell to an average annual growth of about 1% in the 1990s and early 2000s. Until the 1970s, Japan's raw material and technology imports exceeded the value of exports, but beginning in the early 1980s, Japan earned a fast-growing trade surplus, and about half of that trade was directed to the United States. The Japan that Americans recall from the 1980s was an export machine of well-designed and clever consumer products. After the two oil crises, U.S. consumers fell in love with Japan's small, highly fuel-efficient cars that were also more reliable and cheaper to maintain than the much larger U.S. gas-guzzlers. Americans also embraced made-in-Japan office equipment such as copiers and fax machines, as well as cameras, televisions, and stereo systems—so much so that it caused the demise of the U.S. home electronics industry. Japan maintained its trade surplus until the 2011 Tohoku earthquake and Fukushima nuclear power plant disaster, which led to the shutdown of all 52 nuclear power facilities in Japan and necessitated huge imports of coal, oil, and liquefied natural gas (LNG).

In the early 1980s, this burgeoning trade surplus caused grave concerns in the United States, which launched a decade-long trade war. The U.S. pushed Japan to end import protection, open its markets, and deregulate its financial system. These negotiations ushered in the end of Japan's postwar business model. In the 1990s, the nature of global competition also began to change. Beginning with South Korea and Taiwan, other Asian nations began to copy Japan's growth model, and by the turn of the century they had launched the challenge and eventually beat Japan at its own game.

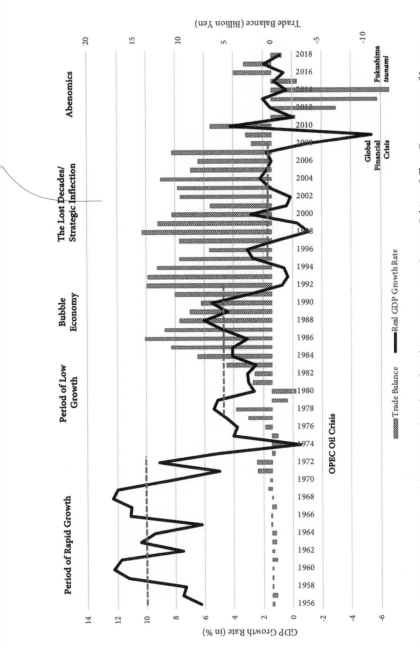

Figure 3.2. Japan's Postwar Annual GDP Growth and Trade Balance, 1956–2018. Source: Cabinet Office, Government of Japan; Customs and Tariff Bureau, Ministry of Finance Japan.

THE SOCIAL CONTRACT

As Figure 3.2 shows, Japan's go-go years were marked by heavy fluctuations in annual growth rates and were often a wild ride. The highly leveraged growth machine was inherently risky, and CEOs were looking for stabilizers, if only to satisfy their own *anzen dai-ichi* (safety first) inclinations. For companies, their first important anchor was the government; picking certain companies and putting them on financial steroids created a certain reciprocal obligation for the ministries to protect their chosen companies in times of trouble. For employees who worked very hard and long hours, an assurance was also needed that their contributions would pay off over time, and this came in the form of lifetime employment. A way to think about lifetime employment is as a core component of Japan's postwar social contract, that is, the tacit agreement of give-and-take within society. Lifetime employment anchored and defined the relative roles and responsibilities of the state and the private sector, as well as of large firms and their employees.

In Japan's postwar social contract, the government pushed large companies toward rapid growth by offering subsidies and other support. And in exchange for this support, large companies were tasked with providing corporate welfare, including not only pensions but also in-company healthcare, along with insurance, training, housing, and of course long-term employment. In this way, the government economized greatly on social welfare provisions, including unemployment insurance, and those savings were recrafted into subsidies for small firms, such as those in the service sectors. The responsibility of employees in this system was to work hard and allow the company to have complete control over their career paths, pay, promotion, and retirement. This helped to reduce the cost for the companies, because being allowed to dispatch workers to different assignments and jobs as needed introduced a certain flexibility into a system where labor was a fixed cost. These agreements extended to the large firms' suppliers, especially in manufacturing, so that overall, the winners' success meant raising the water level for all boats floating in the economy.

Corporate Strategy: Insurance Through Size and Networks

In addition to the close ties with the government, the highly leveraged companies also set up several private mechanisms to ensure their own longevity. The first was the so-called main bank system. In this system, the six largest banks—some with historical ties to prewar holding structures—became the main banks for the roughly 35 core members of each of the six *keiretsu* (horizontal business groups). The main bank got privileged access to each group member's financial information, and in the event a company fell into distress, it was understood that the main bank would come to its rescue and organize a restructuring and turnaround. Illustrating the main banks' stabilizing force, there were fewer than 100 large-company bankruptcies over the postwar period.

For the banks, under regulated interest rates, the key to growth was to furnish more and more loans, while avoiding highly costly bailout events. Thus, they wanted their client companies to grow and diversify. This would require more loans, and would make the companies safer. In line with the strategy wisdom of the time, banks viewed unrelated diversification as stabilizing, because it meant that their clients were operating in multiple businesses with uncorrelated income streams. A decline or disruption in one business would not risk the entire firm. And as long as their borrowers generated sufficient cash flow to pay the interest due on the loans, the banks were unconcerned with efficiency. Profits, margins, or the stock price were quite irrelevant in this equation. What the banks wanted to see were long-term plans for how their clients would continue to grow revenues.

For the large-firm CEOs, this meant that there was one main bank that was their long-standing main lender, shareholder, and financial services provider, and that bank had deep information on the company's planning and financials. There was also an implicit understanding that in times of distress, the bank might interfere or even replace the CEO with a bank official to manage the turnaround. To avoid such interference and keep the bank happy, corporate management focused on businesses that would generate high sales. Thus, many companies turned into complex, sprawling entities that were satisfied with earning profit margins of 5% or less over the entire spread. This size and stability pleased the bankers, but it meant that CEOs never had to make the hard decisions on what businesses they would focus on or which ones they should exit. Corporate strategy in this system was understood not as making a choice but as writing a midterm plan on how to further grow the conglomerate. To this day, this particular legacy of the main bank system continues to run deep in many companies.

In addition to the main bank, Japan's largest 200 firms also derived stability and trade benefits through close relationships with other member firms of their business groups (*keiretsu*). There was an implicit understanding that group members would assure each other of preferential and long-term trades as well as trade credit, especially in times of crisis. For example, the car company Mazda fell on hard times in the early 1970s, when it bet on gas-guzzling rotary engines just prior to the first OPEC oil shock, and this forced a huge write-off. The Sumitomo Bank (Mazda's main bank) moved in with rescue loans and a management revival plan, but what really saved Mazda was a rallying call to all employees of all Sumitomo group companies, as well as their suppliers, to purchase a new Mazda—and many of these "family" members did.[6]

These business groups even offered insurance against the vagaries of the stock market, through stable and often reciprocal cross-shareholding. Business group member firms and trading partners took mutual shareholder stakes, with the understanding that they would not sell, especially not in times of crisis or vulnerability. This meant that each company's main shareholders did not care much about profitability or stock price either. Moreover, cross-shareholding created a highly effective barrier against takeovers. Even though each stake was small, at less than 3% on average, together these stakes accounted for 25% to 35% of all outstanding shares of the group. And there was no "squeeze-out" rule, meaning that minority shareholders did not have to surrender their shares in the event of a hostile takeover. Chapter 6 will show the great changes that have occurred in Japan's shareholder structure since the 1980s, when about 70% of shares were estimated to be in stable, non-traded cross-shareholding arrangements. Dividend payouts were set at very low levels, and typically not associated with performance. This resulted in fairly low returns on the stable shareholders' stakes, which could be viewed as a type of insurance premium to be paid for the stability afforded by group membership.[7]

Cross-shareholding also meant mutual forbearance: group members did not interfere in corporate management, and the task of monitoring was delegated exclusively to the main bank. The resulting system of corporate governance has been labeled stakeholder capitalism, where shareholders are but one of the parties interested in the successes of the company, in addition to employees, suppliers, trading partners and customers, banks, and society overall.[8] And all of these stakeholders had the same primary interests, namely the stability and long-term growth of the company. Boards were internal and management oversight limited to distress events. As long as the company was in good standing with its main bank, it could play in the low-profit zone indefinitely. This worked during the go-go years when the entire Japanese economy was rising, but over time it invited slack, hierarchies, office politics, and a lack of focus and drive that eventually undermined Japanese companies' global competitiveness.

Thus, size became the holy grail of postwar Japan, and size was measured in sales. The ministries afforded access to quotas or technology licenses based on size, setting incentives for large firms to expand their business. Banks were eager to offer loans to these companies that were too big to fail. In the absence of profitability or efficiency performance evaluations by the stock market, every sale was a good sale and every point of market share gained was a triumph, no matter the cost. Newspapers ranked companies annually by size of revenues, assets, and sometimes absolute profits, but almost never on financial ratios. Society held large firms in the highest regard, because they hired the most people, and high rankings translated into high social status for their employees. Keidanren's picking order during the *shūkatsu* hiring season was based on size, and university graduates sought large companies because salaries were determined by the size of the company. CEO salaries, too, depended on the size of the company. Size even mattered for the stock price, as there was a common assumption that a larger company should have a higher market capitalization. The management goal of all companies during the go-go years was clear: sell more, no matter the returns.

As companies grew, they built complex industrial spreads that became Japan's industrial base. Initially, these expansions were extensions of the core, such as when Hitachi Ltd., originally an electric machinery company (making motors, turbines, power generators, and excavators), added household goods (from refrigerators and washing machines to toaster ovens). But over time, new business additions became further removed from the core. By the 1980s, Hitachi had amassed over 1,000 subsidiaries, with an empire stretching from *shinkansen* high-speed trains, electricity gridlines, and steel mill and nuclear reactor construction to semiconductors and storage (supercomputing, DRAM), TVs and LCD displays, medical equipment (MRI imaging, DNA sequencing), materials and chemicals, microscopes, batteries, cell phones, and vacuum cleaners. By the 2010s, more than 30 of these subsidiaries were listed companies in their own right, with Hitachi as the majority shareholder.

To keep up with this expansion, Toshiba, an electric machinery and electronics company founded in 1873, likewise invested in businesses ranging from household goods to medical equipment, power generators and nuclear power plants, radar and broadcasting infrastructure, and computer memory. In the 1990s, Toshiba invented the world's first laptop PC, the Dynabook, as well as NAND, also known as flash memory. Similar to Hitachi, by the 1990s Toshiba operated over 900 subsidiaries. This type of business expansion replicated across industries and companies, and it created a large number of huge companies that were everything but agile.[9]

Lifetime employment was a huge contributor to this conglomeration through adding new business units and subsidiaries. Because it was easy to hire people yet impossible to lay anybody off, companies could exit declining businesses only by slowly phasing them out. But because every sale was a good sale, this was not a priority. What is more, until 1998, Japan's accounting rules did not require consolidated accounting. So, companies would only report on their most important or profitable subsidiaries. In this environment, it was just easier to keep all subsidiaries alive than to tackle the difficult task of phasing out units that were not performing well. Correcting this legacy of the postwar years is the core concern of Japan's current business reinvention.

The Mechanisms of Lifetime Employment

Japan has never had a law that outlined lifetime employment, nor was this stable employment associated with unionization. Rather, employees on a "regular" track have had an employment contract that had no end date, as opposed to "non-regular" workers who had time-limited contracts. The long-term nature of these open-ended contracts was established through a series of court decisions in the 1960s that effectively forbade dismissals unless four separate conditions were all met at once: (1) the company was in economic trouble, (2) non-regular workers had already been dismissed, (3) the company union had agreed, and (4) the worker to be dismissed had repeatedly displayed incompetence. In other words, incompetence alone was not grounds for dismissal. Rather, it was the company's responsibility to find a job assignment commensurate with the worker's competence. This made "hiring mistakes" during the *shūkatsu* process very expensive, and explains the risk-averse approach of HR departments in selecting new company employees mostly on the criteria of being polite and a good personality fit with the company. During the economically taxing years in the late 1990s, the courts began to relax their rulings on dismissals somewhat to assure the survival of firms in distress, and today, fulfilling one of the four criteria may be sufficient to win a dismissal case in court. However, dismissals remain difficult and costly, because the courts still tend to side with the employee, and the reputation costs are significant, as layoffs could greatly damage a company's ability to attract top talent in the future.

THE CAREER PATH OF THE SALARYMAN

The core beneficiary of lifetime employment is the salaryman (and more re-cently also the salarywoman). Even today, in large and medium-sized firms, lifetime employment for these career-track, white-collar wage earners is based on a well-defined reciprocal relationship. The company commits to the em-ployee's education, promotion, health and pension, and the salaryman gives up most rights to career planning, including work hours, geographic location, and assignments. In return, the salaryman is assured a good wage and retire-ment with a pension after around 30 years, at age 55. Typically, the company's HR department also helps the employee to find another job upon retirement, through the corporate network.

The career path is quite predictable: upon being hired at around age 22, the salaryman becomes a member of the new incoming class (*dōki*, "same year employee"), and is trained and promoted in lockstep with this group for roughly the first ten years. Not unlike classmates at U.S. universities, the *dōki* become close career allies and a critical resource for connections to other parts of the large organization. The first two years on the salaryman job are an ap-prenticeship period, with HR practices resembling those in the military—and those in *sumō* wrestling stables and other sports, and even *yakuza* (mafia) families—where all employees are treated exactly the same and put to menial tasks, regardless of pedigree or talent. This is part of the socialization aimed to inculcate the company's values and make employees responsive to directions from above. After this boot camp with repeated in-house training seminars, the following eight years on the job include two-year rotations through vari-ous departments and "on-the-job training" to ensure a full understanding of the company's operations and corporate culture. Pensions vest only after ten years with the firm, creating strong incentives to make it through the initial training period.

In the traditional setup, salaries are determined by the size of the company, and pay is based on tenure with the company, not job category. Performance evaluations are the responsibility of the immediate boss and based on effort and attitude; that is, whether an employee is working hard, does the best they can, and behaves appropriately.[10] As is true in many companies around the world, the best strategy for getting ahead is to work long hours, take orders well, sacrifice personal preferences for the team, and perhaps most importantly, make your boss look good. As we will see in Chapter 8, these human resource manage-ment practices were a critical source of Japan's postwar success in high-quality manufacturing, organizational learning and upgrading, and they continue to be valuable today. On the negative side, in ill-managed firms, the generally passive role of Japanese HR offices and in-house unions have long limited employee recourse in instances of so-called power harassment, and bosses have great power to derail an employee's career. Over time, the boot camp uniformity of this approach across all large firms has made the entire system fairly rigid and ripe for adjustments.

In the traditional system, meritocracy enters not through pay but through the quality of assignments and rotations into important divisions of the company. The brightest employees are given two years of special education, such as studying abroad. When, after about ten years of lockstep promotions, almost all classmates have reached the level of *kachō* (section chief), the race to the top begins. For some there will be no further promotions, while others jockey to make it to the level of *buchō* (general manager), in what is often a fierce competition. After about 30 years of faithful service, at around age 55, all members of the class that came in together are asked to retire, and some move on to second jobs, perhaps with a subsidiary or supplier.

The best of the general managers are rehired to join senior management as a "director," on a new, time-limited executive contract. There are several ranks of directors, and a senior manager could be rehired several times, for promotions into the C-suite, and ultimately the top position of president or CEO. With very few recent exceptions, Japanese CEOs are promoted from within, and there is no fluid market for senior managers. As we will see in more detail in Chapter 6, CEO pay is determined as a multiple of a general manager's salary, which is a big reason for Japan's sense of an egalitarian society. In the traditional way of thinking, CEO pay is a reward for a lifetime of service to the company. A common portrait of the Japanese CEO is as a kind, polite, and humble man who sees himself as responsible for the well-being of the company and its workers, more akin to an officer fulfilling a tour of duty than a visionary leader.

In the traditional thinking, employees are expected to be loyal to the company, with limited individual rights. When companies need to transfer employees into new assignments or locations, they often do not consider the employee's wishes. Assignments might include actions that skirt the boundaries of what is acceptable, such as negotiating a price agreement with a competitor or overstating sales in the bookkeeping, as was revealed in several accounting scandals, such as the one involving Toshiba.[11] However, what is remarkable about instances where such scandals have come to light is that the transgressions were typically done for the employer, not for personal gain. Hugh Patrick, the premier Japan economist in the U.S., has observed that in Japan, employees steal *for* the company, not *from* it.[12] In return for their sacrifices and loyalty, the employees expect reciprocity: appropriate treatment, predictable promotions, stable lifetime income, and a pension. Because the corporate pension is central to old age planning, employees fully expect the company to be managed for stability and longevity.

THE TRADITIONAL FAMILY IDEAL

The centrality of lifetime employment translated into a widely shared concept of the ideal family and the role of women. In many ways, the salaryman was similar to the organization man of the 1950s and 1960s in the United States, as was the setup of the ideal-type family in the suburbs. One important difference, however, was that the American mirage included the Horatio Alger rags to riches dream, with opportunities for upward mobility aplenty. In Japan, aspirations to break ranks and make it to the top were less common; rather, the goal was to achieve a comfortable lifestyle and become a member of the stable middle class, with a house, the ability to pay the children's tuition, and a shared sense of equality and safety.

The picture-book Japanese family lived in a small home in the suburbs, which in Tokyo often meant a very long commute on crowded trains for the husband, who worked long hours. Therefore, the wife and mother of, ideally, two children took charge of nearly all household decisions and duties, including finances and caring for her and her husband's aging parents. She was also university educated, and her main pursuit was to get the children into the right schools—in which function she was referred to as the "education mom." The children's placement in kindergarten would almost surely forecast their successes at the *shūkatsu* 18 years later. As the son would be groomed to follow his father into a life as a salaryman, the ideal role of the daughter was to be gentle and obedient, caring, educated (including in calligraphy, ikebana, and the tea ceremony), and the hope was she would marry a young salaryman to perpetuate the ideal.[13] Until the turn of the century, it was rare to meet women on career tracks in large companies, and society's expectations of the role of women have proven difficult to overcome. As we will see in Chapter 9, however, much of this has now begun to change, including the role of the family man, and this in turn is further contributing to Japan's business reinvention.

Non-regular Workers and Job Changers

Lifetime employment was expensive for companies, because it made labor a fixed cost. This necessitated mechanisms to adjust to temporary economic downturns or upswings, beyond assigning employees to new positions at will. One pressure relief valve was to dispatch people to smaller firms in the supplier hierarchies, where salaries were lower. In the case of the Mazda turnaround in the 1970s, salarymen were dispatched to car dealerships to push sales and support the turnaround. A second relief valve has been the cadre of so-called non-regular workers, whose numbers could be more easily adjusted to the business cycle.

"Non-regular" employment is time-limited, usually to no more than three years, and the employer assumes no benefits or other long-term responsibilities for these workers. Because Japan's postwar economy operated at almost full employment, the largest pool of employees for non-regular positions were women and the elderly. For women, after the children leave home for college, the paths to rejoining the workforce are often limited, given their long absence from the systemic progressions and training in ordinary careers. Thus, the only re-entry path is clerical work, and in Japan this has made women the main group of non-regular workers. As of 2018, of Japan's total private sector workforce of 56 million, 35 million were in lifetime positions, and 21 million were on time-limited contracts. Women accounted for 46% of all employed, but 71% of non-regular workers.[14] These levels are very similar to those in other OECD countries, and career options and attitudes are changing now, as we will see in Chapter 9. However, the relevance of this data point lies in how it has long shaped subconscious biases in the workplace as to what role women are supposed to play. These biases continue to be very difficult to overcome.

Other categories of non-regular work include jobbers (e.g., students working in restaurants) and highly specialized contractors. Beginning in the 1970s, the rise of staffing agencies such as Recruit, Persol Tempstaff, Adecco, and Manpower offered new opportunities to find temporary jobs. Yet, as in other countries, they have also contributed to a bifurcated system for younger workers, whereby the temporary workers are paid less, miss out on the benefits of on-the-job training, and are denied benefits beyond general social security.[15] During the stagnation of the 1990s, the portion of employees with time-limited contracts grew steadily to reach about one third of Japan's workforce by 2000.

Still, it stands to note that even though the U.S. organization man has long been replaced with the transaction man, in Japan, as of today, about two thirds of private sector employees remain in employment positions with long-term job security and defined benefits.[16] This has enormous implications for society and the quality of life in Japan, and explains the careful approach Japanese government and industry have taken to adjust the system to the realities of 21st-century labor markets and changing employee needs.

SMALL FIRMS: SUPPLIERS AND SERVICE PROVIDERS

In most countries, small firms constitute a very large portion of the economy. In Japan, too, over the past several decades and to this day, only about 0.3% of companies in Japan are large (defined as having more than 300 employees or paid-in capital of more than about $3 million). However, large firms account for 30% of total employment and 49% of GDP. Their provision of workforce stability has extended to smaller firms through the large companies' networks of associated, stable supplier hierarchies.[17]

Until the globalization of supply chains of the 1990s undermined the logic of domestic supplier relations, almost 80% of Japan's small manufacturing firms were closely related to one large firm buyer, often as an exclusive supplier.[18] For these smaller firms, stability and predictability came through inclusion in the buyer's vertical supplier network. This extended the large firms' social contract obligations to the many small and medium-sized manufacturers and their blue-collar workers. During the postwar years, this meant that the champions' successes trickled through the entire economy. When global manufacturing and sourcing began to challenge this domestic supplier system, many manufacturers felt just as responsible for these smaller firms' employees as for their own, and proceeded slowly as they began to phase out their supplier hierarchies.

This slow approach often caused problems for the large assemblers which struggled to keep costs down. In 1999, the automobile company Nissan faced failure and was bailed out by Renault, the French carmaker, which acquired 37% of Nissan. The incoming CEO, Carlos Ghosn, became known as the *cost killer*, as he introduced global purchasing, cut suppliers, laid off workers, and demanded a 30% cost reduction from core suppliers. As a foreigner, he was seen as having a license to take such drastic measures. But once the precedent was set, other car companies followed suit. This triggered a large-scale restructuring of Japan's small-firm manufacturing base, and the emergence of cost discipline throughout domestic supply chains. This reorganization at the small-firm level is another important aspect of Japan's business reinvention, as well as another explanation for the measured pace at which large companies are repositioning their business operations.

A second group of Japan's very small firms are in the service sector, ranging from construction firms to self-employed operators of small retail outlets and restaurants, and to dry cleaners and public bath houses. Compared to larger firms and their suppliers, their situation has long been more precarious. In 1963, the Small and Medium-Sized Enterprise Agency was established within METI, with the explicit purpose of helping small firms.[19] This translated into an array of financial aid programs and subsidies, including government loan guarantees to facilitate access to credit. The small firms had significant voting power, by sheer number, out of which grew a plethora of small and medium-sized enterprise oriented policies and public loan programs that propped up even businesses that had long lost a viable outlook or purpose, such as small neighborhood stationery stores or greengrocers.

In economic downswings, small stores were also supported by the goodwill of the salaryman consumers and their wives. Then, and perhaps still today, many Japanese had a soft spot for small firms and traditional businesses, partially for sentimental reasons but also out of a sense of fairness: the thinking was that everybody ought to benefit from economic growth.[20] So, even with the arrival of hyper-efficient supermarket chains and other aspects of modernization, many housewives continued to shop at the local greengrocers. It was the kind and considerate thing to do.

Yet, this aspect of Japanese society is also changing, in part due to a generational shift. Many older shopkeepers face succession challenges, as their children often work for larger firms or are not interested in continuing the family business. As we will see in Chapter 7, this succession challenge has given rise to a new type of domestic private equity industry that is contributing to an upgrading in skills and competitiveness of Japan's smaller firms.

The Bubble Economy of 1987–1991: How the Go-Go Years Unraveled

The great successes of the go-go years culminated in an economic bubble—a four-year period of huge real estate and stock market price inflation fueled by easy money and overconfidence. Japan's government, banking, and business leaders became intoxicated with the idea of becoming "Number One"—the world's largest economy. In hindsight, the bubble was caused by a combination of regulatory mistakes, and widespread corporate hubris and recklessness that resulted in fraudulent lending and hyper-speculative investments. As successes piled up, overconfidence led to asset inflation and a subsequent bust of historic proportions.[21]

The backdrop was the trade war that the United States had started in the 1980s, in response to Japan's fast-growing trade surplus (not unlike its trade war with China beginning in 2018). The trade war with Japan lasted over a decade and eventually turned vitriolic, causing many tensions between the two nations. The U.S. argument was that Japan's highly regulated, closed product and financial markets created barriers to trade for U.S. companies and resulted in a weak Japanese yen; both combined to cause the trade surplus. Japan countered that the comparatively lower quality of American products might have something to do with the surplus, but nevertheless made piecemeal concessions, beginning with financial deregulation, in stepwise fashion to assure the stability of the domestic system. At first, only Japan's largest and best companies were allowed to tap into global financial markets, but over the years the rigid financial constraints of the postwar years were removed one by one. Then, in 1985, at the Plaza Hotel in New York City, yen-dollar exchange rate adjustments were agreed upon, and to compensate for the stronger yen, the Bank of Japan initiated an expansive monetary policy by lowering interest rates, fueling a domestic lending frenzy and real estate bubble.

Financial deregulation meant that the large banks lost their former key customers to global markets, and this forced them to turn to new clients. Previously, banks had mostly catered to their well-known, large client companies, in their function as a main bank, which was a fairly low-risk business. Lending to the new, unfamiliar firms required deep skills in credit risk assessments that exceeded the capabilities of most banks. Soon, they ended up lending to domestic developers and companies that were simply gaming the stepwise financial deregulation.[22] This eventually developed into full-blown financial pyramid schemes, as many believed that land prices would only go up, based on the dubious notion that Japan, as an island country, would face eternal excess demand for space. By 1990, the Imperial Palace in central Tokyo, with a circumference of less than four miles, was valued at more than the entirety of California real estate.[23] Misled by buoyancy, Japan's largest companies wasted shiploads of hard-earned cash on international acquisitions, many of which were simply expensive real estate trophies, such as Hawaiian hotels and shopping malls and office buildings in downtown Los Angeles, and perhaps most famously, Mitsubishi Estates' fateful 1989 purchase of the Rockefeller Center in New York City.

Realizing that easy money had fueled dangerous asset speculation, in late 1990, the Bank of Japan launched a rapid sequence of interest rate increases that signaled the end of the party. Many of the pyramid schemes collapsed, and the heavily leveraged companies were unable to cover their rising interest payments. By August 1990, the Nikkei 225 index had plummeted to half its peak, and asset prices also began to fall. By the time the dust settled, real estate prices had fallen 87% nationwide, and more in the big cities. Most of the bank lending during the bubble years had been based on inflated real estate values and included irresponsible projects, such as loans for a golf course in the steep, snowy mountains of Northern Honshu. As asset prices kept falling, the rug was pulled out from under the entire system, and the banks found themselves sitting on a mountain of nonperforming loans.

The financial collapse then triggered a massive banking crisis that lasted until 2003. Several very large banks were nationalized, others collapsed. So deep ran the shame over the failures that, shockingly, several bank executives committed suicide. The same Japanese banks that just a few years earlier had been among the largest in the world now received government infusions and were forced to merge. The top 20 banks eventually consolidated into six large financial groups. This blurred the previous boundaries of the six business groups. With the exception of the Mitsubishi group, the large *keiretsu* lost their strategic meaning.[24]

The biggest challenge for the newly combined banking groups was how to write off their mountains of nonperforming loans. The full extent of the bad loan debacle was never fully known because Japan at the time had neither a clear definition of a delinquent loan, nor obligatory accounting of subsidiaries, including in the banking system. It was later estimated that the loss of national wealth in stock holdings and real estate alone was equivalent to three years of 1989 GDP—not accounting for the overpaid acquisitions, wasted investments, losses from the creation of deadweight assets, or opportunity costs of not building new business capabilities. In comparison, during the Great Depression the United States lost national wealth equivalent to roughly one year of 1929 GDP.[25]

The nonperforming loans weakened the banks to the point where they could no longer come to the rescue of even their largest clients, and this began to trigger corporate bankruptcies, large and small. The banks began to foreclose on borrowers and, in an effort to gain at least some value, to sell off underlying collateral assets at fire sale prices. Foreign financial firms rushed to Japan to pick up the pieces, and this completely altered the composition and motivation of shareholders in Japan's largest companies, as we will see in Chapter 6.

One may wonder how such a bubble could happen in Japan's tight-culture setting, with its strong leanings toward *anzen dai-ichi* (risk aversion) and slow and careful decision making. The bubble years also brought a series of scandals that were clearly in violation of Japan's norms of appropriate behavior: corruption and graft, even among bureaucrats and politicians, ran rampant; bank officers ignored the rules for loan approvals; the race for market share and the herding behavior it begot lost all nuance; irrational gambling in financial markets exploded; and executives were splurging on expense accounts. If there is one story that captures the extent of the craze, it is that of the Dark Lady of Osaka, Nui Onoe, a bar owner of modest education, who at one point became the nation's single largest individual shareholder after she amassed over $4 billion in investment assets through a Ponzi scheme based on the stock market forecasting skills of her ceramic toad.[26]

One interpretation of this disconnect is that the bubble was a psychological folly that resulted in a mass deviation from Japan's norms, as if the country's entire political and business leadership had loosened up at the beer restaurants and karaoke bars. An economic interpretation might cast the root of the bubble as the result of moral hazard. Businesses and banks overly relied on their mutual insurance schemes for protection from risky financial bets. After 30 years of growth based on well-developed government processes to provide stability, combined with many safety mechanisms through the main banks and *keiretsu*, a perception had been created that risk was socialized across the entire system.[27] During the bubble, politicians, bureaucrats, bankers, CEOs, and managers all lost their normative radar and miscalculated the risk that the system could falter.

The Aftermath

The collapse of the bubble economy around 1991 was initially met with denial: the collapse of stock prices had to be a temporary phenomenon, and robust growth would surely return! To the contrary, the situation continued to deteriorate. In 1995, a sizable regional bank and two major credit unions collapsed, followed in 1997 by a large city bank and a major investment bank. In 1998, two major banks for long-term credit were nationalized. Emergency legislation released about $90 billion to large banks to avoid a financial meltdown. It took until 2005 for the banking sector to consolidate, restructure, and clean up its nonperforming loans.[28]

The tipping point toward business reinvention was reached in 1998, when the banking crisis combined with the arrival of new global competition, a social crisis, and a sudden ineffectiveness of government policies. Together, these revealed that the postwar system had run its course. Large companies suffered from a "triple overhang": too many people, nonperforming loans, and non-core assets. The highly diversified conglomerates they had built during the go-go years were suddenly too large, spread too thinly across too many business segments, and too ossified in their management structures. This translated into dismal performance numbers. In the early 2000s, Japan's listed companies posted a median operating margin of less than 5%, and often zero net income.[29] These poor performers included Japan's flagship companies. For example, for the decade between 2000 and 2009, Fujitsu's consolidated 10-year average operating margin was 2.6%, barely exceeding Hitachi's of 2.1% and NEC's of 1.8%. The only reason these companies were able to weather the slump was that they had recurring profits from legacy clients and government services. In terms of ROE (return on equity), Japan's average for large firms stood at around 8% in 1981, 6% in the early 1990s, and a paltry 3% in 2000, compared to a range of 15% to 20% in the United States.[30] Clearly, the large firms had lost their ability to create value and earn profits.

There are two main reasons why the recovery was slow and such dismal corporate performance continued for two decades. The first is strategic: as we will see in Chapter 4, to adjust to the changing global environment, Japanese companies needed to find new ways to compete. The necessary restructuring, however, required changes in corporate and employment laws, and these were phased in over a long period, between 1998 and 2006. Therefore, companies could not just write off the excesses from the bubble period but had to restructure and then phase them out through attrition.

What is more, at this time of national crisis, the country fully expected companies to stand by their responsibilities for their employees, as much as they could. Large-scale layoffs were an option only if a firm found itself on the brink of bankruptcy. This reflected a societal preference for how best to tackle this crisis, namely a preference for securing the livelihoods of many over seeking a quick recovery with stark social costs. Most companies retained as many employees as they could even if they were no longer needed, and the government tried to carry small firms even if they were no longer viable. In their roles as voters, shareholders, managers, shop owners, and employees, people signaled their preference for a gradual approach. The costs of doing so were high: two seemingly lost decades with low economic growth, low productivity, mounting government debt, a stagnant stock market, and a sinking feeling of being overlooked by the world. But as we look back today, maintaining political, economic, and societal stability as much as possible may have benefited Japan greatly in the long run, due to the cost savings from limiting social displacement.

Distress without Riots

Not all firms and people could be saved. At the turn of the century, layoffs became unavoidable, and many small firms went bankrupt. The bank failures were most acutely felt by small firms that lacked the reserves to carry on when banks closed credit lines. When several large firms collapsed—such as retailers Daiei and MyCal, which had built their empires on private-label goods and multilevel domestic supply chains—they pulled their exclusive suppliers with them into the abyss. In addition, the globalization of supply chains threatened many third- and fourth-tier suppliers. Figure 3.3 shows the number of corporate bankruptcies and the unemployment rate, and also the suicide rate, for the years 1991 to 2018. Between 1998 and 2001, bankruptcies in Japan reached the highest level on record, with over 19,000, and in 2000 alone. Total write-offs exceeded $220 billion. Small and medium-sized firms accounted for roughly 98% of these cases, and 50% of liabilities. The mega failures included two life insurance companies, wiping out a tremendous amount of private savings.[31] This economic collapse caused social anxieties and great distress, as manifested in rising levels of the homeless and of day laborers, and an uptick in robberies, domestic abuse, alcoholism, depression, and suicides.[32]

Yet, in spite of this great personal and societal suffering, the country's social and political underpinnings remained fundamentally intact. Even as a growing segment of society was affected by the fallout, there was no panic, no rioting, no rise of aggressive populism, and no significant rise in income inequality, as we saw in Figure 1.1 in Chapter 1. This reaction was completely different from what was experienced in the United States after the 2008 global financial crisis, including public expressions of anger and activism, the Occupy Wall Street movement, and a turn toward populist politicians. Japan's tight culture played

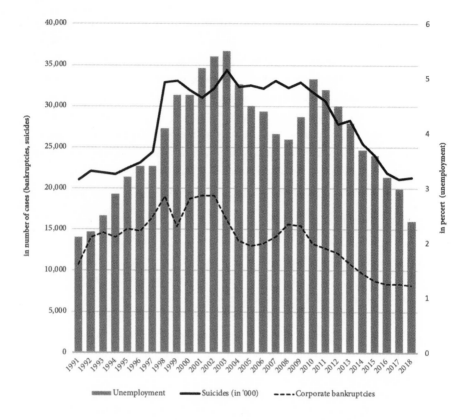

Figure 3.3. Indicators of Social Distress, 1991–2018: Unemployment, Corporate Bankruptcies, and Suicides. Sources: Statistics Bureau, Labor Force Survey Results; Tokyo Shoko Research, Corporate Bankruptcy Situation Nationwide; Ministry of Health, Labour, and Welfare, Suicide Statistics.

an important role here: just as during a major earthquake, most people viewed the economic collapse as a time to suffer as a society, not to look out for only oneself or exploit the crisis for personal advancement. The main agenda was to dampen the blow and limit social displacement for all.

As already mentioned, this slow adjustment led some foreign observers to label the 1990s and early 2000s in Japan lost decades—terminology that was also picked up in Japan, as impatience with the slow recovery grew. In particular, younger people, those born after the bubble years, found it difficult to understand why their fathers or uncles would willingly show up for work on a daily basis for companies that were clearly in dire need of restructuring. A sense began to form among the millennials that they wanted something new.

But upon closer examination, for companies the two lost decades were not lost at all; rather, this was a period of steady, careful, and deliberate transformation. Over twenty years, Japanese business figured out new ways to compete within Asia, and to respond to the rise of China and the globalization of supply chains. At the end of this strategic repositioning, many Japanese companies have reemerged as critical providers of high-technology inputs and components in the Asian supply chains. The slow pace of renewal prevented large-scale social losses, and the entire transition took place with only modest increases in unemployment. By around 2010, the various indicators of social distress began to fall and to return to pre-crisis levels.

The scars of the bubble disaster run deep and have planted a certain distrust, among businesspeople and in society overall, in stock price as a relevant goal to pursue. Of course, a company's stock price is important for global competition and finance, and it can be helpful as a means to compare companies and assess corporate relevance. But as we will see in Chapter 6, stock options are still not an important part of executive pay, and stock repurchases just to increase a company's market cap are viewed with great skepticism. If there is a silver lining to the disaster of the bubble and its aftermath, it may be that it has infused Japan with a sober view of the value of chasing the stock price.

THE CORE CONCEPT

Aggregate Niche Strategy

Prior to the Tohoku earthquake and Fukushima disaster on March 11, 2011, the general global sentiment was that Japan had lost its economic relevance, because its share of global manufacturing output was "only" 10%. But as the world woke up to hear that northern Japan was in a nuclear crisis, it also suddenly realized that a large portion of that 10% consisted of critical inputs needed to make products such as LCD panels, semiconductors, batteries, and medical devices. In some of these products, Japanese companies held a combined 100% global market share. The earthquake threatened these supplies and brought home the point that made-in-Japan inputs were much more critical than the 10% figure might suggest.[1]

In 2011, the Tohoku area was home to more than 30 precision machinery and medical device factories, over ten chemical and materials plants, three large auto plants, and more than 20 auto parts suppliers. Overall, the region accounted for an estimated 10% of Japan's electronic parts and device production, and 3% of its transportation machinery output.[2] In addition to the physical damage to these factories from the earthquake, the region's electricity, logistics, and manpower were interrupted. These companies reacted to the disaster very much in line with Japan's business norms. They apologized for causing an inconvenience, as if the earthquake were their fault. They assured their global customers that they would do everything in their might to quickly rebuild and restart. And miraculously, within three months, they delivered! Teamwork among companies was part of the restructuring effort. For example, weeks of aftershocks meant that the robots in these plants had to be recalibrated repeatedly, which required the dispatch of expert staff. To expedite this process, the engineers at FANUC, Japan's preeminent factory automation company and maker of many of these industrial robots, worked day and night to develop new software so that the robots could recalibrate themselves, and then FANUC donated this innovation to the affected producers.[3]

One example of the global bottleneck caused by the earthquake concerned Renesas Electronics, a company created in 2010 through a merger of the semiconductor operations of NEC, Hitachi, and Mitsubishi Electric. It is one of the world's largest producers of microcontrollers (abbreviated to *mi-cons* in Japan) with a 44% global share of automobile mi-cons. These chips control everything electronic in your car, from the airbags, air conditioning, dashboard gauges, and audio and navigation to the critical engine control unit, without which your car would not run. Mi-cons are customized for each make and model, and these specialized chips cannot be bought elsewhere. In 2011, Renesas operated eight plants in Tohoku, all of which were damaged during the earthquake. Seven were repaired in one month, but in the largest plant, in Naka, the damage was so severe that the CEO thought it would take over one year to rebuild. This plant was known for the highest quality metrics in the world, and its long-term closure would have brought almost half of global car production to a standstill. To avert this outcome, all Tohoku companies, led by the carmakers, asked their employees to volunteer to help Renesas. A steady stream of people participated—at the high point, 2,500 showed up—working overtime day, night, and weekend shifts to rebuild the factory. It reopened on June 1, 2011, less than three months after the earthquake.[4] This was not an isolated incident; similar stories were repeated several times over, so that at most factories, production resumed within several weeks of the earthquake.

One reason for these efforts was the concern that global competitors might catch up and lure buyers away; however, this did not happen. In fact, in many market segments Japanese companies have become even more critical to global supply chains. This was brought to the fore in the 2019 trade spat between Japan and South Korea. Dismayed by continued requests to compensate South Korea for World War II damages, Japan threw a major punch on July 4, 2019, when it removed three specialty chemicals from a "white list" of products previously traded freely between the two countries, meaning they now required an export license, which can take up to 90 days to process. There was much finger-pointing on both sides, but whatever its root cause, the dispute threatened to disrupt global trade. The specialty chemicals in question were fluorinated polyimide, hydrogen fluoride, and photoresist, and they are highly valuable: a gallon of top-notch photoresist can cost as much as a midsized car.

Japanese companies command over 80% of the global market for these advanced chemicals, and 100% at the top end, namely the ultrapure fluoride etching gas needed to make high-performance semiconductors. In photoresists, Japanese companies, led by JSR and TOK, hold about 90% of the world market.[5] In 2019, these materials accounted for $6 billion in annual shipments, or about 12%, of Japanese exports to South Korea. While that may sound small, the impact was huge: the slowdown threatened to hold up the production of current chips as well as the development of next-generation, 5G semiconductors by Samsung and SK Hynix. These components in turn are also indispensable for products made by American companies like Apple Inc.

In response, South Korea's government funded a program to spur the domestic production of such chemicals, but it was widely doubted that this plan would succeed any time soon. Japanese companies have been building their capabilities for semiconductor production since the 1970s and are the world's leading suppliers for a reason. Making specialty chemicals is akin to cooking a very difficult recipe: it is difficult to do at high levels of purity and consistency, and requires significant experience and tacit knowledge that builds over time. The resulting soup cannot simply be disassembled, reverse-engineered, and copied. And unlike cooking a difficult recipe at home, these chemicals are volatile and can be toxic and corrosive.

The above events are all expressions of Japan's new competitive advantage in the global economy: strength in critical input materials and components that others cannot easily copy. Because the value of these components is not fully captured by trade data, or marked by a "Japan Inside" label, these dependencies come as a surprise to many. For Japanese companies, they have been in the making for two decades and are now coming to fruition.

This chapter explains how the rise of South Korea, Taiwan, and China since the 1990s has created new Northeast Asian dynamics in competition and collaboration. This has required Japanese companies to transition from being exporters of consumer gadgets to global "Japan Inside" suppliers. The chapter begins by outlining the changing competitive dynamics in Asia that obviated Japan's postwar growth strategies. It then shows how the strategy of building a string of aggregate niches in input materials came about, and explains its two main components—strategic repositioning and organizational renewal.

Government reforms between 1998 and 2006 enabled the choose-and-focus renewal, and in the 2010s, Abenomics created a new urgency to manage for change. The chapter ends with case studies of Panasonic and Sony that highlight some of the Japan-specific challenges with reinvention: both companies have launched multiple attempts at choose-and-focus and, in spite of steep losses, are still struggling with exiting some of their original lines of business.

We will see that the aggregate niche strategy was not something that was planned or organized; rather, slowly and methodically, one company after the other began to move upstream into technology niches that, in the aggregate, now afford competitive advantage in the new global and Asian market dynamics. This transformation has proceeded slowly. The chapter ends on the question of whether this slow approach, while costly, is perhaps the right way to go about corporate restructuring, as both Panasonic and Sony have not only continued to provide stability in hard times and create value and employment, but are also beginning to reemerge as strong competitors.

The Need to Change: New Competitive Dynamics in Asia

Japan's bubble economy burst just when the global competitive environment changed so dramatically that it rendered Japan's postwar business models obsolete. The rise of South Korea and Taiwan as direct competitors in industries from electronics and semiconductors to steel and automobiles and the rise of China as the "factory of the world" combined to beat Japan at its own game— mass-producing high-quality consumer goods and their input parts, such as semiconductors. Suddenly, Japan's companies were no longer cost-competitive in mainstay household electronics, except perhaps in the luxury categories. Japan's response, in turn, has brought about completely new dynamics of competition and collaboration in Northeast Asia.

In order to compete against South Korea, Taiwan, and China, Japanese companies now have to constantly upgrade into higher technology realms. We can see how this has already happened over the past two decades in automobiles, such as Toyota's Lexus and Prius models, in specialty steel and chemicals, or in high-end infrastructure installations, such as trains and satellites. But upgrading alone is not enough; to stay abreast and make up for the market loss of basic end products, Japanese companies also need to add a new layer on top of this base, one that affords deep competitive advantage. This means advancing into areas where Japanese companies can be leaders in new technologies that their Asian competitors cannot make, at least in the medium run, or do not want to make because they would take too long to scale. Fine chemicals, advanced materials, and high-end components such as sensors are examples of product categories where Japanese companies have strong, accumulated tacit knowledge, experience, and specialized skills. Some of these are fairly small product niches, but they are critical and earn high margins. Japan's new strategy, then, is the pursuit of a series of niches that, in the aggregate, result in a sizable and lucrative presence on the innovative frontier, ahead of the East Asian competitors.

GLOBAL SUPPLY CHAINS

The trigger for this shift was the globalization of supply chains that began in the 1990s. In business strategy, the value chain is a framework for breaking down the production process into distinct stages of value creation, and then analyzing the costs and value capture (profit) of each stage.[6] Until the mid-1990s, most value chains were based within one country and even within one company. Most manufacturing companies relied on in-house production sequences from R&D and product design to actual production to sales. Insofar as they outsourced parts, they relied on local or national suppliers. Since the 1990s, however, a steep decline in the costs of transportation and logistics, modularization of products into fairly standardized components, and increased pressure for cost reductions combined with the removal of political trade barriers to make global sourcing and production more economical. Companies began to locate the various stages of production to wherever in the world they could be performed at the best price-performance ratio, and sourced their parts from global suppliers.

The strategy takeaway from the value chain framework is that not all stages of productions are equally valuable. Unique technologies and mastery of a difficult production process translate into higher value added and earn higher margins, and companies can win in the long run if they can capture a position in the higher value-added, more difficult stages. Thus, the dominant manufacturing model shifted from building in-house capabilities and maintaining a local supplier base to managing a global manufacturing network and outsourcing each input part or stage of production to the best location worldwide. The requisite management skills shifted from local operations management and expertise in exporting to running a vast network of global production sites. This first occurred in industries with high degrees of modularization and standardization, led by electronics and automobiles, Japan's leading export industries. It then extended to tools, plastics and textiles, glass, and ceramics, and by 2000, in industry after industry, supply chains had globalized, upheaving local suppliers and demanding very different purchasing and supply chain operations skills from the large assemblers.

THE SMILE CURVE

The rise of China as the factory of the world then brought tremendous price competition. Industry lore has it that in the early 1990s, this situation led the founder of the Taiwanese computer company Acer to draw the "smile curve of profits" on the back of a napkin (see Figure 4.1.). This curve expresses the profit potential for each stage of the production process of a manufactured item, with the highest margins earned upstream (design, components, production machinery) and downstream (retail). Acer's CEO was concerned that his company was stuck at the bottom of the curve, in assembly, where the margins are lowest, and where mainland Chinese firms would soon dominate.

The smile curve has since become a staple of Japanese government reports and strategy discussions, as it so aptly describes the competitive dynamics in Asia, as well as Japan's specific challenges in repositioning into new areas of core competence. For Japan, being the largest general assembler of a variety of consumer end products has become a losing proposition. Japanese CEOs are realizing that the only way to compete against companies such as Samsung and LG Electronics in South Korea, Acer and Asus in Taiwan, and Haier, Gree Electric, and Hisense in China is to move into the upstream, difficult-to-make, and difficult-to-imitate segments of the supply chain.

The Business Reinvention

While it is easy to see that building upstream core competencies affords new advantages, the management challenges in making this upward shift are Herculean. They can be broken into two separate steps: (1) focus the organization on a set of upgraded or new core competencies, and (2) manage organizational renewal and culture change to build new processes for exploration and innovation. Refocusing means that companies have to design a new corporate strategy, while managing culture change refers to executing the new strategy through an internal redesign of work processes, skills, incentives, and corporate culture so that they foster breakthrough innovation.

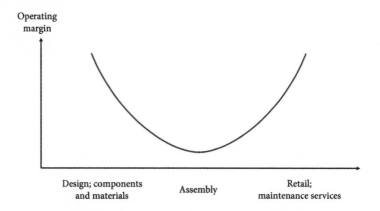

Figure 4.1. The "Smile Curve" of Profits in Manufacturing.

STRATEGIC REPOSITIONING

The first step of Japan's reinvention calls for redesigning corporate strategy and articulating new ways to win. This involves four separate disciplines. First, the company must identify a group of core businesses, which may be existing or new. Next, the company needs to exit all other, non-core businesses, by selling or dissolving them. Meanwhile, the core businesses need to be strengthened, which may be done organically, by investing in facilities and people, or through acquiring market leaders in the business. Once this is accomplished, the new core needs to become the springboard for extension, through stretching and leveraging those core capabilities, into new, competitive businesses. This requires new approaches to R&D.

At the turn of the century, Japan's business buzzword was choose-and-focus (*sentaku to shūchū*), which referred to the first wave of unraveling the postwar conglomerates.[7] Between 2000 and 2006, an estimated 75% of Japan's largest 500 companies conducted at least one measure of reorganization, and 34% reported at least one business exit. Some companies embarked on these reforms right away, while others, such as electronics makers Sanyo, Pioneer, and Sharp, missed them entirely and were eventually acquired by other firms. Those who did launch began by cutting the low-hanging fruit, that is, non-core businesses entered during the delirious bubble economy years—such as Nippon Steel's semiconductor business, or Sony's French restaurant chain, Maxim's de Paris.

But housecleaning alone is insufficient to build new core technologies and stay ahead in Asia. That is why, in the late 2010s, we are seeing a second wave of choose-and-focus for true repositioning and pivoting of core businesses to compete in the digital economy. This requires the much more difficult exit of businesses that used to be the company's core products, and often define its traditional identity. This strategic pivot often runs into deep-seated vested interests within the company and requires clear direction and strong leadership.

For instance, the former Fuji Photo Film Co. is now Fujifilm, a $23 billion company and successful competitor in fine chemicals for electronics, medical devices, and other product categories built on an enduring core competence in surface chemistry. It was founded in 1934 and went on to become one of two world leaders in analog photographic film. At the turn of the century, the company realized that digital photography would soon wipe out the film business, and it began to move aggressively into the chemical films needed for LCD screens, and then expanded into semiconductor materials, medical devices (endoscopes, imaging technologies), cosmetics, and regenerative medicine. Its main competitor, Eastman Kodak, which declared bankruptcy in 2012, was just as cognizant of the disruption coming to the analog film business, but could not overcome internal resistance to letting the traditional business die; Fujifilm was fortunate to have a strong CEO at its helm at the time.[8]

ORGANIZATIONAL RENEWAL

Reorganizing business units is one thing; driving change throughout the organization and building a new corporate identity is quite another. To conquer and defend the high-value niches, Japanese companies have to develop so-called deep technologies, defined as inventions on the frontier of technological breakthroughs. These typically require large investments and are highly uncertain as they may not yet have a defined commercial application. This is very different from existing processes of incremental innovation. Thus, the second leg of Japan's business reinvention is to add new processes that help companies build a culture around speedy, risk-taking, creative research and business development endeavors to complement existing strengths with breakthrough innovation.

Importantly, this is not about replacing old with new, but rather creating a new structure that allows the company the dual approach of keeping and enhancing existing strengths while also building new ways to compete in future business segments. To do this, companies need to build new corporate cultures and new structures that allow the coexistence of mature and path-breaking processes and help employees embrace new diversity. As discussed in Chapter 2, managing this change in a tight culture requires a special playbook and a particular rollout, as well as decisive and visionary leadership. All of these aspects are new to most Japanese companies.

More specifically, this means that Japanese companies need to add to their existing *monozukuri* culture of making things well a new breakthrough innovation culture that pushes the organization further ahead in the East Asian competition. Manufacturing is usually about scaling, cost-cutting, steady low-variance output, and attention to shopfloor process detail. In contrast, pushing the technology frontier requires processes that encourage risk-taking, innovation, diversity, and contrarian thinking, as captured in Facebook's rallying cry to "move fast and break things." As will be picked up later in Chapter 8, it is important that companies do both, under one roof and as a dual strategy, because if they do not constantly explore new opportunities, or do not integrate new businesses into their existing operations, they will not survive in the long run.[9] They also cannot just switch over entirely to a new business, because they need the current business as an anchor, a source for resources to fund the new explorations, and a technology base.

The Move to "Japan Inside"

An important part of the story of how Japanese industry began to move upstream on the smile curve is the technology strength of the supplier hierarchies that had developed since the 1970s. Traditionally, Japan's large manufacturers relied on sizable supplier networks, and their top-tier suppliers were world-class competitors, with skills ranging from materials and components (e.g., camera lenses, glass substrates, masks, disks, memory storage), membranes, and polymers for electronics, to complicated advanced metals and metal parts, connectors, converters, semiconductors, and capacitators. At the turn of the century, even as some of the large brand-name producers were slow to pivot, their suppliers were much quicker on their feet.

The prime example of this dynamic comes from the mobile phone industry. You may recall that in the late 1990s, Japan's cell phone industry was the world's technology leader. In 1999, NTT DoCoMo developed i-mode, the world's first cell phone technology that allowed access to internet websites in html mode, meaning that websites did not need to be formatted for phone use. Industry lore has it that the ideas to attach a camera to a cell phone and to offer text messaging also originated in Japan, because high school girls, known for their consumer savvy, wanted to save their friends' phone numbers with a picture and also be able to communicate constantly, even while in public transit, where talking is considered a *meiwaku* (nuisance). Yet, in spite of their head start, Japan's large electronics manufacturers greatly misread the technology shift in the cell phone industry and lost the smartphone battle by sticking with clamshell flip phones.[10] Still, their suppliers were the best in the world. When Apple developed the iPhone, which launched in 2007, it found a cluster of top-notch technologies in Japan. Even as Sony lost to Apple, Japan's supplier base conquered the inside of the iPhone.

Thus began the "Japan Inside" era in cell phones. In the 2010s, the stereotypical pathway of the new Asian supply chain in electronics begins in Japan, which exports high-tech materials and fine chemicals to South Korea and Taiwan, where input parts, such as LCD panels, are produced (with Japanese production equipment). These parts are then shipped to China for final assembly and exported to global consumer markets, including the United States. In the early 2010s, an estimated 34% of the value added in building the actual phone was generated in Japan, followed by 17% in Germany, 13% in South Korea, 6% in the United States, and only 3.6% in China.[11] And these figures do not include the basic materials or complicated components or the machinery required to build certain parts.

A decade later, in June 2019, the *Nikkei Shinbun* (Japan's leading business paper) did a similar assessment for the top-level Huawei cell phone, and again, Japan was a main supplier of critical components. The total number of parts was 1,631, and production cost was estimated at $364. Chinese firms contributed 38% of the value added in 80 parts, the United States accounted for 16% (15 parts), and South Korea and Taiwan supplied 8% each (562 and 83 parts, respectively). Japanese companies made 23% of the value added, with 869 parts, including all four cameras, made by Sony. Not assessed were filters, oscillators, vibrators, and battery contacts, all from Japan.[12] Moreover, this study did not assess how many of the parts from South Korea, Taiwan, and China were built with input materials from Japan, such as the flash memory and sensors for the fingerprint unit, and the advanced materials needed for the production of chips and batteries.

While the "Japan Inside" impact is difficult to track through the supply chain, it is reflected in trade statistics, as shown in Figure 4.2. As of 2016, Japan had a large trade surplus with South Korea and Taiwan, and both, in turn, had large trade surpluses with China (including Hong Kong) even as the trade between China and Hong Kong on the one hand and Japan on the other was balanced. We will see more on the details of Japan's trade and business relations in Asia in Chapter 5.

THE AGGREGATED NICHES

Japan's centrality to Asia's supply chains is by no means limited to smartphones. "Japan Inside" has since been repeated in industry after industry. Japanese companies dominate global market share in small electric motors in cars, such as for seats, windows, and wipers (estimated at 80%), vehicle power steering (40%), carbon fiber (66%), and advanced sensors (between 40% and 70%, depending on type). For certain areas of medical and office automation equipment, Japan's combined global share exceeds 70%. Although some of these product segments may be small, they are critical for the production of other goods. And in addition to contributing to exports, they also feed into Japan's own industrial base, helping to make Japan's largest companies competitive.

To assess the country's global impact through these niches, for the past two decades Japan's Ministry of Economy, Trade and Industry (METI) has commissioned studies of the combined global market shares of Japanese companies in a variety of product and input categories. The first study was done in 2003, and showed that while Japanese firms had already largely relinquished the market for household electronics, they dominated the inputs, making up 51% in components, and 70% in materials.[13]

This assessment has since been repeated and expanded, and its 2018 edition underscores Japan's dominance in a variety of critical products.[14] An analysis of 931 global markets across a wide range of industries and product categories revealed that, as of 2017, Japanese companies had over 50% of global market share in 309 products, over 75% in 112 products, and 100% in 57 products. In other words, Japanese companies dominate at least 478 distinct, global, high-technology product markets.

All this adds up to a sizable volume of economic value creation. Not counting large end product categories, such as automobiles (where Japanese companies account for almost a third of global sales), the average global size of the 900 input product markets under study was about $4 billion, and Japan's combined average market share across these 900 products was about

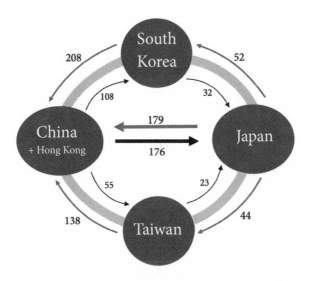

Figure 4.2. Trade Relations in Northeast Asia in 2018, in billions of US$. Sources: United Nations International Trade Statistics Database; Bureau of Foreign Trade, Ministry of Economic Affairs of Taiwan.

50%, or $2 billion per niche. These product markets range from huge to tiny, so there is large variation, and the companies involved also range from huge multinational enterprises that sell into multiple niches to smaller, very focused suppliers. Their names are often unknown to industry outsiders, as they are B2B (business-to-business) suppliers, and the products they supply end up in other products that do not carry their labels. But many of them are Japan's leading global manufacturers, listed companies that are well-known, large employers within Japan. Thus, it would be erroneous to think of these suppliers as small "hidden champions," a concept that refers to small, unknown firms that occupy global niches.[15] Rather, Japan's competitors in Asian supply chains run the entire gamut, and they are often neither small nor hidden. In particular in the chemicals industry, they are well-known within Japan and often operate sizable plants. Moreover, these numbers refer to the combined global market shares of Japanese firms, and not all of these products are made within Japan. Thus, the aggregate niche strategy also explains the growing global production network by Japanese companies.

What is more, most of the product categories where Japanese companies dominate global markets are in critical technology areas, from continuously variable car transmissions and spherical lenses for endoscopes to blanks for the manufacturing of hard disk drives, car batteries, and cell phone parts such as isolators and capacitators. Just counting the upstream materials that anchor the production of other input parts, Japanese companies have a global market share exceeding 50% in 97 top upstream products, and in 212 midstream inputs. Next time you climb on an airplane, note that while the plane itself was most likely made in either the United States or Europe, Japanese companies have a 50% global market share in 18 inputs, ranging from very small items such as fasteners to the carbon fiber for the Boeing 787 fuselage. And when you use a battery-powered device, also note that Japanese firms combine to dominate global markets in 16 essential battery materials.

The aggregate niche strategy adds a new dimension to Japan's global leadership beyond manufacturing. But it is not limited to making things. Companies are now extending this concept into digital economy segments such as systems engineering, digital manufacturing, and edge computing. Chapter 10 will shed more light on these new developments.

EXAMPLE: JSR CORPORATION—
FROM RUBBER SOLES TO PHOTORESISTS AND ANTIBODIES

A representative example of Japan's new type of competitor in the "Japan Inside" sector is the JSR Corporation, which turned itself from a supplier for the auto tire industry into a global leader in polymers, selling a host of materials needed in the production of semiconductors and LCD panels. JSR is also the world's premier producer of photoresists, which put it in the crossfire of the 2019 Japan-Korea trade dispute. The company was established in 1957 as Nihon Gōsei Gomu (Japan Synthetic Rubber) by Shōjirō Ishibashi, the entrepreneurial founder of Bridgestone Corporation, to explore the use of synthetic rubbers in auto tires with the goal of reducing the need for natural rubber imports. Because synthetic rubber is heavily dependent on oil, the OPEC oil shocks of the 1970s threatened JSR's viability. To reduce its dependency on oil, JSR developed new capabilities in polymers, and particularly in fine chemicals for the electronics industry, and today uses this proprietary polymer technology to manufacture elastomers, plastics and materials for semiconductors, and flat-panel displays. This knowledge also served as a gateway into the life sciences in the early 2000s.

Today, JSR runs a global network of plants and research facilities, often located close to main buyers. In addition to synthetic rubber for tires, hoses, belts, and auto parts, JSR makes elastomers for use in soles for shoes such as sneakers, and emulsions such as synthetic latex. In 2019, total sales were $4.5 billion, with elastomers representing 40% of sales and about 15% of total profits. The so-called digital solutions made up 30% of sales and over 50% of profits, and JSR's U.S. subsidiary in Silicon Valley, JSRMicro, has repeatedly been awarded Intel's supplier quality award for the consistent quality of its lithographic materials.[16] The new life sciences segment, while still small with 9% of sales and 5% of profits, forecasts the future with areas such as in-vitro diagnostics and reagents, bioprocessing, and antibodies.

Overall, Japan's chemicals industry is a large, profitable industry that employs over 860,000 people, and contributes 14% of manufacturing shipments.[17] Companies range from the better-known Mitsubishi Chemical Holdings, Sumitomo Chemical, Toray, Teijin, and Asahi Kasei, to the less advertised though equally innovative Nitto Denko, DIC, and Kaneka. Almost all of these firms dominate certain global niches, meaning that the New Japan is taking on a new face and new names. In the digital solutions segments, JSR's main competitors are also Japanese, such as Toyo Ink, Nissan Chemical, Chisso, and Osaka Organic Chemical in photosensitive spacers and protective coatings. TOK, Shin-Etsu Chemical, Fujifilm, and Sumitomo Chemical also compete in related niches. Even though you may not have heard of some of these companies before, you are probably in touch with their products every day.

The 1998 Strategic Inflection and the Koizumi Boom

JSR is an example of successful change over time, but not all companies have fared as well. After the bursting of the bubble economy in the 1990s, many firms struggled to find their competitive edge. In their defense, efforts at strategic repositioning were initially held back by century-old regulations that made even simple moves such as spinning out a subsidiary difficult and costly. The postwar stability maxim had been that companies could add a new business easily, whereas exiting a business was nearly impossible. It was not until the 1998 banking crisis brought widespread distress and pushed many companies to the edge that the courts began to soften their interpretation of when layoffs were acceptable, in order to allow downsizing if it saved a company.

The turn of the century saw a polarization of companies into reformers and laggards. Several of the largest traditional companies were slow to realize that the stability and insurance mechanisms of the postwar years had become liabilities. Continuing their reliance on safety mechanisms such as the main banks and business networks offered a certain insurance even with rapidly declining competitiveness. But their lack of restructuring made these laggards look increasingly bloated, and their business groups less useful for the reformers. For companies that were trying to pivot and create something new, the costs and constraints of *keiretsu* group membership were too high and the benefits no longer as relevant. The withdrawal of the New Japan companies diminished the relevance of these groups, with the possible exception of the Mitsubishi *keiretsu*, which upheld cohesion while pushing the group forward from within.[18] The laggards-reformers division extended into the lobbying groups: reformers began to call Keidanren, the large business association, a "zombie club" and found new representation through the alternative executive association Keizai Dōyūkai. It wasn't until the chairman of Hitachi Ltd., Hiroaki Nakanishi, became chairman of Keidanren in 2014, that it would finally jump on the reform bandwagon.

In the late 1990s, the government had begun to listen to the reformers' requests. Between 1998 and 2006, a series of legal revisions were launched that were so fundamental as to define a strategic inflection point.[19] Literally all laws pertaining to commerce were revised, with the goal of strengthening transparency and disclosure and enabling corporate reorganization. The process began in 1998 with a financial reform program called the Big Bang. Easily the most important of the changes toward financial accountability was the introduction of obligatory consolidated accounting—simply put, listed firms now have to declare all their subsidiaries. This included an obligation to report all nonperforming loans carried by these subsidiaries, and revealed the extent of cross-subsidization across business units. Sunshine, it is said, is the best disinfectant; a new transparency was ushered in.

A second important reform in 1998 was the phasing out of remaining constraints on foreign trade and cross-border financial transactions. In the postwar years, the government had relied on these restrictions for its infant industry protection policies, but over time they had begun to impede trade. Their removal means that Japanese citizens can now freely invest abroad, just as foreigners can freely invest in Japan, including in corporate acquisitions. It also means that the government's tools to protect domestic companies from foreign investors have been severely curtailed, forcing Japanese companies to face the discipline of the global financial markets.

The 1998 Big Bang reform also established the Financial Services Agency (FSA), which combines banking and securities market monitoring authorities. This agency oversaw the banking crisis cleanup of 2002 to 2005, when the largest banks merged into four large financial holding companies, cleared up their nonperforming loans, and repositioned from being just lenders toward becoming financial service providers. The main bank of old has also changed: while many companies may still count one bank as their main bank, the meaning of this relationship is transforming away from the bank's being a shareholder, lender, and rescue agent and toward its being a company's main M&A adviser, project finance syndicator, and asset manager.[20]

Starting in 1997, Japan also began a decade of annual revisions to its Commercial Code and related laws in accounting, taxation, and labor. These laws were old and convoluted, and had become legal obstacles to corporate reforms. In 2006, all these revisions were combined into the new Companies Act (*Kaisha-hō*), in what was called a "once-in-a-century revolution for Japanese company legislation."[21] Each round of the revisions leading up to the new 2006 law chiseled away at former constraints. Also introduced were new bankruptcy rules and new procedures to facilitate business exits, mergers and corporate spin-outs and carve-outs. Shareholder rights, too, were greatly increased, and the 2007 Financial Instruments and Exchange Law—known in Japan as J-SOX—prescribed new internal controls and independent audits. Adding to the transparency push, Japan's corporate law was also drastically reformed in the areas of corporate disclosure, internal auditing, and compliance.[22]

Together, these measures invigorated corporate Japan and resulted in the so-called Koizumi Boom, named after the prime minister who spearheaded them. From 2003 to 2008, Japan reported 17 quarters of positive (albeit low) growth, which brought a new sense of hope. This was abruptly ended by the "Lehman Shock," Japan's term for the 2008 global financial crisis, followed by the 2011 Tohoku earthquake and tsunami and the Fukushima nuclear disaster. Overall, Koizumi's efforts changed the rulebook and thereby the logic of what it takes to win for large Japanese companies. They enforced the cleanup of the vestiges of the bubble mess, by inviting a first wave of choose-and-focus that addressed mostly non-core loss leaders. However, that still left many large conglomerates intact. To accomplish real change, a second round of reorganization was necessary, one that required an actual strategic shift.

Abenomics

In 2012, as Japan was still reeling from the Tohoku disaster, Shinzō Abe was elected prime minister for a second time, and he set in motion a new style of reform program called "Japan is Back." This was rolled out with clever marketing slogans, such as Abenomics and Womenomics, and in addition to legal reforms its execution relies heavily on nudging and shaming based on a series of soft-law guidelines.

Recall from Chapter 2 that regulation through nudging means offering a choice architecture so that people are guided by their own biases to choose the option that is in the public interest. Nudging has already been widely adopted globally; for example, in the United States, more school lunches now exclude unhealthy options, or make them harder to reach or look undesirable. In U.S. retirement saving plans, individuals have to opt out of saving rather than opting in, and a similar setup applies to organ donation in some European countries.[23] The advantages of nudging compared to legislation include speed, as there is no need to write a law, and high rates of acceptance and reduced needs for sanctioning. Combined with positive reinforcement and peer pressure, nudging can be more effective than laws. In Japan's tight culture, nudging and shaming are particularly powerful tools.

Abenomics relies heavily on these mechanisms, and the biggest impact of "Japan is Back" may well be not so much in the individual measures of deregulation, but rather in giving the government's imprimatur to reformers and building social approval for the business reinvention, even where that includes breaking with tradition. For CEOs facing resistance within their companies, Abenomics has greatly facilitated launching a change initiative, as it has given them a license to lead the renewal process from the top down.

Abenomics has also brought a new appreciation of financial markets as conduits of strategic pivoting. The necessary deep-seated transformation in the second round of choose-and-focus requires exiting old core assets that include multibillion-dollar businesses. This is possible only if there is a liquid market in which to sell these assets, and that means having to attract foreign investors. To this end, companies need to change their governance processes and introduce new structures of information sharing, manager-owner relations, and shareholder rights. Abenomics has been pushing this agenda, by reforming these areas and nudging companies to comply with the new, global standards of governance and stewardship, as we will see in Chapters 6 and 7.

The impact of this new mindset of business reform began to show within five years of the launch of this program. Between 2013 and 2019, GDP steadily increased (from ¥476 trillion to ¥549 trillion), and corporate pre-tax profit and private investment hit record highs. Companies listed in the first section of the Tokyo Stock Exchange are becoming more profitable, and in 2018 reported a record average return on equity (ROE) of 10.1% (compared with 14% among U.S. blue chips and about 10% in Europe).[24] After Abe's reelection to a third term in 2017, Abenomics 2.0 presented an even broader program for pro-growth socioeconomic change that included employment and pension reforms, reforms in education and childcare, Womenomics, immigration, and a comprehensive workstyle reform deregulation for 2019 (see Chapter 9).

Despite its apparent successes, Abenomics is not without its critics. From abroad, the reforms are seen as still insufficient and slow, whereas within Japan, many consider them as too drastic and possibly challenging the social balance. Critics belittle the Abenomics slogans, or mistake nudging for a lack of power. But for business, Abenomics will stick, because it is more than legal reform; rather, it is about reinventing the environment within which businesses operate.

The Difficulty of Making the Cut: Panasonic and Sony

Changing global competition, the end of the old business models, legal reforms, a decade of choose-and-focus, and Abenomics have both pushed and pulled many large companies to change. Yet, for many CEOs, change continues to be a challenge. They face obstacles that differ greatly from what CEOs encounter in the United States, ranging from system constraints such as lifetime employment to a widely perceived obligation to remain true to the spirit of company founders. Two companies that exemplify the difficulties of pushing change in Japan are the two best-known electronics firms of the early 1990s: Panasonic and Sony.

At the height of Japan's export-led growth period in the late 1980s, Panasonic and Sony were huge brands that peppered our houses with radios, TVs, cassette players and videocassette recorders (VCRs), turntables, and stereo systems. If you had a Walkman or Handycam, it would most likely have carried the label of one of these two companies, or of one of their Japanese co-competitors. And then they stopped—and missed out on the iPod, cell phones, video streaming, and tablets. With a few exceptions at the very high end, their products were sidelined by those from Samsung, LG Electronics, and Apple. However, unlike

Zenith and RCA, U.S. companies that went bankrupt when Japan's exports arrived in the 1980s, both Sony and Panasonic are still in business, except that they are quite different now. Theirs is a story of the pros and cons of the values of loyalty and obligation to the founders and employees, as well as the tradeoffs between economic efficiencies and preserving employment and key technologies.

PANASONIC

In 1918, the Matsushita Electric Industrial Company, Ltd. was founded in Osaka by one of Japan's most celebrated business entrepreneurs and industrialists, Kōnosuke Matsushita (the company was renamed Panasonic Corporation in 2008). By the 1980s, it had grown to be the world's largest home appliances and consumer electronics company, with five separate brands: Panasonic, Quasar, Technics, JVC, and National. In 1977, *Fortune* magazine labeled it "the most dazzling corporate success in Japan." By 1987, the company had invented the VHS system and conquered global markets for VCRs. The VCR became the dominant product, and accounted for 40% of total sales and 60% of profits, a precarious dependence, similar to the dependence of Samsung Electronics on cell phones today; indeed, in many ways, Panasonic's status in global electronics in 1989 is akin to Samsung's in 2019. Panasonic's other product areas in the 1980s were audio (10% of sales), home appliances (17%), information and industrial equipment (17%), and components (16%, including semiconductors).[25] The company's strategy was to be a fast second and a manufacturing ace: it scouted the market for technologies invented elsewhere, and turned them into nifty consumer electronics and household goods. Videotape recording, for example, was invented in Silicon Valley and first brought to market by Sony with the Betamax. But Panasonic's engineers won the battle for the dominant design by figuring out how to make it more useful with longer run times.

By 1990, Panasonic's sales topped $55 billion, with a 10% operating margin, produced by 190,000 employees in hundreds of domestic and international divisions and subsidiaries.[26] Employees revered Kōnosuke Matsushita's management philosophy, which viewed them as the "treasures" of the company. Panasonic's organization was similar to that of General Electric, with divisions set up as independent profit centers. The company also owned a huge countrywide retail chain with over 25,000 small stores that carried only its own brands. This increased sales, allowed controls over product pricing and positioning, and enabled the beta testing of new designs and pushing products to market while receiving customer feedback and building a loyal user base.

In the early 2010s, however, this former champion was struggling to remain upright. With sales of about $70 billion, Panasonic reported annual losses of about $9 billion in both fiscal year 2012 and 2013, a staggering number. Its decline in the 1990s had been caused by many factors, led by the rise of South Korea's Samsung and LG Electronics, which carbon-copied Panasonic's strategy, except they were quick to transition into the digital world. Panasonic saw its product lines become obsolete and its R&D labs staffed with analog experts unable to respond. New products were developed but none scored: a 1995 game player flopped spectacularly, and a digital camera failed. Quality issues with refrigerators—the flagship product that sustains Panasonic's dominance of the Japanese kitchen—did not help. The globalization of supply chains killed Panasonic's ethnocentric approach of exporting gadgets made in Japan. Domestically, the rise of new sales channels, such as powerful retailers like Bic Camera, wiped out the retail stores. In 1991, Matsushita had bought MCA (which owned Universal Studios and MCA Records), in a move that smacked of imitating Sony's acquisition of Columbia Pictures. MCA was sold off in 1995 at a loss of $1.6 billion. Plants were sitting idle, and leadership was lacking. Yet, through all this, the founder's management principles were held sacrosanct, even as interdivisional infighting and ossified processes caused great inefficiencies. Morale tanked, and business partners reported that the principle of "fairness and honesty" went out the door first.

In 2000, Kunio Nakamura, an operations expert with experience in the United States, took over as CEO.[27] In addition to downsizing by asking 8,000 employees to take early retirement, consolidating the sales structure, and phasing out the retail stores, Nakamura closed 17 large plants globally. He pushed through a revolutionary shift from the company's fabled assembly lines (where the product moves to parts) to cell manufacturing (where parts are moved to the product). He consolidated and streamlined the entire organization, reorganized global operations, and reoriented the central R&D lab with the tag line "in the digital age, there is no room for imitators."[28] He also cleaned up the balance sheet: the staggering $18 billion in losses in 2012 and 2013 were partially caused by write-offs from the 2008 acquisition of Sanyo, a bankrupt competitor that had a strong battery and solar panel business. These acquisitions were supposed to put Panasonic into new businesses away from the bottom of the smile curve, but they were slow to translate into results. But, after all that, the company was still a struggling conglomerate having to make the hard cuts.

Many suggestions were put forward as to why even Nakamura, widely considered an outstanding leader, could not refocus the conglomerate.[29] The organizational structure that the founder built had over time created wasteful duplication and competition among divisions. Legacy HR practices demotivated people and killed initiative. Above all, it was reported, he was tethered by Panasonic's deep-seated values and tight culture. There was a shared sense of obligation to respect and honor the company's original lines of business, and therefore he could not pivot the company away from TVs and semiconductors, which were both loss leaders. To Western eyes this may appear sentimental, or perhaps even silly, but in Japan it reflects a sense of duty to remain loyal to the heritage. The founder's grandson, Masayuki Matsushita, had become a board member in 1986 and was a vociferous defender of tradition. And with the exception of founder firms, Japan's legacy companies are often still run by committee due to the long-standing practice that a CEO serves for six years and then becomes chairman. This means that unless the CEO is backed by the chairman or can somehow find a way to exert authority over his predecessor, his powers in pushing reform may be limited. In the end, Nakamura could not change the company's culture.

In 2012, Kazuhiro Tsuga, a career "Panasonic-man," trained as a computer scientist, was appointed CEO. He found the company in the middle of a deep crisis, but this time around, the Koizumi reforms had been completed, and Abenomics was about the be launched. Tsuga announced a shift away from run-of-the-mill consumer products into a new focus on only high-end consumer products or new B2B segments such as lithium-ion batteries for automobiles and aircraft entertainment systems. In 2013, Panasonic exited the production of plasma panels, followed by LCD TVs in 2016. The company also exited cell phones and sold 80% of its profitable healthcare business. In its place, it acquired Arimo, Inc., a company focused on artificial intelligence (AI). And in 2017, Panasonic made two unusual senior hires: Yasuyuki Higuchi, the former president of Microsoft Japan, to head "connected solutions," and Wataru Baba, a former SAP executive, to run Panasonic's business innovation headquarters, with a mission to "create a new biosphere" for research.

By 2018, Panasonic was once again in the black. However, profits remained elusive as Panasonic's 582 subsidiaries, global factories, and sales offices generated sales of around $70 billion but operating profits of only about $4 billion (less than 6%). Purposefully, the company has forfeited its living room presence, except at the highest end, and has been reorganized into five core business segments: appliances, life/eco solutions, industrial solutions, connected solutions, and automotive. The appliances segment is the only consumer-oriented business, but it still accounts for about one quarter of sales and profits. By far the most profitable segment is connected solutions, which contributes an eighth of sales and almost one quarter of total profits, and is divided into avionics, process automation, and mobile solutions. This is thought of as the future of the company: the new Panasonic is positioning itself in the B2B electronics industry with a renewed reputation for manufacturing and system-building acumen.

Despite all these changes, Panasonic remains a work in progress. The company continues to produce a myriad of consumer products. A sticky culture and resistance to change in middle management have proven bigger obstacles than expected. In 2019, the CEO announced yet another mid-term plan with a new strategy of choose-and-focus, the fifth such announcement in 20 years. But perhaps this time around will be different. Kōnosuke Matsushita's grandson retired in June 2019, and in November 2019, Panasonic announced its complete exit from LCD panels and semiconductors.[30] While we can't be sure how this transformation will play out in the end, Panasonic's 20 years of struggle to make a significant break from its original products illustrates the great challenges of slimming down and reorienting a traditional heavyweight in the Japanese setting.

SONY

Sony was cut from different cloth: it has always been a first mover and inventor, with a "maverick" small-firm attitude, even long after the company outgrew it. The brand has a loyal, global fan base, and many agree that to this day, Sony makes the best TVs, even though it no longer produces the actual panel. Sony's successes are well known. It was founded in 1946, and its first product was a megaphone, followed by a magnetic tape recorder and the world's first transistor radio in 1955. It expanded into TV technology, and in 1968 invented the Trinitron color TV, which dominated global TV sales for three decades. The 1979 Walkman was sheer brilliance: prior to its invention, consumers were unaware that they wanted to listen to music on the go. The camcorder followed in 1985 and was a similar smash hit. In 1989, Sony bought Columbia Pictures, and later added MGM. Today, Sony is the second largest music label in the world, through acquisitions of several record labels, including Columbia, CBS, RCA, Arista, and BMG, between 1988 and 2004.[31]

Unlike Panasonic, Sony seemed to tackle the transition from analog to digital electronics fairly well. In the 1990s, the company brought us the digital Handycam, the Cyber-shot digital camera, and also the Vaio PC. The Trinitron evolved into the Bravia flat-panel TV, and in 2007, Sony built the first full-color, organic, light-emitting diode (OLED) television. Aibo, a robot dog, was born in 1999, and Sony Bank was established in 2001. In 2003, Sony won the Blu-ray disc war against Toshiba. Meanwhile, Sony built a strong global presence in semiconductors, and in 2004 developed the world's first touchless chip, FeliCa (which today powers e-pay services, such as the JR Suica card and Apple Pay in Japan). Its investment in image sensors has resulted, as of today, in a 40% global market share in CMOS chips, which constitute a technology anchor of many of its products.

And then it stopped, and Apple came and ate Sony's lunch. The biggest blunder of all was that Sony missed out on the digital version of the Walkman and lost to the iPod. What is so frustrating about this story is that Sony had actually developed the winning technologies of the day; it simply failed to launch them. The first harbinger of this was the 1975 disaster with Betamax video recording: the product was outstanding technologically but did not address consumer needs. Panasonic won the VCR battle with the insight that Americans wanted to tape three-hour-long football games, even if at lesser quality.[32] In the early 2000s, this repeated several times over. Sony effectively had a prototype of a smartphone as early as 2003 but could not see the potential (Apple's iPhone launched in 2007). It made an e-reader long before Amazon's Kindle appeared in 2007. It failed to catch consumer interest and gutted its early versions of the TiVo and the Slingbox—the initial technologies that allowed you to tape TV shows digitally or watch them from a location other than your home. As for the digital Walkman, again, Sony had developed the technology before Apple made the iPod, but decided not to release it—because it feared that music sharing would undermine sales in its own Sony Music record labels. Rather than creating the expected synergies, the diversification into content had undermined the company's hardware launches.

The blunders underscored that, sometime between 1995 and 2005, Sony lost its stride. To recover from the poor performance of the early 1990s, in 1999, CEO Nobuyuki Idei had launched severe restructuring measures that included layoffs and undermined morale. The R&D lab, long famous for its creativity and freedom to explore, saw its budget cut. It was reported that electronics companies in Taiwan and Korea welcomed disgruntled Sony engineers with open arms, and Samsung in particular profited greatly in the process, even as Sony missed out not only on the iPod but also the smartphone.[33] Idei left Sony behind with huge losses in brand value and without direction. In 2005, a new CEO was appointed in Howard Stringer, who had previously run the Sony movie division in California. He announced a two-year restructuring plan that included withdrawing from 15 businesses, reducing the number of product models by 20%, and eliminating 11 operating bases. The company also sold off about $1 billion of (mostly unprofitable) business at a restructuring cost of $2 billion.[34] Throughout all this downsizing, Sony reported heavy losses in six out of the seven years leading up to 2012, capped by a record loss of $6.4 billion in 2012. It survived this difficult period thanks to the PlayStation and its financial services business. But still, to this day, it has not exited its biggest loss leader, the TV: like Panasonic, Sony has a hard time letting go of the flagship product that was invented by the company's founder.

A whole book could be filled with explaining why Sony committed so many blunders. Hubris certainly played a role, as did the legacy of its founders, who are counted among Japan's most brilliant engineers. Major mistakes included the bubble economy decisions to diversify and advance into real estate (including the Sony building in Manhattan), and a restaurant chain.[35] But above all, Sony was scarred by an eternal war between the engineers, who aimed to make the best technical product, and the sales and marketing staff, who were increasingly exasperated by the engineers' unwillingness to listen to consumer feedback seeking more ease of use. Animosities built to a level where the leaders of the two divisions could not be in the same room—a situation that completely overtaxed the foreign CEO who did not speak their language, and served only to continue the exodus of the best employees. Rudderless, Sony fell out of touch with user needs, and with the markets.[36]

Kazuo Hirai, who took over as CEO in 2012—the same year that Tsuga arrived at Panasonic—brought a strong finance background to the table. He pushed a turnaround and organized significant cost-cutting. He exited all TV businesses except the very high end, restructured the R&D department, launched a buying spree in Silicon Valley for innovative startups and products, and undertook significant financial and accounting moves to improve the look of the balance sheet. This led to impressive increases in net income, from 0.6 billion in 2016 to $4 billion in 2017 and $8 billion in 2019, with sales of about

$77 billion. Together with these record profits, Hirai revved up ROE from –1% in 2016, to 8% in 2017 and 20% in 2019. As we will see in Chapter 6, he retired in 2018 as the highest-paid CEO in Japan that year, and on record for the post-war period. And, it was unclear whether the profit numbers reflected a true turnaround or just an accounting play. As of 2019, in terms of profit generation, Sony is still principally a games company, a music label, and a bank. The product portfolio still covers diverse segments including the PlayStation and Spiderman movies, semiconductors, digital movie theaters, and insurances services. And even though the PlayStation and associated equipment account for a quarter of total sales, the core identity of the company is still the R&D lab, and its sore point is the TV business. Sony's home entertainment earns hardly any profit, and the camera business is under significant pressure as cell phones have obviated most stand-alone cameras.

THE COSTS AND BENEFITS OF SLOW ADJUSTMENTS

Both Sony and Panasonic have held onto their original products for decades, products that earn large portions of revenue but minimal profit. They have muddled through for years on end, launching one midterm plan after another with only incremental impact, and racked up billions of dollars in losses. In the United States, Wall Street would have no patience with such idling. When the erstwhile U.S. electronics companies—such as RCA and Zenith—struggled to compete against their Japanese rivals in the 1980s, they were liquidated within a few years of low returns. This created huge job losses and eliminated any chance that they could recover and direct the vast R&D potential of their organizations toward new inventions. And indeed, Daniel Loeb, the activist investor from Wall Street's Third Point, has repeatedly demanded that Sony sell off parts of its businesses to remove the so-called conglomerate discount and "rerate" the stock price. From his perspective, the inefficiencies caused by holding on and muddling through are simply a failure.

However, an alternative view is to see these two stories as tales of keeping long-term options through reorganization. It is certainly true that both Panasonic and Sony have been incredibly slow—some have even called them incompetent—and have missed out on big market opportunities. The opportunity costs of "what could have been" are astronomical. But in the Japanese business view, foregone opportunities costs are a crying shame, not a kiss of death. Their diverse business portfolios have allowed both companies to weather many years of idling in the no-profit zone, and even survive the gigantic losses during the 2008 global financial crisis.

And unlike RCA and Zenith, today Sony and Panasonic are still standing: as of March 2019, their collective net profits stand at roughly $11 billion, and they employ 400,000 people and bring joy and entertainment to millions around the world. It is probably true that selling off parts of the businesses would increase the stock price, but such a move would not sit comfortably with the tradeoffs that Japan likes to make, where the longevity of the firm, and its history, employment, and technologies are held as valuable and important.

But it is precisely this tradeoff that is now challenged by global competition and the ongoing business reinvention. As we will see in Chapters 6 and 7, there is growing pressure on CEOs to stop the idling and begin to make the hard decisions on how to steer their companies into the future, pressure exerted through governance reform and global stock market influence. Balancing the pursuit of profit maximation with a long-term view that allows safeguarding valuable employees and technologies and upholding the company's role in society is the circle that Japanese CEOs will have to square going forward.

THE IMPACT

Japan's Role in Global Business

In the 1980s, seemingly left and right, U.S. landmarks were being bought by Japanese companies, leading observers to claim that "America is for sale."[1] Among a glitzy array of luxury hotels and office spaces, Japanese firms acquired iconic properties, including California's Pebble Beach Golf Course and New York's Plaza Hotel and Rockefeller Center. These were trophies, hunted down with a "Japan as number one" mentality. But when the bubble economy burst, it wiped out the trophies, as well as some of the banks that had financed them, and left some Americans feeling a certain schadenfreude and saying, "I told you so." Meanwhile, the U.S.-Japan trade war of the 1980s and 1990s had restricted and taxed Japanese exports to the United States, forcing many Japanese car and electronics companies, as well as their suppliers, to invest in production plants in the U.S. From Ohio, Kentucky, and Texas (Honda, Toyota) to Los Angeles and the Mexican maquiladoras just south of San Diego (Sony, Kyocera, Panasonic, Sharp, Sanyo, Nissan), Japanese factories emerged. This influence was much quieter than the real estate deals, but by 2016, 75% of Japanese cars on U.S. roads were made in the U.S., and 17 U.S. states recorded a local Japanese auto plant with investments exceeding $45 billion, producing, overall, 4 million cars and employing more than 460,000 people.[2] And that was just in automobiles. In 2017, Japan's government estimated that 840,000 Americans worked in the U.S. for a Japanese company, in particular in the Midwest, Texas, and California, and that if U.S. employees at suppliers to these companies were counted, the number exceeded 1.5 million.[3] While these investments have reduced bilateral trade, they have also made Japanese industry integral to the U.S. economy.

At the same time, important changes are taking place within Asia that many U.S. observers are unaware of, even though these changes are critically reshaping the role of the United States in the region. A combination of strategic joint ventures and alliances, foreign direct investment (FDI) and mergers and acquisitions in the region, and the growing trade dependencies through the aggregate niche strategy has made Japan the anchor of global supply chains and a central player in Asia. As Japan's growth slowed and America looked away, Asia began to embrace Japan as a model and leader.

In the first instance, Japan's postwar growth model became the go-to development strategy of what were called the NIEs (newly industrializing economies) of Asia in the 1980s: South Korea, Taiwan, Singapore, and Hong Kong. Then, beginning in the 1990s, as Japan expanded its FDI and reach into the smaller Asian economies, Japanese companies became a leading financier of Asia's development. In the early 21st century, three Japanese banks became global leaders in so-called project finance, that is, syndicated finance deals supporting supersized infrastructure projects such as dam construction or energy installations. Japanese capital has also financed Chinese economic growth, directly through loans and indirectly through the offshoring of production. As wages in China were rising, a similar pattern emerged in Southeast Asia. Japan is also a prime financier of global innovation and startup activities, through not just SoftBank's famous investment funds but the over 500 Japanese companies with research and venture capital offices from Silicon Valley to Singapore. All told, Japan is now a critical collaborator for technological innovation across the globe.

Underlying this new economic nexus in East and Southeast Asia are growing cultural ties. Even though the manifestations of Japan's tight culture can at times appear strange to Americans, in Asia the cultural obstacles to doing business are much lower. And while the scars of World War II still sting, millennials carry much less of a grudge than previous generations. They have wholeheartedly embraced Japanese pop culture, beauty products, and fashion, and Japan's brand and reputation for high quality has made Japanese cosmetics, movies, fashion, and style a new symbol of luxury and accomplishment. Traveling to Japan, eating raw fish, getting a Japanese-style haircut, wearing Japanese fashion, and using Japanese cosmetics have become the trademarks of the up-and-coming next generation of young Asian professionals. For millennial Asians, Japan is the place to look up to.

Table 5.1. Japan's Impact in Asia, the United States, and Europe, 2018.

	Exports to (in US$ millions)	Imports from (in US$ millions)	FDI to (in US$ millions) 2017	FDI from (in US$ millions) 2017	Operation Sites (2017)	Travelers to Japan	Students in Japan
China + Hong Kong	178,777 (1)	177,862 (1)	147,663 (4)	11,068 (6)	32,349 (1)	10,587,838 (1)	124,474 (1)
U.S.A	140,664 (2)	83,571 (4)	491,368 (1)	59,212 (2)	8,606 (3)	1,526,407 (6)	2,932 (7)
South Korea	52,482 (5)	32,112 (7)	36,883 (7)	4,067 (8)	945 (8)	7,538,952 (2)	17,012 (4)
EU	83,740 (4)	87,760 (3)	397,711 (2)	113,060 (1)	6,449 (4)	1,548,780 (6)	10,115 (5)
ASEAN	114,476 (3)	112,138 (2)	204,543 (3)	25,765 (3)	12,545 (2)	3,247,526 (4)	95,325 (2)
Other	168,063	254,776	272,640	40,308	14,637	6,742,353	49,112
Total	738,201	748,218	1,550,808	253,480	75,531	31,191,856	298,980

Note: Ranking of Japan in parentheses; first ranks highlighted in grey. FDI are stock data at the end of 2017. Operations sites include production and sales offices. Foreign student data are approximate due to missing data for several countries. Sources: Trade: UN Comtrade Database; FDI: Japan External Trade Organization, "Japan's Outward and Inward Foreign Direct Investment"; Operation Sites: Ministry of Foreign Affairs of Japan, List of Statistics on the Number of Overseas Residents in Japan; Foreigners in Japan: e-Stat, Japan in Statistics; Visitors: Japan National Tourism Organization, Monthly and Yearly Statistical Data; Students: Japan Student Services Organization.

Table 5.1 presents a set of data that underscores Japan's global role in a variety of categories, from trade, investments, and local operations to travelers and students. Japan's impact runs much deeper than trade data might suggest. The table ranks Japan's relevance (in parentheses) for each region or country. China (with Hong Kong) tops five of the seven categories: it is Japan's largest trading partner by far, and currently the country with the most Japanese offices and plants, as well as a source of tourism and students. FDI (foreign direct investment) is expressed as the accumulated total for the 20 years between 1998 and 2017, and the United States ranks first due to the long-standing relations. But note that Japanese companies now have more operations (offices and production facilities) in the area represented by the Association of Southeast Asian Nations (ASEAN) than in the U.S. Clearly, Japan has built a strong global presence in a variety of roles, as a critical trading partner, an investor, a collaborator, a fashion trendsetter, and increasingly, also an educator.

This chapter looks at Japan's relations, as of 2019, with the United States, South Korea, China, and Southeast Asia separately, followed by a few examples of the all-important cultural impact of Japan on next-generation Asians. It ends with an update on Japan's outward-facing M&A activities, which have grown in leaps and bounds and no longer center on trophies. Rather, these new acquisitions are strategic investments to further expand some of the technology niches and to grow the consumer base for Japanese products as Japan's domestic market is shrinking.

Japan and the United States

In 2018, the last year for which data were available at the time of this writing, the United States was the world's largest trading nation and recorded the world's largest trade deficit in goods and services, totaling $621 billion; in manufactured goods alone, the deficit was even larger, at $891 billion.[4] China was the largest trading partner for both Japan and the United States, until the trade war of 2019 threatened to reduce those numbers. From Japan's perspective, total trade with China (with Hong Kong), of $356 billion, was already much larger than its total trade with the U.S., of $225 billion. In the four-year period from 2014 to 2018, 20% of Japanese exports were destined for the U.S., compared to roughly 25% for China, and 15% for Southeast Asia (ASEAN countries).[5]

But the United States is still Japan's most important partner overall. The U.S.-Japan relationship is multifaceted, with a complicated history. After World War II, Japan became the strongest U.S. ally in the Pacific, and to this day the security alliance between the two nations anchors the geopolitical constellations of the Pacific Rim. While this is a topic for another book, this U.S.-Japan alliance also shapes trade flows, resource dependencies, and investments in Asia. On the business side, the two countries are closely connected through trade, foreign direct investments, joint research activities, and a longstanding mutual affinity, respect, and collaboration. However, as we have already seen, when Japan's trade surplus surged in the 1980s, to a whopping 65% of the American trade deficit, the U.S. launched a decade-long, acrimonious trade war that has left Japan with a sense that the United States can also be unreliable.

To reduce the trade deficit with Japan, the United States imposed tariffs and a "local-content" rule, which required that a certain percentage of input parts to a Japanese product assembled in the U.S. be sourced from domestic manufacturers.[6] The industries most affected by these new rules were automobiles, electronics, and steel. Japanese companies began to open assembly as well as part manufacturing plants on North American soil. This resulted in sizable Japanese manufacturing clusters in the Midwest, Texas, and California. As

Table 5.1 shows, between 1998 and 2017, one third of Japan's outward-bound FDI, or about $500 billion, flowed into the United States.

Nevertheless, in the mid-1990s, when Japan's growth rate stalled, U.S. businesses turned their focus to China. Japan's shift of production outside Japan, first to the United States and then into Asia, greatly diminished the direct trade flows between the two countries, and the trade imbalance with Japan became a nonissue for most U.S. voters. Japan was unceremoniously removed from U.S. headlines even when, ironically, its companies had become a much stronger, direct contributor to the U.S. economy. Although happy to get a reprieve from a politically fueled trade war, this downgrading of Japan in U.S. economic and foreign policy at a time of increased commitment to the United States never sat well with Tokyo.

Today, no longer is the United States dependent on Japanese consumer goods exports, nor, with rising affluence in Asia, does Japan depend as strongly on U.S. consumer markets. As of 2018, at the launch of the new U.S. trade war with Asia by the Trump administration, the U.S. trade deficit with China accounted for 46% of the total deficit, while that with Japan accounted for just 8.5%. This was an astounding change compared with the deficit at the height of the trade conflict in 1986. At that time, Japan's trade with the United States accounted for almost 40% of all Japanese exports and 23% of all imports; today, it has declined to about 20% in both. Conversely, for the United States, in 1986 Japan accounted for 12% of exports and 23% of imports, compared to below 5% today.[7]

Rather than trade in highly visible consumer products, the relations between the two countries are now characterized by less obvious dependencies. First, a nontrivial portion of the trade today involves military equipment, some of which is classified. Given the long-standing security alliance, Japan is not only a large purchaser but also a technology collaborator. In the private sector, too, business innovation and collaboration run deep. In the 20th century, many strategic alliances and joint ventures between the countries were driven by Japan's interest in technological catch-up. These were sometimes viewed in the United States as a threat to U.S. technology leadership. But today, Japan is seen as an equal and an important contributor to knowledge creation, and the tone of the relationship has evolved into one of true collaboration and mutual learning among technology leaders.

Examples of sizable private sector strategic alliances in 2018 included a $3 billion joint venture between Qualcomm and TDK on next-generation radio frequency technologies, a $2.6 billion joint venture between Hitachi and

Johnson Controls for advanced air-conditioning, a collaboration on AI between Sony and several Silicon Valley tech firms, and an IBM-Sony project on a magnetic tape system for data storage. There are also numerous alliances and global research projects among pharmaceutical companies in the United States and Japan at all levels. In the area of defense, Raytheon and Mitsubishi Heavy Industries jointly developed a ballistic missile defense interceptor.[8] In the everyday conversations about U.S.-Japan relations, these long-standing and deep business connections and joint ventures, and the mutual appreciation and respect that many American and Japanese companies have for each other, often get overlooked.

In 2018, when the U.S. government turned toward protectionism after years of promoting trade expansion and the globalization of supply chains, the vitriol of the 1990s returned, except this time it was targeted at China. Nevertheless, Japan was caught in the crossfire, because the bilateral trade data on which the trade war was waged did not begin to reflect the degree to which the United States and Japan were connected, nor the realities of the intertwined Asian economy and how any frictions would generate significant regional externalities. This triggered great concern, not just in terms of the security alliance and trade connections between Japan and the United States, but for the stability and economy of the entire region.

Japan and South Korea

South Korea was the first of the Four Asian Tigers (Hong Kong, Singapore, South Korea and Taiwan) to emulate Japan's growth model. Like Japan in the 1960s, South Korea in the 1980s industrialized rapidly, relying on infant industry protection, export promotion, and picking winners among established business conglomerates (the *chaebol*, similar in structure to the Japanese prewar *zaibatsu*). South Korea even mimicked the industries Japan had picked, beginning with steel and shipbuilding, followed by an entry into, initially cheap and low-quality, consumer electronics and cars. Using their comparative cost advantages, this resulted in Samsung and LG Electronics assuming Japan's former global pole position in consumer electronics and household goods.

In the process, the already historically fraught relationship between Japan and South Korea became increasingly competitive. In the 1990s, Japan also lost its semiconductor industry dominance to South Korea. It was said that South Korea stole intellectual property from Japan and copied the production methods that companies like Toshiba, Hitachi, Mitsubishi Electric, Oki, and many others had developed. Just a decade earlier, U.S. companies had accused Japanese firms of the exact same thing, and semiconductors were a long-standing theme in the U.S.-Japan trade war at the time. But once Japan fell on the losing side, it joined the United States in defending against intellectual property theft, as underscored in a series of World Trade Organization cases.[9] Industry observers at the time reported that Japanese companies were so upset with Samsung, LG Electronics, and SK Hynix that they traveled to Taiwan to share their technologies, thereby creating Taiwan's strength in semiconductor production as a balance to South Korea's. Industry lore or truth, the story bespeaks the uncomfortable imbalance that continues to exist between the two countries.[10]

In addition to this tension born of economic competition, the thorny politics of historical memory and apology have colored bilateral relations. Japan occupied South Korea between 1910 and 1945, and during that time greatly affected that country's economic institutions, including even the architectural style of the central bank building. Japan also used forced labor and committed crimes against the Korean people during its occupation of the peninsula and throughout the war.[11] The scars of that colonization still refuse to fade. Contemporary security and trade relations, while close, still regularly devolve into demands for apologies and reparations. Although Japanese culpability was admitted and reparations were legally settled with a sizable lump-sum payment when the two countries resumed diplomatic ties in 1965, these issues came to a head again in 2018 when a South Korean court ruled that, in addition to the Japanese government, Japanese firms, too, owed reparations to wartime Korean laborers. Unwilling to be continually extorted on the matter, in July 2019, Japan removed Korea from its "white list" of free trade countries, meaning that applications for licenses were necessary for trade in specified, high-technology items. These included advanced chemicals, and as we saw in the introduction to Chapter 4, this caused particular concern for Samsung Electronics, which critically depended on Japan for three chemicals needed for the development of next-generation 5G semiconductors.

South Korea retaliated by threatening not to renew a bilateral intelligence-sharing pact called GSOMIA (General Security of Military Information Agreement). This pact forms the backbone of Northeast Asia intelligence for both countries and also feeds into the trilateral cooperation with their closest ally, the United States. The timing of putting the agreement in jeopardy was perplexing, especially in light of ongoing North Korean missile tests. South Korean consumers launched an aggressive "No Japan" boycott, and popular sentiment for Japan reached an all-time low. Meanwhile, the CEO of Samsung Electronics was repeatedly seen in Tokyo, lobbying heavily for a lifting of the restrictions on the three chemicals. After a lot of back and forth, at the last minute South Korea agreed to renew GSOMIA, in exchange for Japan's relaxation of licensing needs for the photoresists, the most critical of the three chemicals.[12]

How these negotiations would end was unclear at the time of this writing. But the event draws attention to the new reality in Northeast Asia: while history and politics are complicated, these countries are considerably integrated economically, with sequenced positions in the global supply chain. And increasingly, business wins the day. We will see later how this is also true for the relations between China and Japan.

By 2018, total trade between Japan and South Korea had grown to nearly $84 billion, and as we saw in Figure 4.2, Japan had a $20 billion trade surplus.[13] Trade with South Korea accounted for 7% of total Japanese exports and 4% of total imports. For Korea, 11.5% of imports came from Japan, compared with 4.6% of exports.[14] By product category, the biggest imports by Korea in 2018 were machinery (including production machinery and parts), chemicals, and precision machinery, while Japan imported mostly agricultural products. It is still rare to see a Korean car in Japan or vice versa. Moreover, partially reflecting the tensions as well as the closed nature of Korea's domestic markets, only 2% of Japanese FDI has been directed toward Korea and relatively few operation sites are maintained (Table 5.1), making trade the mainstay of the relationship.

Also contributing to the tension is the degree to which the entire South Korean economy is increasingly dependent on Japan, due to the aggregate niche strategy. Around 2015, the Samsung *chaebol* accounted for about 20% of the Korean stock exchange's market value, and the group's revenues equaled 17% of GDP.[15] The group's core company, Samsung Electronics, has become the largest cell phone maker in the world, and phones and tablets have reached about 60% of total sales. However, the production of these phones, as well as upgrading the quality to stay ahead of competition from China, requires high-tech imports from Japan. For example, 32% of critical supplies for Samsung's semiconductor manufacturing come from Japan, in addition to the aforementioned photoresists and other chemicals.[16] Moreover, the manufacturing equipment to make LCD screens is also sourced from Japan, as are parts and numerical controls that feed into Korea's machine tool industry, where the dependence runs over 90%

for certain components.[17] These machine tools also affect Korea's automotive sectors. Thus, Japan's aggregate niche strategy has put of a lot of "Japan Inside" into what Korea makes.

Japan and China

As with South Korea, Japan's relations with China have historically been complicated. Japan has borrowed much from Chinese culture: its written language, Buddhism, and even *ramen* noodles have their roots in China. Conversely, Japan's spoken language and grammar, as well as Shintoism and sushi, are as home-grown as Japan's tight culture. World War II left many highly visible scars, and China's recent buildup of military power has strained recent diplomatic relations. But as much as history has complicated bilateral relations, the economic relationship between the two countries has largely been ruled by pragmatism. In 2018, bilateral trade was almost balanced, with roughly $178 billion in exports and imports when trade through Hong Kong is included. China is Japan's largest trading partner, with about 25% of both exports and imports. And for China, Japan is the second largest export destination and third largest import source, after the United States and South Korea.[18]

In addition to its role in trade, Japan is the main source of the direct investment that has funded China's manufacturing boom. Japanese firms are major owners of productive capital, and the main (in many cases the only) source of essential, high-quality input products for the mainland. As Table 5.1 shows, in 2017 Japanese companies maintained over 32,000 sales offices, factories, and partial stakes in companies in China, making Japan's the largest foreign production interests.[19] Although only 10% of Japan's outward FDI was directed to China, nearly 70% of this was related to manufacturing. This underscores, yet again, the division of labor whereby China has become Asia's assembler and Japan the specialized manufacturer of high-tech inputs. The sheer size of China's consumer markets, Japanese companies' significant on-the-ground presence, and the trade dependencies tightly link the two countries' economic successes.

What draws the two economies even closer is that their different positions in global value chains create valuable synergies. China, much like Japan in the 1960s and 1970s, achieved rapid growth through export promotion and low-cost manufacturing of consumer goods. Government subsidies, high domestic savings, and technology adaption were the main drivers, though with the obvious differences that China is not a democracy and most of its large firms are state-owned enterprises. However, whereas Japan had closed its markets to any foreign investment during its initial postwar growth spurt, China's growth has depended critically on foreign capital and knowledge, and China happily became the world's assembler.[20] This means that Japan grew by developing its own, entirely domestic vertical production capabilities, and through constant upgrading and organizational learning built competitive advantage. In contrast, Chinese companies copied the technologies that foreigners brought into the country, but then specialized in the lower value-added, lower cost part of value creation, that is, final assembly. Thus, whereas Japan had developed a complete domestic value chain from product design to final sale, China developed a system built for import, assembly, and reexport.

This proved instrumental for Japan when it came time to move upstream on the smile curve. Having capabilities across the entire value chain meant companies could exit the lower value-added activities and switch into the higher margin, upstream niches. If China wants to do something similar and move upstream, as is proposed in the 2015 industrial policy program "Made in China 2025," it will first need to build the requisite capabilities. Indeed, "Made in China 2025" details how Chinese industry will move away from being the world's factory and move up the value chain into technology fields such as pharmaceuticals, automotive and aerospace industries, semiconductors, IT, and robotics.[21] All of these are large-scale industries and encroach on Japan's bailiwick.

Yet, differences in technology levels and scale of production, as well as development goals, are likely to render China's and Japan's industrial structures more complementary than competitive in the medium term. Given the size of the workforce and pressures to scale fast, China's government is pushing its 2025 plan in industries that promise large volume, usually with huge manufacturing installations. This affords Japan an escape route into niches that require very different capabilities in innovation and manufacturing. Given Japan's shrinking population and labor shortages, scale is no longer as important as profit margins, so Japanese companies can focus their *monozukuri* skills on customized, high-margin, deep-tech niche segments. While some smaller Chinese companies will probably explore some of these smaller niches, they are still behind Japanese companies. And, of course, the Japanese manufacturers are not standing still, but are constantly improving and producing at higher levels of quality, to remain a moving target. Thus, although a rising China looks and in some ways is threatening to Japan, the aggregate niche strategy where Japan focuses on critical segments and continually upgrading and innovating, may allow Japan to stay ahead and out of China's way.

This puts China in a bind: even if the country wants to substitute its reliance on imported technologies, as outlined in "Made in China 2025," it still needs Japan for the niche input materials and products that are small and difficult-to-imitate or difficult-to-make at very high levels of quality. Meanwhile, Japan is not as dependent, because it can substitute Chinese manufacturers for labor elsewhere in Asia. Although moving is costly, reestablishing operations in Southeast Asia is increasingly economical as China's labor costs rise, and this process has been greatly accelerated by the U.S.-China trade war of 2019. For example, in a matter of just a few months in 2019, many large Japanese companies, including Ricoh, Nintendo, Kyocera, Sony, Komatsu, and FANUC, announced they were shifting their production out of China and into Taiwan, Thailand, Vietnam, and other parts of Southeast Asia, while putting further investments in China on hold.[22]

Thus, despite China's industrial policy ambitions, as of now Japan continues to be a creator, while China remains mostly an assembler. Figure 5.1 breaks out bilateral Japan-China trade, and shows Japan's net trade positions with China by industry. Japan maintains sizable and growing surpluses in chemicals, iron and steel products, transport equipment, and optical and precision machinery, whereas it has a deficit with China in agricultural products, electric machinery, and clothing and textiles. This not only highlights the division of labor that Japan and China have pursued but also underscores the nature of their relationship: Japan is dependent on China for some of its food, its desktop phones (where Chinese firms dominate), and the assembly of (mostly Japanese) branded consumer electronics and clothing items, as well as China's consumer markets, while China depends on Japan for advanced chemicals, manufacturing machinery, and specialty materials.

Although soybeans and textiles are important to Japan, these sectors are hardly equal. In sum, in the current economic structure, China cannot substitute Japan, and it will take time to catch up. Conversely, Japan can relocate investment outside China, but needs China's consumer markets for sales. This explains Japan's great effort to expand its presence in Southeast Asia to grow new consumer markets elsewhere. It also explains why China has begun to reach out to Japan, to maintain good relations as the U.S. trade war puts economic stress on the region.[23]

Of course, this economic pragmatism exists at a time of important mili-

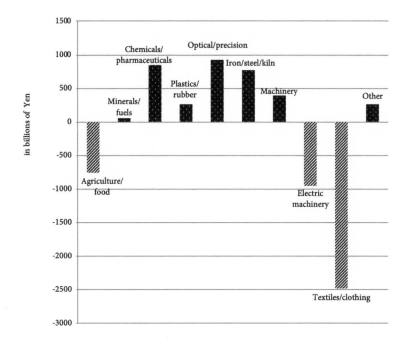

Figure 5.1. Japan's Trade with China and Hong Kong, by Industry, in 2017 (select categories). Source: Customs and Tariff Bureau, Ministry of Finance Japan.

tary and geopolitical power shifts. Just as Japan is worried about a situation of resource or trade dependence on China, China loathes its dependence on the United States. And China's rapid militarization and saber rattling are causing strains in the region and trade disputes that illuminate the consequences and vulnerabilities resulting from deep integration. Since 2013, when China and Japan escalated a long-standing disagreement over the Senkaku Islands, Japan has steadily increased its defense budget and expanded its defense capabilities. On top of this, the U.S. trade war continues to generate uncertainty and a slowing of investment, and threatens to dampen economic activity. How this will develop into 2020 will determine economic and geopolitical relations throughout Asia.

Japan and Southeast Asia

With all the focus on China, the rest of Asia is often overlooked. This is particularly true for Southeast Asia, despite its fast-growing markets and increasing affluence. Today, the region is home to 650 million people, with a nominal GDP above $2.5 trillion ($7.6 trillion PPP) and one of the fastest growth rates of any region in the world.[24] Over the past decade, due to political and economic developments in countries such as Vietnam, Thailand, Indonesia, Myanmar, and the Philippines, Southeast Asia has become increasingly interlinked with Japan, in terms of both trade and culture. Economically, Japan's contributions follow three channels: in-country final production at local plants, such as the manufacturing of cars in Thailand or tires in Vietnam; pass-through assembly or partial production within a larger supply chain; and exports, especially consumer goods, to be sold in ASEAN markets.

Table 5.1 shows that ASEAN countries account for more of Japan's exports than the EU, and are home to 12,545 Japanese offices and plants, a number now increasing due to the shift from China into other parts of Asia. ASEAN is Asia's largest intergovernmental organization, representing ten countries in Southeast Asia: Indonesia, Malaysia, the Philippines, Singapore, Myanmar, Brunei, Vietnam, Laos, Cambodia, and Thailand. ASEAN's 2017 economic report underscores Japan's rising role in the region, led by a growing number of Japanese multinational enterprises (MNEs) that have become major regional employers and growth contributors. Within the manufacturing sector, as of 2016, of the top 20 MNEs in ASEAN countries, seven were Japanese companies. Ranked by overall corporate investments in ASEAN countries, three of the top 20 MNEs were Japanese, namely Mitsubishi UFJ Financial Group (MUFG), Toyota Motor, and Tokio Marine Holdings. As of 2016, these three combined had total assets in ASEAN countries exceeding $100 billion.[25]

Japan's three largest banking groups are building a strong presence in Southeast Asia. For example, in 2013, MUFG acquired a large bank in Thailand, Ayudhya, followed in 2018 by a $6 billion investment in Indonesia's Bank Danamon. Danamon is Indonesia's fifth largest commercial bank, with strong ties to the local auto parts makers that supply Japanese car manufacturers in Indonesia. Meanwhile, Sumitomo Mitsui Banking Corporation (SMBC) increased its holdings in one of Indonesia's largest banks, as well as in banks in Cambodia and Vietnam. Japan's third large banking group, Mizuho, is also building a strong presence in the region.[26] Taken together, over a stretch of just five years, from 2011 to 2016, the loan balances of these three banks nearly doubled, from $110 billion to over $200 billion, making them leading lenders and financial service providers in Southeast Asia.[27] Their role as global leaders in project financing means that they also supply funds for very large-scale installations in the power, energy, transportation, mining, and telecommunications industries of the region.[28]

In terms of incoming FDI, Japan ranks first or second in every ASEAN country except Singapore and Myanmar. In recent years, Japan has accounted for over 60% of FDI in Thailand, 35% in Indonesia, and over 15% in Vietnam, the Philippines, and Malaysia. Japanese companies operate over 3,900 plants in Thailand and almost 2,000 each in Indonesia and Vietnam. Overall, Indonesia is also the largest recipient of government loans from Japan, followed by Thailand, Vietnam, and the Philippines.[29] With the onset of the U.S.-China trade war in 2019, Japan's presence in the form of factories and sales operations is further growing, and Japanese companies are diversifying their beachheads in the region. For example, between 2011 and 2014, 93.6% of FDI in Myanmar came from China, whereas in 2019, Myanmar is increasingly looking to Japan, and Japanese FDI there grew by a factor of five in 2017 alone.[30] As Japan grows its economic presence in the region, it is also aiming to create a geopolitical base that might help balance the complicated relationship with China.

Japan as the Aspiration:
Pop Culture and Consumer Goods

James and Deborah Fallows, in their 2018 exploration of the U.S. heartland, observed that China looks better from a distance than up close, whereas the United States looks bad from a distance but gets better the closer you get to the ground.[31] Similarly, the further away you are from Asia the better China looks, but the closer you get, the more you realize how central Japan is in Asia today.[32] This goes way beyond trade and investment, and Japan's impact on Asia in terms of culture, fashion, pop music, leisure activities, games, TV, and entertainment will be a huge factor for the region's future geopolitical alignment. Japan has become the quiet power of Asia, and many young Asians have embraced this new reality with enthusiasm.

At the ground level, Asia is embracing Japan due to a generational change. A pattern that has already emerged between South Korea and Japan is replicating with China and Southeast Asia. For example, China's "animation generation," meaning people younger than 40, is quite drawn to Japanese culture. In 2017, the value of the anime market in China was estimated at $21 billion and rising.[33] The affinities have grown as China's Japan-bound tourism has grown by leaps and bounds (Table 5.1). This is perhaps nowhere more important and visible than in the increase in the number of Chinese eager to learn from Japan, including in areas such as culture, sports, and business, and studying and working in Japan. As shown in Table 5.1, Chinese students account for almost 40% of foreign students in Japan, followed by students from Vietnam, South Korea, Indonesia, and Myanmar.[34]

The rise of Japan as the place to look up to is also reflected in various countries' surveys. Table 5.2 shows the most recent favorability ratings of Japan, the United States, South Korea, and China from the Pew Global Values Survey. Japan ranks as most favorable in Indonesia, Malaysia, the Philippines, Thailand, and the United States, and also ranks highest all combined. In South Korea and China, Japanese favorability is considerably lower, reflecting historical grievances. A separate survey in 2019 showed that, of the 50% of Koreans who held a negative impression of Japan, 75% cited resentment over Japan's failing to properly reflect on its own history.[35]

Meanwhile, Japanese cultural exports are voraciously consumed by young people across Asia. In the second half of the 2010s, when Asia grew more ambivalent toward the United States, an increasingly affluent Japan with its luxury brands became the new attraction. Admiration for the high quality and reliability of ingredients in "Made in Japan" products was joined by a new "cool Japan" conception of hip, way beyond anime and concepts of *kawaii* (cute, as in Hello Kitty dolls). Japan has taken on new meaning as a status symbol, and at least for the millennials, this overrides postwar resentments toward Japan. The desire of young Chinese and Southeast Asians to emulate Japanese fashion, style, and brands has started a groundswell that is difficult to express in numbers. One indirect expression is the fast rise in Japan-bound tourism, to over 3 million visitors from ASEAN countries in 2018, with visitors from Thailand alone topping 1 million.[36]

A prime example of the cultural underpinnings of the new Asian consumerism is the cosmetics industry. An increasingly affluent Asia has grown its own vibrant companies, which are eroding U.S. and European status and brands. The previous trade surplus the United States enjoyed in this industry has turned into a deficit. Meanwhile, Japan's high-end cosmetic exports have tripled between 2012 and 2017 to $3.7 billion (not counting shampoos and lotions), as Japan has conquered Asian cosmetics with brands such as Shiseido, Kao (Bioré), Kanebo (Sensai), Kosé, Shu Uemura, Koh Gen Do, DHC, Skin Inc, and Hada Labo. While high-end cosmetics are yet another niche in the aggregate strategy, the cultural impact is deep, as throughout Asia Japanese brands have earned a

Table 5.2. Favorability Ratings of Japan, the United States, South Korea, and China in Asia, 2014–2017.

	Japan	United States	South Korea	China
Bangladesh	71%	76%		74%
China	14%	50%	54%	-
India	43%	49%	21%	26%
Indonesia	76%	48%	54%	55%
Japan	-	57%	25%	13%
Malaysia	84%	54%		79%
Philippines	81%	79%	69%	54%
South Korea	30%	74%	-	33%
Thailand	81%	72%		72%
United States	75%	-	62%	43%
Vietnam	86%	85%	82%	10%

Source: Pew Research Center Global Values Survey. Data are from various years between 2014 and 2017, and are the most recent available figures for each country.

reputation of superior quality and prestige. Trying to get into the action, new U.S. boutique brands such as Tatcha and Boscia are positioning as Japanese, claiming a deep spiritual connection to the rising sun.[37]

South Korea is also becoming a powerful competitor in this segment, and is positioning one level below Japan's high-end target in price points. This competition is increasing the hipness factor and revenues all over Asia for both. A similar story is unfolding in movies and TV dramas, where South Korea has also become Japan's major rival for Asian screen times. Japanese TV soaps often have a moral story that will make many watchers teary-eyed, whereas the Korean variety is said to be better at romance; either way, together with fashion magazines and foodie exchanges, Japan and South Korea are competing powerfully for the hearts and purses of young Asians, making each other better in the process.[38]

Japan's Global Mergers and Acquisitions

The final aspect of Japan's growing impact on the world economy is the new business growth through global acquisitions. Unlike the trophy hunting of the 1980s, Japan's recent shopping spree has been guided by clear strategic goals. For example, in reaction to a shrinking domestic market, Japanese life insurance companies have begun to acquire insurers in larger markets with more young people, and beverage companies have bought out competitors in growing markets. Moreover, technology firms are buying up startups that add to their core competencies or can help them extend into new markets, while also acquiring established companies in order to consolidate their dominance in niche markets.

Figure 5.2 graphs Japanese M&A activities, expressed in billions of yen. These are divided into "in-in" (Japanese acquiring Japanese firms), "in-out" (Japanese acquiring foreign firms), and "out-in" (foreigners acquiring Japanese firms) activities. Of particular interest in this chapter are the in-out deals. In Chapter 7, we will revisit this chart expressed in the number of annual deals, and see that the number of Japanese acquisitions of foreign firms doubled from 371 deals in 2010 to 777 deals in 2018. In Figure 5.2, we are looking at the value of these deals. In terms of money spent, the in-out category accounts for the lion's share of recent Japanese M&A activities. Between 2010 and 2018, Japanese companies invested a total of roughly $800 billion in outward-bound M&A, with a record year in 2018. There were strong indicators at the time of this writing that the upward trend of M&A would continue for 2019 and beyond.[39] Note that these numbers are approximate, as not all of these deals are public, and values differ by data source.

The year 2018 saw a total of about $300 billion (¥30 trillion) spent on mergers and acquisitions in Japan, of which two thirds were Japanese acquisitions of a foreign company, totaling $210 billion. The list was led by the largest ever overseas acquisition by a Japanese company on record, top pharmaceutical company Takeda's acquisition of Dublin-based Shire for $62 billion. This megadeal was followed by semiconductor maker Renesas's purchase of Integrated Device Technology (IDT) of Silicon Valley for $6.3 billion, Hitachi's acquisition of ABB's power grid business for $6.4 billion, and Recruit's acquisition of Glassdoor, the U.S. job-website operator with a vast database of company reviews and salary data, for $1.2 billion (see more in Chapter 9).[40]

All this makes Japan a leading player in global M&A. From 2014 to 2017, the country ranked fifth, behind the United States, China, the United Kingdom, and Canada, until the 2018 deals catapulted Japan to being the second largest M&A nation after the U.S.[41] Even before the banner year of 2018, Japan's acquisitions included many other purchases of companies that you might be surprised to learn are now Japanese; for example, Sprint (SoftBank), Jim Beam (Suntory), American Standard and Grohe (Lixil), the Financial Times (Nikkei

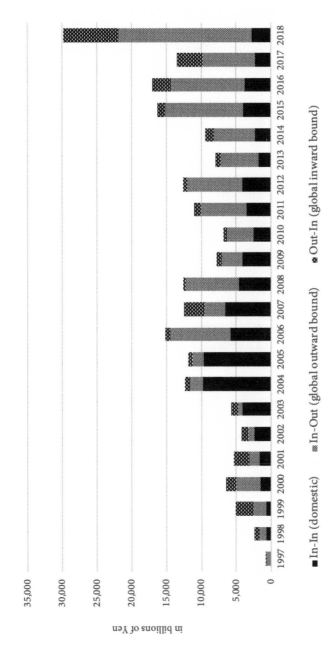

Figure 5.2. Mergers and Acquisitions, 2006–2018, by Value. Source: Constructed with M&A data from MARR online.

Shinbun), Dell Services (NTT Data), and StanCorp Financial (Meiji Yasuda Life) are all now majority owned by Japanese companies. Nor was this a one-time event. Activities continued into 2019, when Asahi Group Holdings, the owner of Asahi Breweries, spent $11.9 billion to buy Anheuser-Busch InBev's Australian unit, following its previous purchases in 2016 and 2017, worth $11.1 billion, of European breweries including Italy's Peroni Brewery and the Czech Republic's Pilsner Urquell.[42]

The uptick in global M&A has coincided with a mindset change vis-à-vis mergers and acquisitions, and a new strategic purpose.[43] Acquisitions of foreign firms have become an integral part of the second wave of choose-and-focus. Following their exit from non-core businesses, many companies proceeded to invest resources in building out their newly defined core. Abenomics is highly supportive of outward-bound M&A, and has brought in several tax reforms and deregulation in regard to stock conversions and other remaining hurdles to acquiring foreign companies.[44] The rebirth of Japan's banking sector has also added fuel to this fire. The large banks are an immediate beneficiary of the new M&A boom, because it has opened two new avenues for growth just as they were in the process of rewriting their business models. First, the banks themselves are acquiring foreign banks. And, they are developing new and lucrative M&A advisory businesses, and in fact are now seen as pushing their clients to make bolder and more decisive deals.[45] This further unties the hands of Japanese companies in expanding abroad, and unlike the trophy purchases of the 1980s, the new global expansion is often part of a thought-out strategy.

To illustrate the new strategic flavor of Japan's overseas acquisitions, con-sider Bridgestone's $1 billion purchase of Telematics, a business unit of TomTom, the Dutch navigation system company. TomTom wanted to exit this business in order to focus on its battle with Google Maps in the development of digital maps for self-driving technologies. Telematics offers vehicle-related data for fleet management and connected car services, and Microsoft, Daimler, and Michelin had been rumored as bidders. Bridgestone, the world's largest tire company, emerged victorious. It is now building new capacity in intelligent cars, by combining tires and sensors to collect road conditions and tire in-formation. Bridgestone CEO Masaaki Tsuya explained that the tire industry was now a so-called CASE industry—connected, autonomous, sharing, and electromotive—and that Bridgestone had positioned itself to capitalize on this shift.[46] We will see in Chapter 10 how many leading Japanese manufactur-ing firms are pivoting into new capabilities that straddle the boundaries with digital manufacturing and data-based services, and global acquisitions are an important element of this new development.

Thus, the surge in outward-bound mergers and acquisitions by Japanese companies further contributes to Japan's growing global impact. Not all of this is obvious to the casual observer, but Japan's impact on the world economy far exceeds standard measures of trade balances or product sales. And these new M&A activities also feed into the larger current of Japan's business reinvention and choose-and-focus: companies sell off yesterday's businesses and pivot to compete for tomorrow. In addition to growing the requisite new capabilities and markets domestically, they are also acquiring global technology leaders. These M&A activities serve two goals: to build out their new technology niches, and to move into new markets to increase their customer base. As this happens, Japanese companies are building beachheads in various regions of the world, and are becoming much more global. This, in turn, requires new management skills and business processes, as we will see in Chapter 8. Quietly but certainly, Japan's global business impact keeps growing.

MANAGEMENT CHANGE

Governance, Stewardship, and Executive Pay

In February 2015, Daniel Loeb, founder of Wall Street's activist investor Third Point LLC, made a significant investment in FANUC, a world leader in factory automation and robotics and one of Japan's most profitable and successful companies. Loeb was notorious for his approach of publicly excoriating his targets' CEOs to force their capitulation. In this instance, once vested he requested that FANUC change its "illogical capital structure" and fix its "blatant" capital inefficiency so the company could "significantly re-rate," Wall Street–speak for a stock price increase. Further, he believed FANUC should open up and be more forthcoming with corporate information, and use its $8 billion in cash holdings to increase dividends and launch a stock buyback program. FANUC was already a success, yet Loeb was scheming to make a quick buck by reaching into the company's cash jar.

Known for its ubiquitous use of yellow on its corporate campus in the foothills of Mount Fuji, FANUC has indeed long been known for a cult-like secrecy. The company is also known for paying high wages to its hardworking workforce that lives on its distant campus and rarely interacts with the outside world. Employee business cards do not list a phone number or email address, and the company is paranoid about hacking attacks. When Third Point knocked on the door in 2015, FANUC was paying a fixed dividend, had no debt, and carried a significant amount of its sizable earnings in cash. But the CEO—son of the founder Dr. Inaba and like Loeb a University of California, Berkeley alum—had already considered some of the measures Loeb was demanding. In 2013, FANUC had opened up its management board and invited in an outside director, and it was preparing several acquisitions. As we will see in Chapter 10, the company was also launching its FIELD open platform to compete in digital manufacturing. Already poised for change, within a few months of Loeb's investment the company had built an investor relations department, doubled dividends, and conducted share buybacks, leading the activist investor to comment that "the whole *zeitgeist* in Japan is shifting."[1]

Loeb had previously tried his luck in Japan in June 2013, with a $1.4 billion (7%) investment in Sony, which he sold 14 months later at a nifty 20% gain. Sony was bleeding red ink and had reported its fifth annual loss in six years. Loeb demanded that Sony sell off its entertainment and electronics businesses, a proposal that raised eyebrows on both sides of the Pacific, as it would have left Sony as little more than a shell with a bank. George Clooney, who at the time owned a business backed by Sony, joined the opposition, stating, "There is no conscience at work…it is only about creating wealth. A guy from a hedge fund is the single least qualified person to be making these judgments, and he is dangerous to our industry. Hedge fund guys do not create jobs, but we do."[2] Sony's board of directors considered but ultimately rejected Loeb's proposal. But Sony's CEO and former CFO, Kazuo Hirai, did launch a drastic cost-cutting campaign in Sony's movie units and sold the Vaio PC business, which gave the company's financials a nice facelift.

Nevertheless, many in Japan shared Clooney's unease. Certainly, a good dose of investor pressure to modernize and globalize may be the jolt that many Japanese companies with large cash holdings and low capital efficiency need. But activist pressure motivated solely by increasing the stock price to make a quick buck through short-term financial engineering was surely detrimental to a company's future, and such activities did not sit well with widely shared Japanese preferences for corporate stability and longevity. As corporate governance underwent a major overhaul, it was accompanied by a keen sense that Japan needed to design new mechanisms to defend against attacks by short-sighted activists, termed "vultures" (*hagetaka*).

During the postwar period, Japan's boards were almost entirely internal, and the main bank was the primary monitor of corporate health. However, this approach no longer works in an era of global finance, and it has also produced some spectacular scandals, such as the massive accounting fraud at Toshiba, brought to light in 2015. Moreover, to execute the aggregate niche strategy of refocusing through exiting non-core businesses and carving out corporate units, a liquid financial market is needed. The only way to attract global finance to Tokyo is to conform with global expectations of shareholder rights, management transparency, and financial disclosure. Thus, Japan's challenge with corporate governance reform is how to balance the needs of global financial markets with what has long worked well for Japan's companies, namely a concern for employees, a commitment to customers and clients, and the pursuit of long-term value creation.

To confront this challenge, in the late 2010s, just as the United States began looking to incorporate more stability and stakeholder representation into its Wall Street–dominated system, Japan began to turn toward shareholder capitalism.[3] Behind this apparent paradox is a new global soul-searching for a modern definition of the purpose and social responsibility of the company. Should it solely focus on maximizing profit, as the Chicago School of Economics posits, or should it contribute to societal interests, as reflected in calls for ESG (environmental, social, and governance) considerations, SDGs (sustainable development goals), and CSR (corporate social responsibility)? And what structures and mechanisms of corporate governance are required to pursue these goals without falling prey to the vultures? Japan informs this debate by offering an alternative approach to corporate governance, one that begins with the assumption that companies and investors are not contrarians but partners with a shared interest in creating long-term value.[4]

This chapter introduces Japan's newly emerging processes of management oversight, stewardship, and executive pay. It begins with the significant changes in Japan's shareholder structure since the 1980s. To meet the demands of institutional and foreign investors who now represent 50% of the shareholders in companies listed on the Tokyo Stock Exchange, new means of participation and interaction between shareholders and managers had to be built. These were constructed through a two-pronged—or sandwich—approach: governance reform opened the boardrooms and introduced new transparency, and a new stewardship code invited active participation by asset managers. This sandwich approach has linked internal controls with external oversight. The rollout of governance reforms and the new stewardship code has relied heavily on soft law, nudging, and shaming, which has proven highly effective in Japan's tight-culture setting. Governance reform has also subjected executive pay—which remains at about one tenth the U.S. level, albeit rising—to new transparency rules and board of director controls.

As of 2019, Japan's new system has two remarkable features. First, the penultimate goal of the ongoing reforms is to introduce new discipline. In addition to monitoring, this also means pushing senior management toward organizational renewal, through making the difficult strategy decisions to pivot into new businesses. Second, in my interpretation, the new stewardship code represents Japan's attempt to make the new system resilient in the face of short term–oriented activists, by requiring institutional investors to build the capacity to participate in the governance process. As Japan's large asset managers build new expertise in overseeing companies, they will shift the governance zeitgeist even further. As a result, Japanese CEOs are now facing a completely new set of pressures, opportunities, rights, and responsibilities vis-à-vis their shareholders. Together, the sandwich reforms may result in new defenses against the financialization and the hypermobility of money that have come to characterize the United States. While Japan's corporate governance system is changing, it has placed itself on a trajectory very different from that of the U.S.

What Is Corporate Governance For?

Japan's conceptualization of corporate governance has long contrasted with that of the United States. In the U.S., corporate governance has been deeply influenced by agency theory, which begins by assuming a conflict of interest between principals (shareholders) and their agents (managers). Because managers are driven by "self-interest and guile," shareholders need to be shielded from their inclination to betray and self-enrich.[5] Under this paradigm, the role of corporate governance is to protect shareholders through monitoring, intervention rights, and representation via the board of directors. In postwar Japan, the view has been the exact opposite: because markets are unpredictable and uncertain, managers need to be protected from the market, and this was accomplished by forging long-term, mutual shareholder relationships with trading partners.

Agency theory has come under criticism lately, due to mounting evidence that other theories of motivation are more powerful in explaining outcomes, and agency theory predictions often do not hold up empirically.[6] And the 2008 global financial crisis, with its many instances of ruinous financial engineering and wrongdoing committed by banks and companies, brought to the fore what had long been simmering: the way governance, oversight, and executive pay are structured in the United States incentivizes managers to take actions that are short-sighted and often detrimental to the long-term well-being of the firm and its employees. The schemes of activist investors to assume seats on the board and demand payments smack more of extortion than governance, and astronomical levels of executive pay contribute to fast-rising inequality.

Judging from the language used in recently revised governance codes in the UK and by the OECD, a new approach is emerging that begins with the assumption that shareholders and managers want the same thing: a healthy, stable, and successful company that creates value in the long run and contributes to societal matters such as sustainability and social responsibility. From this vantage point, the role of corporate governance is to create mechanisms for interaction and collaboration between shareholders and management, and safeguards to balance their interests.

These are also the new goals in Japan. Recall from Chapter 3 that corporate governance was seldom an issue before the turn of the century. Large firms and banks held mutual cross-shareholdings, making for stable shareholders with aligned interests in an environment where everybody wanted more sales with little concern for profits or efficiency. Boards consisted of internal directors who were known to rubber-stamp decisions already made by top management. And the only publicly accessible corporate information was what senior managers fed to journalists. The only outside actor with any power to intervene was the main bank, which was satisfied as long as sales were solid.

In the 2010s, for Japan to compete globally and attract global investors, this system needed a major overhaul. Governance reform would require creating new mechanisms of transparency, structuring new boards with external members, defining new processes for board discussions and annual shareholder meetings, and establishing new norms of appropriate behavior for board members and senior managers.

A second area of reform was to empower boards of directors to prevent scandal. This is an important function of any governance system, and perhaps the one where such systems fail most often. Japan has seen a series of scandals where, with hindsight, it appears that more transparency and independent directors would have made a difference. Perhaps the most telling was the 2011 financial scandal at Olympus—the camera maker that held a 70% global market share in endoscopes—which wiped out three quarters of the company's stock market valuation and was globally lambasted as evidence of Japan's secretive management practices. The scandal emerged when Olympus's British CEO, hired to restructure and reorganize the company, learned of accounting irregularities and money laundering stemming from the bubble years. When he blew the whistle, he was fired. His subsequent attempt to mount a proxy fight against the entrenched management was thwarted by limitations on shareholder rights.[7] Between 2015 and 2016, at least 58 other cases of accounting irregularities were reported in Japanese companies. There was also a series of quality misreporting cases, including scandals at Kobe Steel and Toa Corporation, a construction company.[8] In 2018, the Carlos Ghosn scandal (discussed later) added yet another aspect. Whether better oversight by a board could have prevented these cases remains uncertain. But these cases have been instrumental in shaping the reform debate, and their disclosure and public discussion are, in and of themselves, already a sign that the system is changing.

Japan's reforms are also about creating new, constructive means of interaction that allow CEOs to make bolder decisions regarding refocusing and repositioning. The vast majority of Japan's top executives are internal managers who have worked their way up the corporate ladder and were selected for their loyalty and dedication to the company. And to this day, many see their roles as, first and foremost, protecting the careers of those beneath them. This has translated into a strongly shared *anzen dai-ichi*, or risk-averse, approach to decision making in senior management. For example, as we saw with Panasonic and Sony, many firms are still hesitant to close down traditional business units, even if they are loss leaders. Insofar as the traditional mindset of these CEOs needs to change, it is not so much in terms of reining them in but rather encouraging them to be more aggressive and decisive in their strategic decision making.

In addition to the three main goals for Japan's governance reforms—to create new structures of management-shareholder interaction, empower board oversight, and push corporate reforms through market discipline—Japan's government also has a fourth goal of its own: in light of an aging and shrinking society, Japan's large pension holdings urgently need to earn higher returns. Corporate governance reforms are seen as essential to make Japan's financial markets attractive for domestic and global investors, so as to increase liquidity and returns on investment. This made corporate governance a core item of the Abenomics reform agenda.

The New Shareholders

New mechanisms of shareholder-management interaction became necessary because Japan's shareholder structure has changed dramatically over the past 30 years. Figure 6.1. shows the results of annual shareholder surveys by the

Tokyo Stock Exchange (TSE) of the relative percentages of groups of share-holders of its listed companies. Individual shareholders (far left) have held steady at around 20% due to comparatively high numbers of very large, blue-chip founder and family firms in Japan, such as Uniqlo, Nidec, SoftBank, and Rakuten. In the other categories, a sea change has occurred. The upper line, reflecting the situation in 1986 at the height of the postwar system, shows that roughly 70% of all shares on the TSE were held by domestic banks (21%), in-surance companies (21%), and corporations (29%). These were mostly loyal or cross-shareholders; in the case of corporate stakes, they also included partial stakes in the companies' own, listed subsidiaries. In contrast, the lower line shows that today, more than 50% of shares are held by institutional investors, namely foreigners (30%) and so-called trust banks (20%), which represent large asset managers. Today, shares held by banks and insurance companies combine to less than 10%, and corporations hold about 22%.

The decline in the role of banks as shareholders is seen as a main contribu-tor to the long-term stagnation of the Nikkei 225 stock market index. To im-prove capital adequacy in the banking sector after the banking crisis of 1998, the government capped the amount of equity banks could hold. But given the post-bubble slump, when banks began to unwind their substantial cross-shareholdings, nobody wanted to buy them. This influx of shares for sale greatly depressed the stock market throughout the early 2000s, even as global equity markets, including those in the U.S., were booming. In this view, Japan's long stock price depression had less to do with corporate performance than with a sound policy to reduce the risk exposure of the banking system. While this policy made the stock market look sluggish, for the banking system it turned out to be a stabilizing factor during the 2008 global financial crisis.[9]

It is important to appreciate that the survey numbers reported in Figure 6.1 represent averages for a large number of listed companies. The reality is much more polarized. As of 2019, the Tokyo Stock Exchange had roughly 3,500 firms, of which about 2,000 were listed in the so-called First Section (TSE1). Only about 500 of the TSE1 companies are truly large and global, with several thou-sand employees. And whereas the smaller firms tend to be owned by domestic interests, the shares of major companies are often majority held by trust banks and foreign shareholders, to a much higher degree than Figure 6.1 suggests.

The category of trust banks was separated out in 1988 to capture the rise of Japan's institutional investors. These trust banks come in several flavors. The first group contains the six large trust banks associated with the financial groups

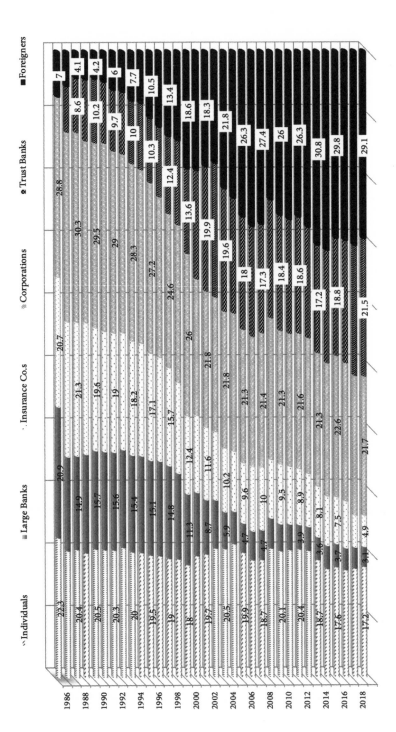

Figure 6.1. Changes in Japan's Shareholder Structure, 1986–2019. Source: Japan Exchange Group, Inc.

of Mitsubishi, Sumitomo-Mitsui, Mizuho and Resona, as well as Nomura Trust and Banking and Norinchukin Trust and Banking. They manage assets ranging from corporate pension funds to individual mutual funds, and their core clients are large companies and their employees. Industry observers estimate that as of 2018, these four institutions alone managed assets of about ¥16 trillion (roughly $160 billion). These large trust banks are the nominal shareholders for the assets under management, and they vote at annual shareholder meetings as instructed by the asset owners. Some of these banks have historical ties with long-standing, loyal clients, but increasingly, they compete for business through their investment track record.

The second group of players in the trust bank category consists of roughly 500 asset managers of varying size that occupy certain niches, including private wealth asset management. The third group is made up of the so-called re-trusts (*sai-shintaku*), or "master trusts." These are similar in function to Wall Street's "street names," such as State Street Bank & Trust, and they offer administrative services for the first two groups. In Japan, there are three such re-trusts: the Master Trust Bank, the Japan Trustee Services Bank, and the Trust and Custody Services Bank. Legally and on paper, they are listed as the shareholders for the over ¥100 trillion ($1 trillion) they administer. In reality, they are strictly IT administrators that trade and hold electronic shares on behalf of other asset managers, including trust banks, pension funds, indexed investments, and also foreign funds. They, too, vote at shareholder meetings only as instructed. The fact that they become the official holders of the shares they administer greatly obscures the real identity of shareholders. This has forced Japan's largest companies to hire investigative services from specialized investor relations advisory firms to identify their true shareholders.

For the CEOs of large Japanese companies, the rise of anonymous yet powerful asset managers and foreign investors requires a new mindset. While they may still count on the allegiance of some of the domestic financial institutions, they must assume that the asset managers are oriented toward earning returns. Rather than being quiet and loyal, if dissatisfied with a portfolio company, these asset managers may simply sell. This may depress the stock price and invite activist investors who smell a bargain. For the company, the best defense against these events is to run the company well, including communicating with large owners and reaching profitability targets. For Japanese senior managers, this is a completely new task. Identifying how to attract and engage with the new investors while also upholding Japan's preferences for stability and safeguarding against activists has become one of their biggest new assignments.

What tipped the balance from a preference for stability and protection to opening up to global investors was the need to introduce more liquidity into the markets. This was done to accommodate the two "Tokyo Whales"—mega-shareholders estimated to own about 11% of the entire TSE.[10] The first whale is the country's central bank, the Bank of Japan, which came to the commercial banks' rescue and bought up a lot of their cross-shareholdings in the early 2000s. Then, as part of the Abenomics quantitative easing program in the 2010s, the central bank invested massively in ETFs (exchange-traded funds). This makes it one of the top ten shareholders in 40% of Japan's listed firms.[11] The second whale is the Government Pension Investment Fund (GPIF), which is the single largest institutional fund in the world, with assets of $1.5 trillion in 2018. About 25% of these assets are allocated to domestic stocks, which in 2018 translated into roughly 7% of the entire stock market. Most of these funds are held in indexed investments and managed by the large domestic and foreign asset managers and investment banks in Tokyo.

Both of these whales need more water to swim in, so to speak. Eventually, the Bank of Japan will have to unravel its sizable stakes to phase out quantitative easing, and this can only be done without harm in a liquid market. Meanwhile, given Japan's quickly aging and shrinking population, the pension fund is concerned about its reserves. In 2006, the GPIF hired a globally experienced, aggressive chief investment officer who became part of the push for increasing corporate performance and investor returns. This has turned the GPIF into a long-term, yet vociferous investor advocate for ESG considerations, sustainable development goals, and asset managers' engagement with companies. The sheer size of these two whales and their calls for profitability and new forms of investor relations are forcing Japan's senior managers to think more carefully about the power of market forces and how to present themselves to the global investor community.

Corporate Governance Reform

The government's intellectual roadmap for governance reform was the 2014 *Ito Review*, a report that set out a reform package combined with a rallying call for companies to review their profitability and capital efficiency. Leaning on the 2012 *Kay Review* in the UK, which identified short-term rent-seeking and a lack of asset owner interest representation by large institutional investors as main causes for the 2008 global financial crisis, the *Ito Review* sought to reform Japan's corporate governance system in ways that would prevent excessive short-termism and support long-term value creation.[12]

PROFITS, NOT SALES

The *Ito Review* became famous for suggesting that companies strive for a minimum "8% ROE." For better or worse, return on equity was anointed as the holy grail of performance, and an increase in this metric by all firms was seen as tantamount to market rejuvenation. While the 8% hurdle was perhaps taken too seriously and triggered some counterproductive management decisions, as we will see later, the true purpose was to shift corporate Japan's mindset away from the focus on sales that remained entrenched in many CEO offices around the country.

To further nudge companies to focus on profitability, in 2014 the Tokyo Stock Exchange launched an index called the JPX400.[13] This index consists of 400 companies, based on annual revisions of a ranking of profitability (measured by ROE), profits, and size. The main purpose is not to offer another investment index so much as to shame companies that miss the cut. The index is purposefully designed to be quite large, so that any company not included is clearly not a top player.[14] For employees, too, the index can be a wake-up call: working for a company not included means you may be wasting your talent. The beauty of the mechanism lies in its gentle shaming: nobody has to say it, yet everybody knows. Especially in a tight-culture setting, this level of shaming is often sufficient. In 2015, the unfathomable happened: Sony dropped out of the JPX400, sending shock waves through the organization and the entire country. The company wasted no time in responding: as we saw in the previous chapter, it appointed its chief financial officer as CEO, and within a year, Sony was once again a member of the top 400.

By 2019, most large companies had answered the call. In 2012, the average ROE of Japan's listed companies was 5.3%, compared with 10.5% for U.S. companies and 15% for European firms. By 2017, this had risen to 8.55% in Japan, compared to 16% in the United States and 13% in Europe. And in 2019, Japan surpassed the 10% mark, at least momentarily, even as trade wars and exchange rate changes were threatening to depress revenues for the next fiscal year.[15] This significant increase would be nearly impossible to accomplish simply through accounting magic, so it must represent true increases in profitability.

Alas, the JPX400 also had unintended consequences. As intriguing as the "8% ROE" marker was in helping companies improve, it raised widespread concerns for leaning too much on the U.S. benchmark. Many viewed ROE as too crude a measure for international comparison, given significant accounting differences across countries. But what really raised flags was the insight that the shame index had created a perverse incentive. An econometric study of the index showed that companies at the cusp of the 8% threshold began to "manage for ROE," and in many instances, they did so by cutting R&D expenses. This raises the return in the ROE equation but undercuts long-term value creation.[16] Certainly this was not the intended effect, as innovation is critically important for the strategic pivot. Subsequent revisions of the governance guidelines have toned down the relevance of the 8% hurdle. Still, the shame index has become a global example of the power of nudging as a policy tool.

Boardroom Reform: The 2015 Corporate Governance Code

The 2014 *Ito Review* was also the opening bell to ring in a series of reforms regarding the constitution and responsibilities of boards of directors and investors, the rights and duties of management, and transparency and disclosure. State Street, the U.S. asset manager, viewed these as so fundamental as to mark a "watershed moment."[17] Foreign critics, commenting on these reforms from the agency theory perspective, found them to be lacking rigor.[18] By Japanese standards, however, by the mid-2010s, reform had brought a palpable sense of change. Not only were the provision of corporate information and the diversity on corporate boards increasing, but the style and content of board and annual shareholder meetings had also changed significantly in many large companies.

Given the closed nature of the previous system, a top reform goal was opening boardrooms and increasing the number of outsiders on corporate boards. This move began in 2009, when the Tokyo Stock Exchange recommended that boards have one "independent" outside member, that is, not dispatched from an affiliated company such as a bank or main trading partner. Due to the historically strong role of networks, long-term relationships, reciprocity, and obligation, the definition of *independent* became an important aspect of reform. By 2010, 70.5% of TSE1 firms had an independent director or compliance officer, in terms of the early lenient interpretation of that word.

In 2015, a triple reform push was launched by way of a new Corporate Governance Code (modeled after the OECD's *Principles of Corporate*

Governance), new TSE guidelines on board membership, and a substantial revision of corporate law (the Companies Act). Regarding board composition, the new prescription is that a board should include at least two truly independent outside directors (now defined much more strictly as having no business relation at all with the company). More active participation by women and foreigners was also specifically recommended.[19] One could take issue with the effectiveness of quotas for board composition, whether specifying gender or any other characteristic, in bringing about true system and mindset change. However, in entrenched situations, quotas are nonetheless a positive first step to begin to move the needle. Considering the average TSE1 company had fewer than nine board members at the time, appointing two from outside the firm was significant, as it meant that one fourth of the company's directors would be independent. By 2017, 95% of TSE1 companies had at least one outside director (compared to 45% in 2008 and 55% in 2012), and 87% had two truly independent directors, signaling that the quotas did indeed affect behavior.[20]

However, this raised a new challenge for companies: where to recruit these independent directors? Owing to the stricter definition of what constitutes an independent director, they had to recruit outside their corporate networks. And given the previous restrictions on women's careers, there were few candidates for female directors. The custom of holding monthly, half-day board meetings, carried over from the postwar practices of internal boards, also kept meetings too short for substantial discussion. This, in combination with the Japanese norm that attendance in person is truly important, unintentionally limited the number of foreign candidates. Initially, companies drew on former bureaucrats, CEOs in unrelated industries, accountants, and academics. Some companies even agreed to conduct web-based conference calls to permit foreign board members to attend. For senior managers, all this has combined into a sea change in how to run a board meeting, and initially caused great uncertainty and discomfort regarding the appropriate conduct and level of interaction with these outsiders.

In the early days of growing board diversity, many senior managers and board members reported that everybody was at the steep end of the learning curve. Concern about inadvertently violating behavioral norms in an unfamiliar setting translated into scripted meetings that seemed perfunctory, with the CEO lecturing, the accountant commenting on the monthly profit and loss numbers, and an agreement by all to keep up the good work. But the situation improved quickly: as new practices and processes permeated the system, companies adapted, board meetings became longer and less formulaic, and deliberation increased. Insiders report that the "conversation in the boardroom has changed," with much more true discussion of corporate strategy.[21]

Adding outside board members seems to have made a positive impact. Early research on the relation between boards and performance has found that Japanese companies with independent directors report better performance and that a company's stock price increases in response to the first outside director joining the board.[22] Even though causality is difficult to establish in this type of research, these findings added further power to the reformers' push and increased acceptance of outsiders in the boardroom.

Soft Law and Nudging

In spite of significant initial resistance from traditional large companies and their main lobbying association, Keidanren, between 2015 and 2019 the ratio of TSE1 companies with at least one outside director increased to almost 100%. This success was unexpected even within Japan and is best explained by the main regulatory approach chosen to phase in these changes: soft law (i.e., guidelines) combined with nudging and shaming. Although some of the governance reforms are now baked into hard rules, the initial approach was to leverage Japan's tight-culture and rely on the power of social proof—our human tendency to want to fit in and mimic the behavior of those around us—as a main tool of implementation. The approach was to make suggestions without sanctions, and slowly change the common views of what constitutes a modern and global boardroom by showcasing and celebrating early adopters.

In the soft law approach, the government issues a guideline—not a law—that declares a desired policy outcome and invites companies to "comply or explain." Companies can choose to follow the guideline or not: if they do, that's great; if they don't, they must explain why. The approach rests on the notion that in policy areas such as governance, diversity, and inclusion, the market itself provides strong discipline, and therefore nudging is often more efficient than pursuing change through the legal system.

Noncodified elements are part of almost all regulation, particularly in its implementation. This is captured by the long-standing notion of using "carrots" (inducement) and "sticks" (punishment). Within monetary policy and banking systems, regulation through inducements is known in the United States as "moral suasion," and in Japan as "window guidance" and "administrative guidance."[23] After the scandals during the bubble economy, which revealed too much informality, soft guidance had fallen out of favor in Japan. But along with some European and Asian countries, Abenomics enthusiastically introduced the 21st-century version of this regulatory approach. Soft law for governance reform was first used in the UK for its ease and speed. Guidelines issued by a ministry can bypass political review and afford flexibility, unlike "one size fits all" regulation. And when this type of nudging is done right, compliance can be greatly increased, even in the absence of monitoring and sanctioning.

When Japan first employed this soft law approach in the early 2000s, with the guideline on outside directors, resistance was initially high. Very successful companies, led by Canon, Toyota, and Honda, were steadfast that there was nothing wrong with their boardrooms. They pointed to the benefits of inside boards in a system of lifetime employment, such as ease of deliberation thanks to a shared, deep understanding of the company's needs, and also intellectual property protection. However, due partially to the government's nudging and partially to quality scandals and declining performance after the 2008 global financial crisis, by 2014, all three companies had succumbed to peer group pressure and added an outsider to their boards. As they complied, a new normal was created in which not having an outside director now meant a company was deviant.[24] Holdouts became outliers and risked embarrassment in their search for a compelling reason why an outsider was not acceptable in their company's boardroom.

High compliance rates notwithstanding, in 2018, the Asian Corporate Governance Association demoted Japan's corporate governance rating due to this over-reliance on soft law. This may be an instance where frameworks and research insights related to nudging, as well as to tight and loose cultures, could be helpful in understanding the differences in the needs and realities of regulation across countries. For a tight-culture country like Japan, high compliance rates suggest that soft law a is highly effective and speedy way to bring about reform. In fact, as we will see in Chapter 8, Japan has since found a wider application for nudging in the push for workplace diversity and inclusion.

The Stewardship Code:
Empowering Asset Managers

Some readers may recall the case of Bull-Dog Sauce, a well-known brand of Japanese condiments. In 2007, a U.S. activist investor called Steel Partners launched a hostile bid for the Bull-Dog Sauce Company, after management had resisted Steel Partners' advice on performance improvements. A long battle ensued, and Bull-Dog launched a poison pill, the legality of which Steel Partners challenged in court. The Tokyo High Court ruled against the fund and labeled it an "abusive acquirer," viewing its goals as detrimental to the company. This labelling reflected fears, at the time, of management intervention in Japanese companies by Wall Street firms. Interestingly, just over ten years later, foreign and domestic fund managers as well as CEOs in Japan agree that this event would not be repeated today because the rules, perceptions, and needs of the financial markets have fundamentally changed. What does remain, however, is a concern that even though activist investors may bring much-needed discipline, they could also be detrimental to the long-term viability of a company.

Japan's new answer to the challenge of defending against potential vultures, perceived or real, is to hold asset managers—such as the trust banks, fund managers, and insurance companies—responsible for the representation of asset owner interests. Compared to the United States, where the asset management industry is fairly fragmented, Japan's institutional investors are very large, and the six large trust banks account for a large portion of the business. Not involving them in governance means letting sizable shareholder interests sit idle. If these voices could be heard, they might positively affect governance. So, activating this lever and appealing to the stewardship responsibilities of asset managers became the second side of the governance sandwich.

In the traditional Japanese system, institutional investors, such as life insurance companies and banks that managed corporate pensions, did not consider the necessity of representing asset owner interests. In a system dominated by cross-shareholdings within business groups, their main task as shareholders was to be stable and loyal. They may not even have attended the annual shareholder meetings. In those days, activism was viewed with suspicion (it was considered to be "noisy" or, worse, "rocking the boat"). But as the shareholder structure diversified and activist investors, both domestic and foreign, arrived in Tokyo, the annual shareholder meetings became less formulaic and sometimes even contentious. To build mechanisms through which asset owners are heard in these new discussions, Japan became the first country to follow the UK's initiative in issuing a stewardship code that laid out the role of institutional investors in corporate governance. It was issued in 2014 (and revised in 2017) as soft law regulation, under the title "Principles for Responsible Institutional Investors."[25] The goal was to turn institutional investors into more active and engaged shareholders who would not only advise portfolio companies on management decisions but also represent asset owner interests in times of activist investor attacks.

The "comply or explain" prescription of this code is that institutional investors are to formulate a clear, open policy on how they, as asset managers, will fulfill their functions as active shareholders representing asset owners. This includes regular announcements on how they will work with the board, their position on corporate policies such as dividend payouts, their potential conflicts of interests, and perhaps most importantly, how they voted on each agenda item at the shareholder meeting. The code eschews the word "monitor" and instead asks asset managers to engage so as to "properly grasp the circumstances of the portfolio companies."[26]

Thus, the stewardship code is a call for institutional investors to build a staff that is observant and knowledgeable about a portfolio company's goals and progress. To comply with this call, institutional investors must build or acquire new internal talent and knowledge in order to issue advice, take positions on matters such as CEO succession or executive pay, vote, and then report these activities to their asset owners. This has already begun to change the operations and staffing of the large trust banks, away from simple administration to building a knowledge base in financial analysis and research.

The underlying assumption of the stewardship code is that if an activist investor's request appears to be detrimental to the long-run interests of the company, asset managers representing asset owner interests will block the proposal.[27] But even in Japan's setting of strong obligations and reciprocity, and even in light of the risk-averse leanings of insurance companies and pension funds, CEOs can no longer be certain how institutional investors will vote. When it comes to poorly managed companies, the newly informed and empowered institutional shareholders might well side with an activist fund. Data that tally asset manager votes at annual shareholder meetings have already shown an increase in items where asset managers opposed company recommendations, including items on CEO succession, CEO pay, and board of director appointments. Thus, the stewardship code is not a guaranteed safety net for senior management. Rather, it adds yet another group of shareholder interests CEOs must consider.

As of April 2019, 246 institutional investors had signed up to adopt the code, of which 183 were asset managers, 23 were insurance companies, and 33 were pension funds. Moreover, about a quarter of the signatories were foreign. The Financial Services Agency regularly polls asset managers, and a majority of the large players have agreed to disclose their voting behavior at shareholder meetings.[28] One big exception consists of the managers of corporate pensions funds, who sense a potential conflict of interest if they have to vote on their own companies' proposals. And some of those who have signed on might have done so just for compliance on paper, rather than to take a true participatory stance. As the system is still evolving, uncertainty runs high, which is uncomfortable to many and, in and of itself, propelling further reforms. The full effects are yet to be seen, and it will be interesting to follow the evolution and market consequences of institutional investor activism in Japan.

Executive Pay and the Carlos Ghosn Scandal

On November 19, 2018, Carlos Ghosn, the chairman of the Nissan Motor Company, was pulled out of his private jet at Haneda Airport and arrested, initially, for underreporting his executive pay and compensation package by $80 million. Over the subsequent five months, he was indicted three more times, for personal use of company assets (for such items as houses, a yacht, and his own wedding) and aggravated breach of trust, such as improper money transfers for personal benefit. This included a complicated deal with a large Japanese bank whereby Nissan guaranteed personal loans to Mr. Ghosn to cover his significant private investment losses stemming from the 2008 global financial crisis. It also became clear that Nissan's board of directors had been sitting hamstrung, with board meetings lasting no longer than 30 minutes and shallow in content.

As the indictments piled up, Ghosn was held in solitary confinement, in ways that seemed overly harsh by international standards and greatly worried the foreign CEO community in Japan. The fall from grace of one of the world's best-known auto executives sent shock waves through the industry. Ghosn had come to Japan in 1999 to manage Japan's flagship automotive company, which had been bailed out by Renault. Known as the "cost killer," he pushed Japan's entire auto industry toward higher efficiencies and global sourcing. In 2004, Ghosn became the first foreign business leader to receive the Emperor's Blue Ribbon Medal.[29] How this scandal would end was unclear at the time of this writing, as Mr. Ghosn fled Japan for Lebanon on New Year's Eve 2019 in spectacular fashion, leaving behind $15 million in bail and a great mystery in how he had escaped tight 24-hour surveillance.

Ghosn's executive pay from Nissan in Japan, as reported in March 2018, was about $7 million, and he ranked 18th in CEO pay in Japan. This was twice as much as the CEO of Toyota received, but not outrageous. At issue was a side contract in which Ghosn granted himself lump-sum retirement pay of $82 million in the future, and this was not reported in Nissan's annual financial statement. And while retirement pay is commonly a sizable portion of CEO pay in Japan, this was exceedingly high. At almost the same time, a domestic scandal involving the Japan Investment Corporation (JIC), a private-public investment fund, ended with the resignation of its anointed CEO, senior managers and the entire board, allegedly over the matter of excessive executive pay. This had been set at about $1 million each, and an even higher but undeclared amount for managers of JIC sub-funds.[30] Even though the depths of both situations were still murky at the time of this writing, it seemed that pay was not necessarily the real, and certainly not the only, reason for the exits of these two CEOs. Nevertheless, the pay aspects of these scandals triggered domestic soul-searching regarding ongoing changes in Japan.

One important function of the governance system is to represent shareholder interests in regard to executive pay, on the grounds that without oversight, managers may be tempted to vastly overpay themselves. In the United States, most boards appoint a special compensation committee, which tends to be guided by the postulation of agency theory that people will not work unless paid, and that more pay triggers more effort. To incentivize CEOs to exert effort, their pay is tied to the company's performance, and this is assessed by the stock price. Typically, the pay for a large-firm U.S. CEO has several components: a predetermined fixed salary and a variable portion consisting of a bonus, stocks, and stock options. These options can be converted into cash after a certain period and at a certain price. Critics have long pointed at the severe shortcomings of this system, beginning with the false assumptions of what motivates people, and the use of the stock price as a metric to assess management performance. What is more, the focus on stock price sets incentives that are deleterious to the company. CEOs are incentivized to forego long-term investments in employees, R&D, and strategic change that may take time to show results. Worse, they may be tempted to engage in financial engineering to jack up the stock price, by taking on more debt or launching a stock buyback. While performance thresholds can be useful and can help in implementing tough decisions, if overdone a short-term focus on the stock price will surely undermine the long-term viability of the firm, to the detriment of other stakeholders.[31]

One reason for the high CEO pay in the United States—which exceeds other senior managers' pay within the same firm by multiples—is the highly liquid market for CEOs. As the anointed superstars, CEOs move around, and they use the salaries of other high-paid CEOs as a comparison to demand ever higher pay. This means CEO pay is determined horizontally, and CEOs can squeeze companies for salaries that seem detached from the capability of any single person to contribute to corporate earnings. This has also made U.S. CEOs the highest paid in the world, and over the past decade has greatly contributed to rising inequality in the United States.

In contrast, in Japan, CEO pay has traditionally been structured toward the long-term. Almost all Japanese CEOs are internal candidates who grew up through the ranks of lifetime employment. At the turn of the century, 82% of senior managers in large Japanese companies had never worked for another firm, compared to 28% in Germany, and 19% in the U.S. Outside CEOs were exceedingly rare: between 2000 and 2009, only 4% of Japanese CEOs were out-siders, compared to 20% in U.S. and 25% in Europe and Asia.[32] Furthermore, when a CEO resigns, they typically become chairman of the company. All told, the most successful Japanese senior managers occupy the C-suite for almost two decades before they fully retire.

Senior manager pay is determined vertically within the firm, and to this day, it is typically set as a modest multiple of the company's general manager salary. Traditionally, Japanese companies have set overall pay scales based on company size, and there is high parity across the entire organization. The typi-cal salaryman's annual salary consists of a standard wage and a company-wide bonus, typically also equal across the organization. So, even though so-called allowances (reimbursements for transportation, extra pay per child, and so forth) introduce a modicum of individual variation, pay for lifetime employees is quite egalitarian. With each promotion, all employees also receive a similar raise, meaning that all general managers earn roughly the same amount.

When their lifetime employment contract ends after the typical 30-year career, the best of the general managers are rehired as executive directors. No longer salaried, their remuneration is now determined at the very top and ratified at annual shareholder meetings. This pay is usually set as a multiple of their previous general manager salary, and the variable portion remains below 20%.[33] In the mid-1990s, with limited pay competition among executives, the chairman received 4.2 times the manager salary, and the CEO 3.6 times that amount. As we will see shortly, this has begun to change recently due to global pay competition and the arrival of foreign managers in the executive suites. Still, in terms of the domestic market for executive leadership, horizontal price setting remains limited. An external market for CEOs exists, consisting of so-called professional managers, but their number is small, and because they are not viewed as the establishment, they generate little price competition.

As of 2017, a salary above $100,000 (¥10 million) was considered high in Japan, and it was estimated that only about 5% of all Japanese employees earned more than $100,000 (not counting bonuses or allowances). The "$1 million" club was truly exclusive, with only 704 senior managers of listed Japanese companies earning more than $1 million. In comparison, in 2017, there were a reported 102,000 people in the United States who earned a salary of more than $1 million (not counting stock options or other variable pay), although unlike the data for Japan, this number included not just business executives, but also athletes, movie stars, and other high earners.[34]

In the Japanese system, the way in which Japan's CEOs are rewarded above scale is through multiple retirement packages, paid at each level of senior management, and as a big retirement bonus after they serve their standard six-year term as CEO, followed by another six-year term as chairman.[35] Although executive pay remains comparatively low, total remuneration adds up over these multiple retirement payouts to multiples of the annual salary. Together with their long stays in the C-suite, pay through pension payouts incentivizes management toward ensuring the longevity of the company, with a time horizon of almost two decades. Of course, CEOs have already dedicated their lives to the company, have worked their way up the hierarchy, and have been selected for their concern for the company and its stakeholders. But insofar as they need further nudging to care about the company's future, scheduling pay at the end of their tenure further induces long-term planning.

In most companies, these cumulative deferred payments and the end-of-career bonus, paid upon retirement, are determined by the CEO. It was this cumulative pay that got Carlos Ghosn into trouble at first. The necessity to declare this pay in the annual financial statement was introduced only with the recent governance reforms, and Ghosn maintained that his retirement pay had been determined prior to the rule change. This caused talk of a possible witch-hunt aimed at the foreign CEO by traditional Japanese interests, until other allegations surfaced that indicated a variety of dealings in possible violation of the law.

In 2018, the 25 highest paid U.S. CEOs earned a total of $1.3 billion, or on average $52 million each. Note that these numbers are so-called fair values, or nominal pay, not the actual realized gains which can be up to three times higher.[36] This average of $52 million also excludes Tesla CEO Elon Musk, who chose to pay himself $2.2 billion in 2018, when the median income of his employees stood at $56,123 and the company was bleeding red ink. Excluding Tesla, median employee earnings at the U.S. firms with the top 25 highest-paid CEOs were $89,200, meaning that the average ratio of CEO pay to employee pay was 843x (again, nominally). Overall, there were 82 CEOs in the U.S. earning nominally over $20 million in 2018.[37]

By Japan's own standards, 2018 was also a record high year for salaries in Japan. Although orders of magnitude smaller than U.S. pay, and containing a variable portion of less than 20%, the 2018 figures nevertheless caused outrage and accusations of greed within Japan. The shocker was that Japan's highest-paid CEO in that year, by far, was Kazuo Hirai at Sony, at $25.5 million, of which $11 million was a pension payout.[38] Computing numbers parallel to the U.S. data, Japan's top 25 highest-paid senior executives earned a total of $250 million, or $10 million each on average. This translates to just one fifth of the average nominal pay of their top 25 highest-paid colleagues in the U.S. The Japanese companies that awarded their senior managers these high salaries also paid comparatively high wages, with average employee pay of $81,427, resulting in a CEO pay ratio of 182x.

Importantly, of the ten senior managers who were paid more than $10 million in Japan in 2018, seven were non-Japanese, indicating that Japan's new wave of high pay is driven by foreign executives. The companies where they work have attracted global talent that has introduced horizontal pay competition to Japan, and this has led to the unusual situation in which Japanese CEOs are not always the highest-paid people in their organizations. The three highest-paid SoftBank executives combined make about $50 million in annual pay, and overall SoftBank had nine executives earning more than $1 million. Yet, SoftBank's CEO and largest owner, Masayoshi Son, paid himself a salary of only $1.4 million and ranked 402 on Japan's top-paid executives list. The legacy companies also are not stingy by any means. In 2018, Hitachi reported 18 people among the top 100 highest-paid executives, and the leading companies in the Mitsubishi business group a total of 22.[39]

Looking only at the top 25 offers an extreme version of the story. Below the top 100 highest-paid executives, Japan's CEO pay and corporate salary, while inching up, is still marked by significant wage compression. A 2017 comparative study of disclosed CEO pay data for 400 major companies underscored this. By level, U.S. CEOs nominally earned ten times more than Japanese CEOs.

By compensation structure, the average U.S. CEO pay consisted of 10% base salary and 71% stock options, setting strong incentives to manage toward the market. In contrast, in Japan, the fixed salary made up 58% of CEO pay, annual incentives were 29%, and long-term incentives 13%.[40]

A main reason for the continuing wage compression in Japan, even in the face of higher executive pay for foreign managers, is that Japanese CEO pay continues to be driven by norms of fairness and a keen sense of appearances. Insiders report that rather than employing the mechanisms of governance and compensation committees—which do not seem to be working effectively in the U.S. anyway—Japanese CEOs refrain from asking for higher salaries, as they do not want to be seen as greedy. Even as the number of high net worth individuals in Japan is rising, demanding high pay or flaunting wealth is still considered inappropriate. Excessive executive pay is widely considered as unfair to the employees, who also work hard, and inappropriate in light of society's expectations of the social role of the corporation. And although stock options were introduced in 1997, a 2012 study of 200 large listed firms revealed that even though 32% of TSE-listed companies had adopted stock options, these options remained small and many executives were reluctant to convert them.[41]

Yet despite these norms, executive pay in Japan is clearly increasing, giving rise to demands for more transparency and oversight. Previously, executive pay had been shrouded in secrecy. A rule change in March 2010 has made it obligatory for listed companies to annually report all executive salaries exceeding ¥100 million (roughly $1 million), including fixed and variable cash payments, severance pay, and noncash compensation such as stock options.[42] As of 2017, accrued pension benefits, health insurance, special allowances, and nonmonetary benefits did not have to be reported, an exemption likely to play into the Ghosn case as it tests the definitions of these various types of pay. Meanwhile, shareholders, and especially institutional and foreign investors, are pushing for more transparency on executive pay and succession, and corporate governance reform includes pressure for companies to introduce a compensation committee.

Even though today the values of loyalty and obligation still have a certain currency, there is a new undercurrent in Japan toward higher pay. This is bound to rise only further, especially if a job market for CEOs develops and horizontal price negotiations replace the use of vertical multiples to determine pay levels. This is likely to bring further governance reforms, in the form of a larger role for compensation committees, and further transparency regarding the internal operations of Japanese firms.

$$\textbf{7}$$

FINANCIAL MARKETS

Private Equity and M&A

In April 2019, Hitachi Ltd., Japan's largest IT, electric machinery, infrastructure, and energy equipment technology company announced the sale of Hitachi Chemical, a listed firm in which Hitachi Ltd. held a 51% share. This was a watershed event in Japan's business reinvention. Not only was it a sign that Japan's diversified conglomerates were getting serious about consolidating their subsidiaries. It was also the first major case of a large Japanese company pivoting its core into a new industry. Hitachi Chemical was one of Hitachi's three inner core subsidiaries, and a very successful global company with advanced technologies in lithium-ion battery and semiconductor materials. In fiscal year 2018, it accounted for $6 billion, or 7%, of Hitachi's total sales of $85.5 billion.[1] The sale of a crown jewel so integral to the Hitachi brand stunned Japan. And no sooner had this announcement sunk in than Hitachi followed with another shocker, namely that it would sell all its listed subsidiaries. By December 2019, in two deals valued at more than $8.8 billion in total, Hitachi had sold its 51% stake in Hitachi Chemical to Shōwa Denkō, and its business in diagnostic imaging devices, Hitachi Medical, to Fujifilm.[2]

These deals were part of a larger, assertive plan to reposition and consolidate, and increase profitability. Whereas before Hitachi had large stakes in 22 listed subsidiaries, by late 2019, this number had been reduced to only three. For example, in 2017, the company had sold Hitachi Koki (power tools) and Hitachi Kokusai Electric (semiconductor equipment) to the private equity firms Kohlberg Kravis Roberts & Co. (now known as KKR) and Japan Industrial Partners, for a total of $3.6 billion.[3] Then, in 2018, Hitachi sold Clarion, a car navigation system company, to a French car parts maker for $800 million. Over the previous decade, Hitachi had already exited businesses spanning logistics, finance, wind turbines, cell phones, and hard disk drives.[4] The strategic intent with these activities is to chart a new course focused on the digital transformation, and to compete in advanced systems solutions for digital manufacturing, as well as electricity and other energy-related operations and smart infrastructure (more on this in Chapter 10). This new strategic focus also involves acquisitions. In late 2018, Hitachi acquired the U.S. power grid business owned by Swiss heavy machinery maker ABB, and in 2019, it bought JR Automation Technologies, a U.S. robotic system integrator.

Hitachi's repositioning is having a huge impact on Japan's reinvention. What may look fairly standard to U.S. eyes—a series of carve-outs and acquisitions in the process of business reorganization—is new to Japan. If Hitachi, Japan's largest, most diversified electric machinery company, the standard-bearer of Japan's manufacturing sector, can change its course and steer toward agility in the new digital economy, then any diversified Japanese company can. Hitachi's reinvention nullified the excuse of being "too big to change." What is more, while many Japanese companies have tried to shed smaller non-core businesses since the late 1990s, the Hitachi reorganization of 2019 was the bellwether of a new wave of strategic repositioning, the second wave of choose-and-focus. It represents a new approach of shifting existing corporate assets out, and instead focusing resources on new business segments to deploy the aggregate niche strategy—even when that means relinquishing highly successful and profitable business units if they no longer fit. In Hitachi's wake, other large Japanese companies are now getting ready to make the hard decisions. At the same time, these decisions still must follow the basic tenets of Japan's business norms: carve-outs need to be done in carefully structured ways that are considerate of the business legacy and the employees of the spun-out units. The crown jewels cannot just be taken to the pawn shop.

To carve out such big pieces requires a large, liquid market, and this market began to build up in Japan in the late 2010s. Japan's offerings of high-quality corporate assets attracted foreign investors, and they arrived in the form of private equity (PE) funds. Unlike activist shareholders who buy stakes in listed firms to push a reform agenda, PE funds operate off-market: they invest either in businesses that are not listed, or take their acquisitions private. They then invest in their restructuring and manage a business reorganization before they put them up for sale, ideally at a gain. Until the 2010s, Japanese CEOs had viewed

PE funds as predatory vultures and a noxious outgrowth of Wall Street greed. But as choose-and-focus became real, PE funds have come to be considered in more balanced ways. Their presence is seen as providing needed discipline, as they are often right when they identify a firm as a candidate for restructuring. This discipline is also helping to push Japan's reform agenda, as the best defense against unsolicited activist investors is to run a great company. Moreover, the PE funds have emerged as constructive and helpful financiers of the second wave of choose-and-focus.

Not all PE funds are the same. They fall across a spectrum of length of investment horizon (short to long) and profile (high to low). You could also think of this as a two by two matrix, with the two dominant cells being the long-term, engaged, low-profile funds on the one hand, and the short-term, aggressive, high-profile ones on the other. Another way of expressing this spectrum is to think about high-quality, long-term owners on the one end, and financial engineers (aka vultures) on the other. In a 2017 interview, the chief investment officer at Yale University described the former as "intelligent capital investment" and labeled their "buy-make better-sell" activities a "superior form of capitalism." In contrast, he found the activist approach to be "a naïve playbook that is destroying the quality of companies and the market overall."[5]

Nevertheless, it is not always easy to tell the difference, as even within one company, fund managers may have different approaches. The world's largest private equity funds—KKR (oldest), Blackstone Group (largest overall), Carlyle Group (largest PE), and Bain Capital Private Equity (largest restructuring)— have assets under management exceeding $100 billion each and operate in multiple market segments with different objectives. They have been associated with both value-creating turnarounds and corporate destruction. Naturally, as Japanese companies invite PE investors to buy their subsidiaries and business units, their goal is to bring to the table only the high-quality value creators and to build barriers against the financial engineers.

This chapter describes how Japanese companies are building a value-creating private equity industry, with the help of tight-culture norms and various levers of ostracism. After offering data on the size of private equity, globally and within Japan, the chapter reviews the growth of private equity in Japan, as well as its challenges, and then shows how Japanese companies have set up structures to deter deleterious behavior by these investors. However, private equity is only one of several market-based activities related to the choose-and-focus activities of Japanese large companies. The final section examines the other types, including activist investors, a Japanese version of such investors in the form of "public equity," as well as domestic mergers and acquisitions.

The takeaway is that Japan has developed its own culture and norms of appropriate behavior for these market transactions, and through a variety of mechanisms, including exclusion, is nudging participants into assuming more long-term, value-creating strategies. Selling highly valuable assets means parting with businesses that are near and dear, and Japan's keen sense of responsibility for employees and a legacy often makes such trades difficult. Selling these companies is not just about money but also about accountability and reputation. Of course, CEOs are fully aware that this is not always rational in market terms, but they nevertheless proceed slowly and demand assurances that the units sold off will not simply be stripped of their assets and discarded. As they try to find a new home for their assets, they are looking not for the highest bidder but the right owner.[6] Trust is not usually a word associated with global private equity, but for many of Japan's CEOs, trust is a precondition, to assure that their business units end up well. Through this insistence, slowly but surely, Japanese companies have developed a new set of rules, and even hard-core Wall Street players are abiding by them.

The Private Equity Industry

Recall from Chapter 4 that refocusing options for a company include selling a certain business unit to another company, merging it with other companies' units into a new company (a type of spin-out), or selling it to an investor (a carve-out). In a carve-out, the investor is usually a private equity firm, and the company may retain an ownership stake in the unit. A high-quality, long-term PE firm then brings in a seasoned CEO who invests in and rebuilds the organization. This is akin to flipping a house, and based on professional management skills and accompanied by hard decisions on how to restructure. This corporate remodeling usually takes four to seven years. These funds attract investments from institutional investors and asset managers interested in earning returns through restructuring these corporate assets. The risk associated with this activity is that if the turnaround effort falls short, it will wipe out the entire investment; the reward comes from selling the remodeled firm at a much higher price.

In contrast to this high-quality approach, a financial engineering PE firm (a short-term vulture) does not invest much in the object; like a chop shop, it sells the underlying assets, pays itself an enormous fee, and shutters the firm. One example of such deleterious engineering is for the fund to invest in a retail chain that owns its stores, sell the real estate (and take a fee for that), and then force the retailer to lease back the stores, which will eventually drive the retailer into bankruptcy; this was the sad turn of event at Mervyn's, an erstwhile leading U.S. retail chain.[7]

Functions of Private Equity Investors

The best-known form of private equity is venture capital (VC). Similar to the high-quality PE funds, VC funds operate with a long-term view of building value. But whereas VC funds focus on startup companies, corporate buyout funds focus on the acquisition of corporate business units. Just as VC funds guide startups, set milestones, and perhaps bring in a new CEO, corporate buyout funds introduce new management systems, additional funding, and consulting expertise. Many PE funds have their own consulting firm or in-house consultants, in addition to access to a network of professional CEOs.

For a large company that wants to divest a business unit or subsidiary, in addition to selling to a PE fund, choices include selling it to or merging it with another company, or taking it public by listing it on the stock market. In the late 2010s in Japan, selling a carve-out to a PE fund was often the faster and more lucrative option. And what has really made private equity a preferred route in Japan's second wave of choose-and-focus is the very fact that it is off-market. That is, private equity allows the company to refocus without having to worry about the share price of the carved-out unit, or even its own share price. And in the ideal scenario, private equity enables managers to make consequential divestitures by taking the middle road between Japan's traditional *anzen daiichi* approach and the more brutal U.S. way of downsizing through layoffs and closures.

Japan's rapid growth in private equity activity in the 2010s was driven by two main categories of activity: choose-and-focus carve-outs and succession deals. The corporate carve-out market was the largest in dollar amounts invested. As of 2019, Japan still had more than 250 conglomerates, defined as firms with more than 50 consolidated subsidiaries, and in total they had more than 30,000 subsidiaries.[8] One quarter of firms listed on the JPX400 had more than 100 subsidiaries each. The arrival of foreign shareholders, as seen in Figure 6.1, generated concern about the so-called conglomerate discount, Wall Street speak for depressed stock prices due to diversification, which in turn might invite activist shareholders who would force divestitures to raise the stock price. Rather than facing the vultures, companies turned to PE firms to help them consolidate at their own pace. In 2015 alone, there were 842 spin-out cases worth over $50 billion, followed by 850 cases in 2016 worth over $30 billion.[9]

The second large category of Japan's M&A activity in the late 2010s was associated with the "succession challenge" caused by the massive retirement wave of post–World War II founders of small firms that lacked a successor. Between 2000 and 2018, the median age of managers of small firms increased from 47 to 66, and it has been estimated that, by 2023, over 300,000 small firm owners will reach the age of 70, with 62% having no succession plan.[10] Closing these companies would be costly to society: they employ an estimated 6.5 million people and contribute about ¥22 trillion (roughly $220 billion) to GDP. Their banks and surrounding regional economies may also depend on them. To facilitate restructuring in this middle market, a 2018 tax reform related to corporate succession offered incentives for PE funds to invest. This has opened a new market opportunity for domestic and foreign PE funds to bring capital, advice, and management experience to small firms. Succession deals accounted for about 50% of total PE activity in Japan in the late 2010s.

PE funds also engage in turnarounds and distress deals, where they invest in companies in trouble. In Japan, it often happens that small and medium-sized companies face bankruptcy, despite having strong projects and a loyal customer base, because they lack the management wherewithal to escape a temporary crisis situation. Coming to the rescue of such companies has become a growing business for Japan's domestic PE funds. Finally, there are also the so-called management or leveraged buyouts, where a company chooses to delist from the stock market, perhaps to escape a vulture attack, and invites a PE fund to structure the financing of buying back its own shares. This was the original PE fund activity that gave the industry its vulture image, as chronicled in detail in the 1987 book and movie *Barbarians at the Gate*, about the ruthless destruction by KKR of the U.S. conglomerate RJR Nabisco.[11] In Japan, these activities are still rare; when they do occur, they often entail smaller firms.

Private Equity by the Numbers

The PE industry is huge. In 2017, globally, the industry was estimated to consist of about 4,800 PE firms, with about $2.5 trillion in assets under management and more than $900 billion in "dry powder" (funds ready to be deployed). Most of this global industry is headquartered in the United States. By 2017, Japan stood at roughly 10% of the U.S. market in size, but the market was growing fast.[12] As of 2019, global savings from pension, mutual, and sovereign funds, plus capital from banks and insurers, continued to flow into these funds, which had outperformed stock markets, fixed income, and even hedge funds since the 2008 global financial crisis. At a time when global interest rates were low, the PE industry found itself in a major boom.

In the reporting of business statistics, PE investments are considered mergers and acquisitions. Figure 7.1—which is similar to Figure 5.2 but expressed in number of deals as opposed to dollars—shows that 2018 was a record-setting year for Japan's M&A market, with 3,850 deals. Of these, roughly one quarter were cross-border deals (either in-out or out-in). As we saw in Figure 5.2, the total value of all the deals was about $300 billion, and two thirds of that was spent in cross-border mergers and acquisitions. In contrast, Figure 7.1 shows that in terms of number of deals, domestic activity dominated: of the total of 3,850 transactions in 2018, 2,814, or 73%, were domestic, and they were worth roughly $3 billion. According to industry estimates, about 50% of domestic mergers and acquisitions were succession deals, followed by 20% in both divestitures and management buyouts (carve-outs and spin-outs) by large firms.[13] A smaller number, though an important portion in terms of value, were mergers between large Japanese firms.

This increase in activity has made Japan, once again, a lucrative and attractive market. In addition to the domestic players, global PE funds have begun to enter, or re-enter, Tokyo. Between 2006 and 2016, while the stock market was stagnant with returns of 1x, Japan's PE industry earned an estimated 2x on the large deals and 4x on deals under $55 million. The market had reached a sweet spot: it had enough liquidity to allow big deals but was not so competitive as to drive down the returns. Entry multiples (i.e., the price paid for assets expressed in relation to earnings) were around 7x EBITDA, much lower than in the United States (10 to 14x) or Europe (10 to 12x), but this 7x EBITDA was about 25% more than the seller could earn through other divestiture options.[14]

Private Equity, Japan-Style

Japan's experience with PE funds began in the mid-1990s when the growing banking crisis attracted U.S. financial firms to Tokyo. GE Capital was one of the first major entrants, followed by Ripplewood Holdings and Cerberus Capital Management, which arrived in 1998 and bought out two of the former long-

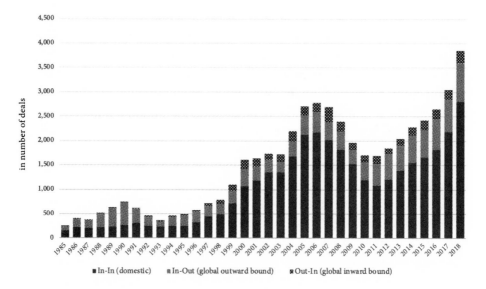

Figure 7.1. Mergers and Acquisitions, 1985–2018, in Number of Deals. Source: Constructed with M&A data from MARR online.

term credit banks that had gone into receivership. When the former flagship Industrial Bank of Japan (IBJ) was merged into a new financial group called Mizuho, many of the best and brightest jumped ship to join foreign PE funds. The struggling banks tried to salvage at least some value from nonperforming loans and sold collateral to these funds, often at 10 cents to the dollar, making entry relatively easy and lucrative. The initial bonanza ended in the early 2000s, and by then some of the Japanese bank employees had established their own funds.

Even though they helped to alleviate the banks' nonperforming loan burden, these early funds were seen as barbarians at the gate, as they benefited from Japan's post-bubble crisis. Between 1997 and 2002, in the first round of choose-and-focus after the 1998 banking crisis, PE funds bought more than ¥30 trillion ($250 billion) of distressed assets and real estate. In 2007, a hit NHK-TV drama series titled *Hagetaka* ("Vultures") portrayed buyout funds as rapacious invaders from Wall Street that destroyed Japan's inefficient small or family-owned firms and undercut the country's business values of trust, loyalty, and responsibility for employees. In the show, a foreign PE fund employed takeover schemes unknown to Japan to bring financial efficiency and discipline to corporate Japan. The series triggered heated discussions of the costs and benefits of the discipline of the market versus Japan's traditional style of stable ownership and management protection. It also highlighted the need for corporate Japan to change and learn the global ways of finance.[15]

The Koizumi boom triggered "leave it to the market" deregulation and invited a second round of PE growth. Between 2002 and 2007, the number of annual deals nearly quadrupled, from 23 to 90, for a total value exceeding $10 billion in 2007. Still, most of these early deals were non-core divestitures and turnaround investments.[16] While the market was growing, Japan's CEOs nevertheless remained cautious: foreign funds were still seen as vultures and dealing with them was stigmatized. After the 2006 Bull-Dog Sauce "abusive acquirer" debacle, as we saw in Chapter 6, the global financial crisis hit, and many U.S. firms retrenched and exited Japan. In 2018, a Japanese fund manager reflecting on that case commented that "there has been a complete change since the Bull-Dog case in 2006. This would take a completely different path today."

Abenomics invited the third PE boom, when Japan emerged as an attractive, fast-growing PE market in the mid-2010s. A larger portion of the new inflow of money is domestic. Between 2013 and 2017, the PE industry in Japan raised roughly $3 billion annually, and in 2017, assets under management were estimated at around $30 billion, with over $10 billion in dry powder. Then, in 2017 alone, Japan-focused PE funds raised $5.7 billion, and regional funds that included Japan raised $22 billion, twice the amount raised in 2016.[17]

In contrast to the United States, where pension funds (43%) and insurance companies (13%) dominate among the PE investors, in Japan, 53% of PE investments are sourced from corporations and banks.[18] The corporations use PE investments to deploy a portion of their large cash holdings: in early 2019, they were estimated to hold $4 trillion in cash reserves, with a capital-to-asset ratio exceeding 40%, and these assets were partially fueling the PE market.[19] But the largest domestic driver, by far, consisted of the so-called policy investments (*seisaku tōshi*). This term refers to three main investment categories: (1) pension funds (including the Government Pension Investment Fund), (2) the Japan Post Group, through its own fund JPIS (in addition to being a postal service, Japan Post is a bank and insurance company and holds $1.85 trillion in assets, of which 40% are earmarked for alternative investments), and (3) so-called public-private funds. The largest of these public-private funds are the Innovation Network Corporation of Japan (INCJ) and its 2019 successor, the Japan Investment Corporation (JIC), with $20 billion in assets under management.[20] As of 2019, these funds occupy such a large fraction of Japan's entire investment pool that, in addition to entering the market themselves as general partners, they have to distribute their funds over a large number of asset managers. This has spawned a new, rapidly growing asset management industry.

Family offices of wealthy individuals, mutual funds, and other private asset management funds are a less publicized but quickly growing source of liquidity for the emerging PE industry. As we saw in the introduction, Japan now has many wealthy individuals, and as of December 2016, total Japanese household financial assets were estimated at over $15.4 trillion.[21] While details are unknown, asset managers report that a growing portion of their assets is being channeled into alternative investments, and in particular private equity.

This activity has created a positive feedback loop. As the stock market now puts pressure on management to increase profits, CEOs look to refocus their conglomerates; they lean on PE funds for divestitures, which pulls more liquidity into Japan. This new liquidity brings more discipline for managers, which fuels further carve-outs. By the mid-2010s, the world's largest PE funds all had committed billions of dollars to the Japanese market, and a domestic industry was flourishing. In 2016 alone, KKR declared Japan its "first priority" outside the United States and invested $10 billion in Japan.[22]

Patience and Partnership

There are now three large categories of PE firms active in Japan: (1) global portfolio PE firms that pursue a variety of goals, including exchange rate diversification; (2) foreign (mainly U.S.) PE firms with a large office in Japan, either as part of a wider Asian strategy or with a country focus; and (3) Japanese-owned domestic PE firms. For the purposes of Japan's business reinvention, the latter two are of most relevance.

The Japanese PE funds range from large to small. The largest, with more than $500 million of assets under management as of 2018, include Advantage Partners (the oldest and largest), Integral Capital, Japan Industrial Partners, Polaris Capital, Tokio Marine Capital, Marunouchi Capital, Unison Capital, and Nippon Sangyō Suishin Kikō (NSSK, an offshoot of TPG Capital). The next tier consists of about 20 funds with assets over $100 million, including

CLSA Sunrise Capital, New Horizon, Rising Japan, Whiz Partners, AZ-Star, Globis Capital Partners, and i.Sigma. In 2018, the entire domestic industry was estimated to have 235 PE funds, up from 175 a year earlier; in other words, an average of one new PE fund was created per week in 2017.[23]

The leading foreign PE firms in Japan are known as the Big 4: Bain Capital PE, KKR, Blackstone Group, and Carlyle Group. Carlyle has been in Japan since 2001, and in addition to its global assets, has raised more than $3 billion in Japan. Even though Carlyle experienced three major failures, with telecommunications provider Willcom, Toshiba's ceramics business Covalent, and display panel company Avanstrate, it has been steadfast in its commitment to Japan. Bain and KKR have come, gone, and around 2016, come again, with a large war chest.

What all these funds have in common—and also share with the Japanese PE funds—is that almost all of their fund managers and heads of office are Japanese. Industry observers sense that the truly foreign funds are much less successful, because most Japanese CEOs are still suspicious of short-term financial engineering.[24] As Japanese CEOs base their deals on their deeply ingrained preferences for long-term relations and reciprocity in deal making, they tend to rely more easily on other Japanese. In deals where the main PE fund is a foreign firm, there is typically a Japanese co-investor, to create a sense of balance, even if that makes little sense from a financial perspective.

The Japanese fund managers have a variety of backgrounds, but the stereotypical career path of the most important ones—from the heads of Integral, Advantage, and JIP to their counterparts at Carlyle and Bain—is a former career in traditional Japanese banking. Within Japan, these Japanese fund managers are sometimes seen as outsiders, as they are "rocking the boat" with their reformist approach to corporate restructuring. But within Japan's PE industry, they are successful because they know how to navigate Old Japan's business norms. They typically started their careers at the beginning of the bubble at a bank, and then jumped the sinking ships during the banking crisis of the 1990s. Some of them joined a foreign PE fund right away, while others gathered more experience in an M&A advisory or foreign consulting firm before they became PE fund managers. Having been groomed as bankers in the 1980s, they know what it takes to be (or appear) polite and appropriate, and they also understand—and often genuinely share—the seller's preferences for long-term value creation. Meanwhile, they also know how to be responsive to conservative Japanese asset owners such as pension funds.

These Japanese PE fund managers have helped craft the new rules of Japan's PE industry in line with the preferences and demands of Japanese CEOs, and have established new PE business norms that frame the transaction as a "partnership," rather than a one-off deal.[25] These fund managers are result-oriented and profit driven, yet also want to improve Japan's economy. This combination positions them to bridge the gap between the long-standing concerns of legacy CEOs and the new needs of the market. And they have established Japan's two main ingredients for success: respect the seller's assets and employees, and deliver on the long-term value creation.

A U.S. observer might wonder why the financial engineers, domestic or foreign, don't just cut in, win the deal, and make their play. While that is of course always a possibility, as of 2019, they were being deterred by a very effective defense mechanism: ostracism. Any fund that violates a company's trust greatly diminishes its own chances of succeeding in another bid. Tokyo's financial industry is well networked and news travels fast, so CEOs know which fund managers deliver. They are also prone to being unforgiving and have long memories. To be successful in Japan, a PE fund must build a reputation for reliability. One fund manager reports that making a PE deal in Japan takes "years of courtship." This is especially true for the smaller succession deals that are often proprietary (and not auctioned off), where it is common that only one PE fund works with the company. To get this exclusivity requires a convincing value creation plan, and an ability to deliver on the promise. And because the sellers are looking not for the best price but the right owner, they will simply not deal with vultures, no matter the price they offer. Foreign investors have realized that the rushed deal making of Wall Street is not a winning strategy in Japan, and even activists such as Daniel Loeb are said to be toned-down when they come to Tokyo, as they have learned that nudging and shaming are more effective than issuing demands.[26]

Unlike the practice in the U.S., at least until 2019, Japan's corporate assets are rarely auctioned; if they are, bids are by invitation only. Deals require long cycles of interaction between the seller and the fund. Sometimes sellers demand that there be two buyers, ideally with one being Japanese, in the hope that this will introduce a better power balance, and an additional layer of insurance against short-termism. All this has resulted in the emergence of a private equity market that differs greatly from the U.S. market, not just in tone but also in durations of deal making and expectations of value creation. As another fund manager remarked: "Of course, the occasional fake long-term proposal happens, and then they go in and break the company apart or flip it right away, that's a social reality. But those guys can do it only once—they will never get another deal in this town."[27]

EXAMPLE: THE TOSHIBA DRAMA

In 2017, the CEO of Western Digital learned this lesson the hard way. He thought himself the clear winner in the bid for Toshiba's NAND flash memory unit, but was outdone by a six-party consortium led by PE fund Bain Capital. Valued at $18 billion, this deal was the largest on record in Japan, and the largest in Asia, that year.

Toshiba invented flash memory technology in 1987, and you may recall its launch in consumer markets as the USB "thumbstick" in 1991. Since then, semiconductor technology has made great strides. By now, flash memory has replaced the hard disk drive in our computers, it stores photos in our cameras and music on our phones, and it is expected to be a core infrastructure component of the digital transformation. In the mid-2010s, with a 35% market share each, Toshiba and Samsung Electronics ruled the global flash memory market, and the business was growing and profitable. Then Toshiba was struck by a management crisis, in the form of an accounting scandal in 2015, followed by the collapse of its nuclear power business, caused by an ill-advised, multibillion-dollar investment in Westinghouse. To avert bankruptcy, in 2016, Toshiba sold its medical business (including CT scanners and MRI machines) for $6 billion to competitor Canon, which, incidentally, paid a hefty surcharge following a price battle with a PE fund.

Toshiba then put its flash memory unit up for sale. What ensued was an intense battle for the business that culminated in a lawsuit by joint venture partner Western Digital, whose brash CEO, Steve Milligan, had prematurely appeared on Japanese TV to declare victory. As a business partner who shared global production sites with Toshiba, Milligan assumed his company had first dibs on this highly prized business. But he had alienated Toshiba executives by repeatedly violating all of Japan's business norms. This included the utterly inconsiderate decision to make a low-ball offer, which was seen as insulting at best, and a breach of trust and friendship at worst. When rival bidders appeared, Western Digital threatened to sue all of them, in an effort to scare them away. There was no way Toshiba could entrust a crown jewel to somebody who was so inappropriate, brazen, and out of line.[28]

At that moment, Bain Capital entered the mix, almost as a white knight. With its global reach, it was able to rally a group of foreign investors to finance the $18 billion deal, including Dell and Apple, who are among Toshiba's largest customers. Toshiba and Hoya (a leading Japanese materials supplier to the technology) maintained a combined majority of the voting stock in the new company, Toshiba Memory Corporation, which was incorporated in April 2017. In the end, while this deal was about getting the highest price, it was also about etiquette, the longevity of the business, and a transition that would leave everybody's dignity intact.

The Challenge: Professional Managers

The biggest challenge for Japan's PE industry is the lack of a deep pool of managerial talent. It is reported that there is some exceptional talent in the Tokyo PE offices, individuals who have spent time abroad and bring to the table both global experience and a local network. But they are rare, and there are many fund managers who are still learning the ropes. Because there are not yet many established case studies or accumulated experience on how to structure a PE deal in Japan, they cannot draw on an established toolkit or provide a long track record for investors to assess.[29]

Moreover, the PE fund managers—who tend to come from banking or consulting backgrounds—are often inexperienced in managing a business turnaround. When the industry was small, this was not as much of an issue, because the portfolio firms could be left to their own devices, or perhaps a competent manager could be found and promoted from within the company. But as more, and more advanced, deals are struck, the PE fund managers have to oversee the activities of their portfolio companies in more hands-on ways.[30] Consultants, too, are scouting for talent to advise new managers on executing a turnaround strategy.

Underlying these challenges is a lack of experienced turnaround CEOs and also consultants and professionals in other supporting industries, such as lawyers and accountants. However, as we saw in Chapter 3, there is still no liquid market for CEOs, and large firms tend to hold on to their leadership talent. At the general management level, few Japanese managers have gone through outside leadership training, and few hold an MBA degree. If hired by a PE fund, the experience they bring to a carve-out tends to be confined to how to run a manufacturing operation, meet targets, and produce midrange plans. Very few general managers in Japan are trained by their large-company employers on how to lead a business. While running operations is an important skill, it does not translate into the capabilities needed for successful turnaround management.

There is a pool of so-called professional managers (*puro keieisha*), and even a Wikipedia entry with that title, which in 2019 listed only 47 names. Tokyo businesspeople think that the actual number is probably closer to 1,000 managers, in their 50s, who have a background in consulting, investment banking, and management and could be hired to run PE portfolio companies. However, these "pro managers" are often not considered part of the establishment, nor do they necessarily have the career path and experience that would prepare them for the traditional CEO role.[31] Even though they may be quite capable in the smaller succession deals, they may not have the network and access to be successful leaders of large portfolio firms. Thus, the biggest pain point in Japan's young PE industry is the lack of management experience, at the level of both the PE funds and their portfolio firms.

This managerial talent scarcity may ease as the PE industry itself becomes more mainstream, and there are some indications that this is beginning to happen. In 2018, TV Asahi launched a new version of the drama *Hagetaka*. Whereas the 2007 original portrayed ruthless foreign investors and Japanese inexperience and angst, in the new version private equity is portrayed as a positive force that rescues corporate Japan and even protects it from evil market forces.[32] This also reflects a new attitude by the employees of these carved-out or spun-out entities. As salaries are no longer determined by the size of the company and the mid-career job market has opened up, employees no longer see reorganization as a calamity. Some even embrace it as a new beginning with better working conditions and more upward mobility, as opposed to muddling through at a non-core business of a struggling giant company.

Activist Investors

A growing concern for Japanese companies is the rise of unwanted investors, that is, the market for corporate control. Such shareholders proactively demand management change or divestitures aimed at increasing the company's stock price, and thereby the value of their shareholding. In Japanese, they are referred to as "speaking shareholders" (*mono-iu kabunishi*)—meaning they are "noisy" (*urusai*), including the connotations of shrill and bothersome. As Japan's market for corporate assets grows and corporate governance increases the rights of shareholders, such activism is becoming much easier and more profitable. Increasingly, Japanese CEOs have to worry about becoming the target of activism.

Unlike PE funds, activist funds target listed companies that they identify as underperforming. They assume shareholder positions which can be as small as 5% or upward of 20%. The intent is to use the rights associated with the shareholder stake to demand substantial changes from management. And just as with PE funds, activist investors fall on a spectrum from truly constructive to entirely self-interested. For example, they may demand a higher dividend payout, or pressure the company to repurchase its own stock to drive up the stock price. A certain respect for the existence of such noisy shareholders can be healthy for sparking proactive restructuring and upgrading. But the question remains whether Japan can balance this desirable discipline with sufficient protection against harmful raiders.

This fear is directed not only at foreigners. The first Japanese activist fund was founded in 1999 by Yoshiaki Murakami, a former government bureaucrat who came to be known as the "scourge of Japan's boardrooms," and was jailed in 2007 for insider trading in the so-called Horiemon scandal.[33] Murakami was labelled a *meiwaku* (nuisance) for his self-declared efforts to change the country. It was perhaps thanks to him that activist shareholders earned the label noisy. Still, over the years, his financial successes attracted other funds into the markets, including from abroad.

In 2019, there were a reported 25 activist funds in Japan, up from eight in 2014. These included Hong Kong–based Oasis Management and Argyle Street Management, and U.S.-based Elliott Management, King Street Capital Management, ValueAct Capital, and Fir Tree Partners. These funds aim to exploit low valuations of undermanaged listed companies by using the "power of capital" (a phrase used by ValueAct). They are doing so with growing frequency: in 2016, there were a reported 20 cases of activist intervention in Japan, and by 2018, this number had jumped to 47. This was much higher than the 36 reported in 2018 in the UK, or Germany's 19. It was also the highest in Asia, with China ranking second with 13.[34] In the past, some of these activists have been described as being outright rude at annual shareholder meetings, and their proposals have included substantial demands, such as removing a CEO, adding a new independent director (including themselves) to the board, selling off a business, or engaging in financial engineering.

Yet here too, a new "Japan style" is beginning to show. According to industry observers, the tone of the activists in these negotiations began to change around 2018. Perhaps this was due to learning that polite and appropriate were the norms by which business was run in Japan, and reflecting a desire to fit in. And just as PE funds had, the activists realized that the best way to succeed in Japan was to be persuasive, not pushy. Perhaps ironically, the fastest route to success was often the slow route, taken patiently in a manner that was respectful and reasonable. It also helped that Japanese companies had something that these investors dearly wanted: cash and huge upward stock price potential. To everyone's surprise, by 2019, even Yoshiaki Murakami had adapted and was advocating a new approach of finding what he called win-win solutions. And in a great reduction from its usual noise levels, in 2019, ValueAct kindly requested that one of its partners assume a board position at Olympus, and this was presented as being done out of concern for the company, with the goal of building a brighter future.[35]

Regardless of whether this more polite approach is always genuine (*honne*) or perhaps just a façade (*tatemae*), it has attenuated the tone, if not the actions, of the noisy investors. As of 2019, it appears that Japanese tight culture is shaping activists, not vice versa. The activists have bought into the norms of Japanese business culture, at least to some degree. While it is unclear whether this can be upheld in the long run, in the late 2010s, social pressure on the markets has opened the door to a new type of investment activism characterized by civility.

Public Equity Funds and Misaki Capital

An idiosyncratic element of Japanese private equity has also emerged in the form of companies that act like long-term, value-creating private equity funds, but deal with listed firms. This is explained by the very large number of very small firms listed on the Tokyo Stock Exchange—about 2,000 companies on the TSE have fewer than 500 employees. Some of these companies have great assets—a market position, a technology, or a brand—but either face succession issues or lack the management depth to take their business to the next level, such as through a global expansion.

Misaki Capital was founded in 2013 by Yasunori Nakagami, who came from a consulting background and realized that this public small-cap market was much larger than private equity at the time. He set out to deploy the mechanisms typically seen in value-creating PE deals in the public market. At one level, Misaki is an activist shareholder: the firm takes on a small equity position of about 5 to 10% in a small company, then introduces new operations and management processes with the help of its strong staff, many of whom have a consulting background. Misaki exits after a few years of management improvement, with the hope of a higher stock price by that time. The difference here from a more short-term activist approach is the hands-on involvement in management change, as if the small company were a private equity portfolio firm. To distinguish itself from activist funds, the noisy shareholders, Misaki calls itself a "working shareholder" (*hataraki kabunishi*) and a "constructive activist."[36]

Misaki's recipe has three distinct ingredients. First, the focus is not on turnarounds but on an upgrading of operations and management improvement. Portfolio companies are picked for their solid source of competitive advantage in an industry with fairly high barriers to entry. Further, because Misaki's goal is to be constructive and collaborative, the company's management team needs to be open to change and fully embrace the joint effort; there are no unwanted investments. Further, the portfolio company needs to have potential, such as existing management skills or easily trainable staff, especially in areas such as accounting, logistics, or finance.[37] Unlike ValueAct's motto about the power of capital, Misaki's business approach is to use the power of persuasion—in other words, nudging. Misaki works intensively with a small group of select portfolio firms, and hopes to build a trust relationship with each. Misaki thinks of this as a "triple win": the target company is strategically upgraded, Misaki's asset owners earn high returns, and the Japanese economy overall benefits from the productivity boost among small companies. This triple win strategy has also turned out to be highly lucrative.

The case of Misaki underscores how polite, considerate, and constructive investments can make economic sense. The impact of players like Misaki is similar to that of Japan's PE funds, in that they show it is possible to earn high returns in Japan without being a vulture. It is not necessary—and could be counterproductive—to be aggressive in trying to effect management change. Japan's business norms of civilized interaction work well even in finance and governance. Yet, polite does not mean being weak or overly forgiving. These funds are just as oriented on increasing returns on investment as any other investment fund. Rather, they represent a clever marriage between U.S. market ideas of efficiency and performance upgrades and Japan's tight-culture preferences for long-term, polite, and considerate investor relations. As Yasunori Nakagami puts it, "the concept is, let's blend the good things of Western management with the needs of the Japanese business setting."[38] As more players join the fray, Japan's business reinvention is also happening at the level of the smaller firms.

Mergers and Acquisitions:
Friendly or Hostile?

In addition to the rise in Japan's PE markets, Figure 7.1 also reflects an increase in domestic M&A activities. Since 2011, the number of domestic (in-in) mergers and acquisitions has steadily increased, reaching 2,184 in 2018. The bulk of this activity has involved mergers of smaller regional companies that had jointly hired a professional manager in order to scale up. While detailed information on these deals is difficult to collect, one of the leading advisory firms in this market reported consulting on 650 cases in 2017 alone, and in most instances, retiring CEOs sold their firms to a similar or neighboring business directly.[39]

During the postwar period, and still to this day, many Japanese CEOs have viewed a merger with a competitor as a tragic, one-sided defeat, especially for large companies. Typically, the CEO feels responsible for protecting jobs, especially in the absence of a liquid, mid-career labor market. And even if employees were to keep their jobs, their identity, career tracks, and job security would likely be wiped out. Thus, even a merger among equals is typically seen as a dereliction of duty, a failure by senior executives to manage the company for longevity. And in this line of thinking, the CEO is responsible for this failure.

When asked to estimate how many of Japan's large, domestic mergers are unwanted, if not hostile, a veteran M&A specialist at one of Japan's largest banks replied: "Almost all. There are no mergers in Japan, only acquisitions, and none are friendly."[40] Traditionally, Japanese mergers and acquisitions were triggered by financial concerns, never strategic ones, such as to create win-win synergies. One side was usually the weak one and the other the rescuer. Therefore, counting the number of officially hostile takeovers in Japan is not a useful exercise, as most of these events were unwanted, even though they are not labelled hostile to avoid embarrassment. A better yardstick for change is counting the frequency at which such combinations occur.

And in the late 2010s, domestic mergers have increased dramatically. Between 2012 and 2018, the total number of M&A deals roughly doubled, from 1,848 to 3,850. Of these, domestic mergers jumped from 1,219 to 2,814. Nor were these all deals among small firms. Choose-and-focus oriented mergers among large companies have also become a steady occurrence, such as the 2012 merger of Nippon Steel with Sumitomo Metal to create the third-largest steel company in the world. Steel is a scale industry and joining forces would increase market pricing power and allow for streamlining and increased capacity utilization while pushing market leadership in specialty steel segments.

Recently, some of these domestic M&A deals have become more combative, with juicy battles played out in public, for all to see. In 2019, following a surprising shareholder fight over leadership at Lixil, which confirmed the new shareholder rights through corporate governance reforms, a bitter fight emerged between the Itochu Corporation and its partially owned, listed subsidiary, Descente. Descente is a maker of sports apparel, with global brands including Marmot, Arena, Umbro, and Le Coq Sportif. As Descente refused management guidance from Itochu, its main shareholder, Itochu unceremoniously increased its stake in the company and appointed a new CEO. Many in Japan were surprised by the sudden surge of this new style of public merger battle, which was seen as further evidence that the new governance rules and market mechanisms are taking hold.[41]

Underlying this recent activity is a change in how the society, government, and companies in Japan view mergers, including acquisitions of Japanese firms by foreign companies. In the postwar period, such deals were rare because Japan's market was mostly closed to foreign investors, and this was a hot topic during the U.S.-Japan trade wars in the 1980s and 1990s. Through the 1990s, most attempts by foreigners were thwarted by corporate cross-shareholdings and the absence of a so-called squeeze-out rule that obligates minority shareholders to surrender their stakes in a takeover attempt. And where the cross-shareholdings failed, the government had often stepped in, such as by finding a domestic "white knight" to take over the company before the foreign interest could.

All this, too, has begun to change. After the 1998 banking crisis, cross-shareholdings began to unravel and several of the former main banks merged across business group boundaries, which removed the previous group protection. Then came the failure of Nissan, which brought Renault and Carlos Ghosn in as saviors. The need for choose-and-focus repositioning and the governance reforms of Abenomics then began to reshape the thinking about the opportunities created through asset sales and mergers, as well as the market necessities of clearing out vestiges of the past. The arrival of foreign acquisitions is reflected in the rise of the out-in deals in Figure 7.1. Between 2012 and 2018, these roughly doubled, from 112 to 259 deals. In Figure 5.2, we saw a more dramatic, more than tenfold increase in the value of these deals, from barely $6 billion in 2012 to over $80 billion in 2018. This marked a significant break with the past. These acquisitions included high-profile cases that highlighted a new willingness by Japan's government to let even erstwhile flagships go to foreign interests.

The opening bell of this new era was rung with the 2016 case of Sharp Electronics, which, after a contested battle that involved a Japanese public-private investment fund, was bought by Taiwan's Foxconn (Honhai) for $3.8 billion. This came as a shock to the business community because Sharp was Japan's only remaining large, flat-panel display manufacturer at that time. Similarly, in April 2019, a Chinese investment group acquired a substantial share of Japan Display Inc. (JDI) for $2.1 billion.[42] JDI was the result of a 2012 merger of the LCD panel operations of Sony, Toshiba, and Hitachi, and a main supplier of small, high-tech touch screens to Apple. There was no mistaking the message: Japanese companies are no longer protected, regardless of their legacy or industry, by domestic interests. Those that cannot compete in the new global economy may not be saved.

Overall, the growth of private equity, the arrival of investor activism, and the rise of foreign acquisitions in Japan bespeak a fundamental reorientation in Japan's financial markets. The new pressures to compete through deep-technology leadership have propelled corporate strategic repositioning, and this is accompanied by a new embrace of financial markets to support this reshaping of industry. This in turn has attracted new investors to Japan, and they soon realized that Japan's markets continue to operate differently. The easiest path to success is to conform with Japan's business norms. This has created a different type of market, one that shows private equity need not be noisy or destructive, and it has also created lucrative markets that are bound to grow as Japan's reinvention continues.

MANAGING THE REINVENTION

Culture Change

It is often said that changing a company's culture is like turning a super-sized commercial cargo ship. Really big ships need five miles to stop, and five to ten miles to turn, and the turn leaves a huge wake. Moreover, once a ship commits to a turn, it will not waver.[1] This is the challenge faced by the CEOs of large Japanese companies as they try to reinvent their firms—and do so within a tight country culture, with a plethora of deeply ingrained notions about what is acceptable. Apprehension in the face of uncertainty is amplified by the lifetime employment system that ties an employee's fate to the company's, making any drastic change an anxiety-inducing event. Intertwined among these preferences and nuances is Japan's focus on the appropriate process, with its attention to detail and sensitivities about deviating from protocol. All these beliefs and emotions form the labyrinth through which CEOs have to maneuver to bring about change. As they do, just as during a time-out call in a Japanese baseball game, they need to carefully negotiate the next moves for all to agree. Nevertheless, even as mid-level managers nod their heads, some still may quietly boycott the turn in an effort to slow it down enough that it occurs only long after their own retirement.

Many of Japan's leading companies are now in the middle of making this turn as part of their internal management reinvention—a change in corporate culture. While some companies are still unsure about what direction to steer in, others are in the midst of complicated maneuvering to prepare for the turn, and several are nearly ready to switch to full speed ahead. This chapter lays out some of their challenges, and the measures reformers are taking to bring about culture change within their organizations. It begins with an introduction to the alignment model, a framework that brings structure to the discussion of Japan's current management challenges. It then introduces concrete examples of three ways in which companies are introducing culture change: organized change events under the heading of "open innovation," workspace and office redesign, and the introduction of individuality to the workplace. It ends with a discussion of the leadership challenges through the case study of AGC Inc., formerly known as Asahi Glass. The takeaway is that in a tight culture, managing change toward less rigid processes requires a highly structured approach, and this takes a long time of careful preparation and nudging before it comes to fruition.

Managing the Dual Strategy

The implementation and execution of the aggregate niche strategy necessitates new management approaches for innovation and global operations. During the postwar period of catching up, corporate strategy was about taking technology invented elsewhere, commercializing it by building new consumer products, and exporting these products. The long list of products generated in this way includes videotape recorders, fax machines, and liquid crystal displays. This approach required ingenuity around finding commercial applications, new product design, and topnotch manufacturing. Japanese companies advanced these in their central research laboratories, with a focus on applied R&D, and through sophisticated manufacturing processes that built on continuous improvement (*kaizen*). In contrast, to build out global technology niches in advanced materials and components, robotics, or manufacturing equipment, companies have to employ processes conducive to original breakthrough innovation. They also need to gain speed to stay ahead of the competition, and must manage global research and sales operations and collaborative research efforts around the world. Importantly, they will be successful only if they also maintain and further hone their critical strengths in difficult-to-imitate and difficult-to-make deep technologies.

Accordingly, the execution of the aggregate niche strategy rests on a dual strategy: *monozukuri*, the art of making things, on the one hand, and cutting-edge innovation on the other. The dual strategy means that a company has to simultaneously "explore" new activities while it "exploits" existing core competencies and products.[2] For Japan today, this means discovering future technologies and global markets, and manufacturing highly complicated materials at consistently high levels of quality that cannot easily be copied. To win, companies need to be able to do both in one company, under the same roof; that is, they have to be ambidextrous.

In 2019, the concept of ambidexterity—the execution of the dual strategy— became a business catchphrase in Japan. It provides a framework for managing the addition of a new layer of discovery and global management onto existing operations. While it may sound easy on paper, implementing this dual strategy touches upon the core identity of the company as well as the self-identity of employees and their understanding of their skill sets. Adjusting the norms of the organization is a Herculean task that companies everywhere struggle with. And in a tight-culture environment, with its preferences for schedule, structure, and predictability, managing this change requires a process of its own. Given that changing the country's culture is impossible, companies have to work within it. Perhaps ironically, this means they have to roll out a structured approach for transitioning to a less structured system—to introduce looser aspects of creativity, innovation, and change, companies need to design tightly organized events to overcome resistance to change.

The Alignment Model

A helpful tool to structure the discussion of what type of changes and new processes Japanese businesses need is the alignment (or congruence) model.[3] This model posits that in order to successfully execute a certain strategy, a company must build a strong fit, or alignment, in the nexus of four critical components: (1) the critical *tasks* needed to execute the strategy; (2) the *people* who will do these tasks, referring to skills, competencies, and mindset; (3) an organizational *structure* that sets metrics and incentives focused on accomplishing these tasks; and (4) a corporate *culture* that creates buy-in and encourages the attitudes and behaviors needed to accomplish the critical tasks. It is the role of leadership to organize and proactively manage these four components on a daily basis, as discussed in the following paragraphs.

Critical tasks refer to the economic and competitive realities of the company, and what it takes to execute the corporate strategy. How will profits be generated? If cost leadership is the goal, how will it be achieved and sustained over time? Or, in an industry with high fixed costs, where high capacity utilization is key, how can shift runs be optimized and worker productivity increased? In Japan, because lifetime employment makes labor a fixed cost, maximizing labor productivity is almost always a critical task and, in one interpretation, explains the many hours of unpaid overtime that lifetime employees are expected to work in return for their stable jobs.

The *people* component encompasses the skills, competencies, and attitudes to help the workforce accomplish the critical tasks. It is shaped through selection and training of employees and building a workforce consisting of the types of people who will work well to accomplish the task. *People* also refers to a mindset and approach to work, including engaging in teamwork and being detail- and process-oriented or creative. If senior management wants to steer the ship in a new direction, they need to be sure to take the employees with them, by creating excitement for new assignments and offering opportunities to build new skills and change work habits.

Structure refers to the HR system and the standards and metrics for promotions and rewards. Employees have a very keen sense of the true metrics by which they are assessed, and any misalignment between stated goals and metrics applied is likely to cause confusion and demoralize the workforce. Thus, incentives such as pay, benefits, and individual performance assessments should be designed to steer employees toward accomplishing the required tasks. Also included here is the organizational design of the company, including hierarchies, lines of command, and the accessibility of leadership.

Culture refers to the behavioral norms within the company. As we saw in Chapter 2, there are three dimensions to culture: content, consensus, and intensity. A strong corporate culture is marked by high levels of consensus regarding the content of the norms (e.g., whether it is all right to be late to work, or to wear flip-flops in the office), as well as how strongly people feel about deviations. The Japanese word *yarikata*, "the way things are done," encapsulates this shared behavioral code. Importantly, corporate culture can be managed and changed because its content is defined by the organization. But the more ingrained the culture, the more careful attention to the change process is required.

As an example of a good fit among these four elements of strategy execution, imagine a company that sells a differentiated, high-end product, such as a luxury car. This makes innovation and design critical tasks. People (the employees) include excellent engineers with a constant drive to push the envelope. In terms of structure, rewards and promotions should be given to employees who create new hit products, and the corporate culture should be about creativity, risk-taking, diversity, teamwork, and speed. In contrast, a poor fit would be a company that claims to push for innovation, but in reality budgets are cut, people are fearful of their bosses and reluctant to try new things, the structure emphasizes hierarchies and mistakes are punished, and the culture discourages teamwork. The strategy takeaway from this framework is that managing a company well requires a close fit of the tasks-people-structure-culture nexus. Managing change cannot be done simply by announcing a new strategy, but requires management to guide the company toward a new alignment of these four components.

Thinking about the execution of strategy as a function of alignment also affords another insight, the success-to-failure paradox. The stronger a company's tasks-people-structure-culture nexus, the larger and more successful it becomes. This success then cultivates pride in established patterns and processes, and over time the *yarikata* ossifies. Entrenched bureaucracies and rigid lines of command develop. Overconfidence in the company's successes may make people blind to new opportunities or emerging external shocks, such as global competitive shifts or technological disruptions. In fact, in the face of a disruption, strong culture companies often double down on the ingrained behaviors that made them successful in the first place, even though they clearly no longer work. The paradox is that the entrenchment of what made the company a success is what leads to its downturn.

This is exactly what Japanese business experienced, en masse, in the 1990s: confronted with new competition from South Korea and Taiwan, many large Japanese companies tried to do more with the old recipes. The strong culture, overlying the country's tight culture coupled with risk aversion, led to an over-adherence to the critical tasks of the old alignment. And even where managers saw the need for change, they often encountered huge resistance, as we saw in the case of Panasonic, where a perceived need to be loyal to the founders' philosophy stymied change.

The Legacy Nexus: *Monozukuri*

We have already seen that Japan's postwar business strategy was to export and build global market share in high-quality, mass-produced consumer products. Figure 8.1 shows the alignment for this *monozukuri* (manufacturing) model. The management task is to create an organizational alignment anchored on the critical tasks of steady increases in efficiency and quality through learning, and high yields through hard work and few errors. This necessitates optimizing operations and building continuous improvement (*kaizen*) into the production process. The type of workers that such a manufacturing company needs to hire and train includes people with functional expertise (e.g., in electronics), skills in process engineering, a willingness to follow orders, short feedback loops, and a knack for operational excellence. Metrics and incentives emphasize exact compliance with rules and PDCA (Plan-Do-Check-Act) cycles, adherence to standard operating procedures, and the initiative to quickly identify and fix mistakes. The emphasis is on long production runs, constant upgrading, rules and processes, and not causing trouble, for example by making a mistake, slowing down the production line, or missing a day of work.[4]

A great way to structure this, from the HR perspective, is to provide lifetime employment with lockstep promotions where all are treated equally, with high wage parity. Lifetime employment is also supportive of a culture of strict procedures, conscientious and detail-oriented adherence to rules, and disciplined, hard work, often expressed in long hours. Leadership has to be clear in terms of metrics and output goals, norms of behavior, the celebration of results, and motivation through clear numerical goals, such as production targets. The result of this alignment is a very powerful and successful system that is constantly improving. At the risk of spelling out the obvious, this alignment is a perfect match for Japan's tight-culture preferences. And it worked.

The New Japan Nexus: Breakthrough Innovation

To win at the technology frontier that anchors global supply chains, Japanese companies now have to be agile and adaptive, and spearhead technological disruptions. These new critical tasks necessitate a new organizational alignment (presented in Figure 8.2). The critical tasks for breakthrough innovation include the ability to sense and respond quickly to new technology trends and global market changes, to predict future technologies, and to build new innovative businesses through technical excellence. This requires that people are open to acquiring new skills and competencies and also open to change and experimentation. They need peripheral vision, a tolerance for deviation and failure, and an ability to work on diverse teams and assignments.

For HR and organizational structure, these new tasks necessitate new metrics and incentives that are conducive to this new mindset and foster innovative behavior. This may require new cross-functional interdependencies and processes for learning across boundaries. Failure needs to be accepted

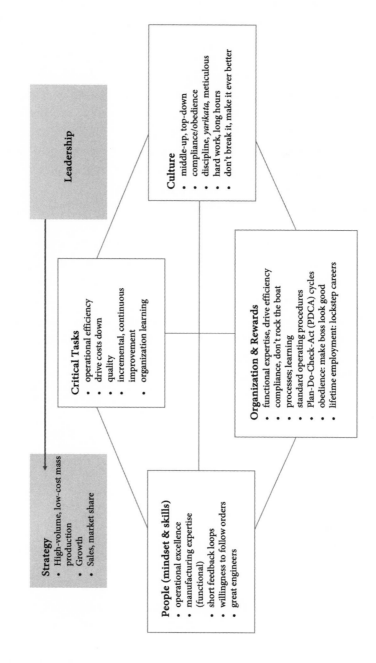

Strategy
- High-volume, low-cost mass production
- Growth
- Sales, market share

Leadership

Critical Tasks
- operational efficiency
- drive costs down
- quality
- incremental, continuous improvement
- organization learning

Culture
- middle-up, top-down
- compliance/obedience
- discipline, *yarikata*, meticulous
- hard work, long hours
- don't break it, make it ever better

People (mindset & skills)
- operational excellence
- manufacturing expertise (functional)
- short feedback loops
- willingness to follow orders
- great engineers

Organization & Rewards
- functional expertise, drive efficiency
- compliance, don't rock the boat
- processes; learning
- standard operating procedures
- Plan-Do-Check-Act (PDCA) cycles
- obedience: make boss look good
- lifetime employment: lockstep careers

Figure 8.1. The *Monozukuri* Alignment Model.

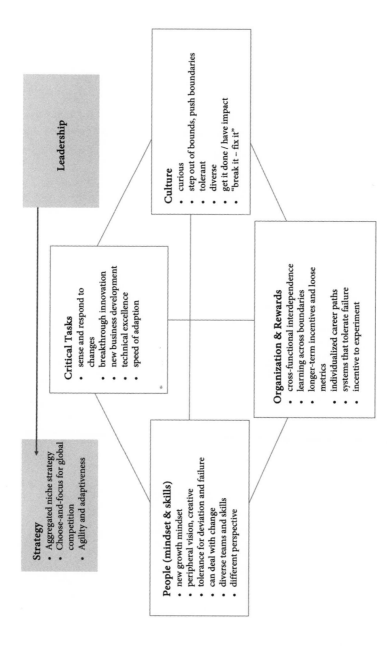

Figure 8.2. The Breakthrough Innovation Alignment Model.

as a corollary to risk-taking. Outcomes will be more difficult to measure and slower to materialize as new technologies gradually translate into new products and businesses. Therefore, performance evaluations need to be longer-term, with a reduced emphasis on short-term metrics and process-orientation, and more consideration of impact and contribution. Individualized career paths and personal skill formation that allow for specialization are also needed. A corporate culture that can pull all this together is characterized by curiosity and a tolerance for diversity and risk-taking, or a "move fast and break things" mentality. In this setting, leadership is about encouraging discourse, ideation, and creativity; empowering people to take initiatives; and supporting the allocation of resources toward new ventures.

Ambidexterity

At first sight, this breakthrough innovation alignment is clearly at odds with Japan's tight-culture preferences. So how can companies in a tight culture with preferences for order and predictability create these new structures that allow for agility, diversity, and innovation? Suddenly adopting a loose-culture approach—announcing a new *yarikata*, for instance—would likely be perceived as introducing chaos, and many employees would anxiously recoil to their ordered processes and resentment would build. The tight-culture answer to this question is to launch renewal carefully, by slowly nudging people into embracing a new identity for the company and a new view of appropriate behavior at work. This redefinition of the norms and behaviors of the organization can be brought about with the help of a series of meetings and events that include all employees and steadily increase acceptance of new processes. This need for a structured rollout is the main reason why it is taking even the reformers in Japan so long to steer their ships in a new direction.

What makes this transition even more difficult is that both, the *monozukuri* and the breakthrough alignments, are necessary for success. To succeed at the technology frontier with products and materials that are both innovative and high quality, the legacy nexus needs to coexist with the innovation nexus. Therefore, the reinvention of the internal corporate processes is not a switch from the old to the new, but the creation of something entirely different: an ambidextrous company that can do both: exploit existing strengths (in scaling, learning, and cost-cutting, for example) and explore new opportunities (innovative technology and new global business).[5]

One example of a Japanese company that is turning ambidextrous now is

Hitachi Ltd., Japan's premier infrastructure, electric machinery, and electronics company. As we already saw in Chapter 7, Hitachi is known for its turbines, escalators, elevators, steel plants, power plants, electricity grids, electronic systems and equipment, trains, refrigerators, chemicals, medical equipment, and much more. Even though many of these businesses are now being carved out, energy systems and social infrastructure installations remain important components of the company's core identity. At the same time, Hitachi is proactively building out new capabilities to explore future business applications in AI and data system management, such as Hitachi Vantara and the company-wide IoT Lumada platform. These new segments require a new culture centering on innovation, which is being introduced under the motto "Inspire the Next."[6] Clearly, constructing infrastructure installations and making trains run on time requires a different mindset and skill set from building out AI capabilities. But for Hitachi to be competitive in the future, it has to find ways to manage the dual strategy, make both alignments work together, and create synergies across the entire organization.

Implementing Change in a Tight Culture

During the 2000s—the second allegedly lost decade—turning ambidextrous and implementing change through the dual strategy is exactly what Japan's leading companies started to do. They began to introduce new processes to nudge the workforce toward accepting an additional, new, and different innovation alignment within their organizations. To change their strong corporate cultures and employee behavior, they have developed many different tools and processes. All of these aim to introduce new thinking, emphasize openness and tolerance, and expose employees to alternative settings and ways of doing things. In particular, three levers of change have become quite common: a push toward open innovation, office redesign, and adjustments to workplace behavior.

INNOVATION TOURISM

Part of the push to change employees' mindsets and encourage risk-taking occurs through organized events, trips, meetings, and other structured activities. Whereas Japan's catchphrase at the turn of the century was choose-and-focus, the buzzword in the 2010s was "open innovation." The original concept included various processes of free innovation exchange, including crowdsourcing.[7] However, in Japan, open innovation acquired a narrower meaning, namely, the opening of companies to global processes of change. This phrase came to be used to push not only the traditional Japanese in-house corporate R&D labs but the entire workforce toward more openness. In the R&D labs, lifetime employment had caused ossification and a "not invented here" syndrome, meaning that employees often refused to incorporate ideas that had originated elsewhere. A 2017 government report estimated that more than 70% of all large firm innovation was done completely in-house, in what was called the "self-sufficiency syndrome" (*jimai-shugi*); only 0.7% of large-firm innovation activities was based on collaboration with startup companies.[8] In most companies, employees were more concerned about protecting their careers than building something new. Open innovation, in the Japanese sense of the term, was the idea of shaking up established processes and encouraging people to infuse new ideas and methods into the encrusted structures. Concrete measures to support this shift included a rise in mid-career hiring, to bring in new ideation from the outside, as well as acquisitions or investments in startup companies and foreign firms.

In the early 2000s, more than 200 large companies launched their own corporate venture capital (CVC) funds. Between 2008 and 2018, domestic CVC investments more than tripled, from an estimated $600 million in 2008 to $2.2 billion in 2018.[9] Over the same decade, large Japanese companies invested in more than 2,000 Silicon Valley startups.[10] More than 500 Japanese firms now have "innovation offices" in Silicon Valley, San Diego, and other U.S. innovation clusters, and many more have contributed funds to U.S. venture capital companies.

The Silicon Valley innovation offices, in particular, spearhead CVC investments by scouting tech startups in the Valley. But perhaps more importantly, they are also loose-culture ambassadors, charged with changing the corporate culture in headquarters, one employee at a time.[11] Prime Minister Shinzo Abe's visit to Silicon Valley in 2015 further stoked the innovation fire and generated a new wave of what is now often referred to as innovation tourism. Some local VC funds and incubators have come to resent the many curious visitors longing for insights into the innovation mecca, and describe their behavior as "4L": look, listen, learn, leave—meaning that these visitors do not bring anything to the table. Signs have popped up in front of Google, Facebook, and the Stanford University campus to guide tourist buses away from central parking locations where they are seen as causing a *meiwaku*.

Undeterred, some Japanese companies doubled down on these innovation trips and asked their Silicon Valley offices to build out structured, professionally coached training programs for the short-term visitors. Some of these "innovation labs" have become quite large, with 50 or 100 employees. In addition to conducting their own research, they run digital transformation and design thinking workshops and brainstorming exercises, and some even host incubators for startups. Several have evolved into stand-alone, new consulting businesses that also offer programs for innovation tourists from other companies. A new cottage industry has emerged where Japanese innovation labs in Silicon Valley run training programs, in Japanese, for Japanese managers.[12]

According to several companies that operate such labs in California, the idea behind the large amounts of money and effort spent on innovation tourism is to invite people to leave their comfort zones. Because California is known in Japan to be culturally loose, and to "own the brand" of loose-culture approaches to workshops, design thinking, and brainstorming, many program participants have a different mindset from the time they step off the airplane. The change of scenery gives them cultural permission to be different: the space and pace are different, as are the people, the weather, the meetups and events, and of course, the exercises that involve brainstorming. Structured conversations about employees' visions of the future and their fears and opportunities are possible in California, in ways that would be inconceivable in Japan due to the rigid norms that govern office behavior there. Although these innovation tourists may not be able to transpose California workplace culture to Japan after just one short visit to California, the hope is to expand their horizons and encourage new outside-the-box thinking.

Office Redesign

In Japan, too, changes are being made to pull people out of their rut. The purpose is to encourage new initiatives and a new focus on outcome over process. Tools to nudge people into embracing new behaviors include changes in workplace rules and changes in office layout that require new behavior. Early attempts at workplace innovation can be traced back to former Prime Minister Koizumi's Cool Biz campaign of 2005. From the old days, you may recall images of armies of salarymen dressed in full suits, dress shirts, and ties, being pushed into super-crowded subway cars by station employees, and doing their utmost to make it through their long commutes in 95-degree heatwaves without becoming sweat drenched. An entire industry of light suit materials and footwear developed around this, such as Uniqlo's AIRism and HeatTech products.

The Cool Biz initiative grabbed this opportunity for change. To respect traditional views of appropriate office attire, Cool Biz was officially presented as a measure to save energy, which would be good for the economy. The new guideline was to set office building thermostats at 28 degrees Celsius (82 degrees Fahrenheit) during the summer months, which can be exceedingly hot and humid in Japan. Workers were explicitly encouraged to adjust to this higher setting by not wearing jackets or ties, and some companies, including large traditional ones, even allowed client meetings in Cool Biz outfits.[13] True to tight-culture apprehensions about uncertainty, corporate HR departments carefully structured the transition, through compulsory information meetings and revisions of their company's "code of conduct" to outline the new rules on allowable attire. Their guidelines triggered a huge boom for the casual business dress industry, to the detriment of the domestic tie makers. Cleverly, the apparel companies extended their marketing into an unofficial "warm biz" campaign for the winter months. After the nuclear power reactors in Japan were shut down following the 2011 Fukushima disaster, a new Super Cool Biz campaign allowed polo shirts. As of 2020, ties are rare in normal Japanese business settings. Cool Biz can be credited for ending the era of the obligatory suit as the office uniform, and the rise of both office fashion and a very slow yet steady increase in expressions of individuality at work.

In a next step, companies have begun to address the office space itself, to orient daily routines away from order-taking to personal contribution making. The traditional large Japanese company office—which is sometimes credited with inventing the open floor office plan—has a very structured layout that makes it possible to assess the entire office hierarchy in just one look. There are no cubicles or privacy. Desks are small and compact. The general manager's and section chiefs' desks are in the far corner from the door, and from there they can constantly watch their entire unit at all times. They know who is working hard, and who is asleep at their desk, how long employees are out to lunch, and how early or late they are in the office. One outgrowth of this tight supervision is the practice whereby all junior employees have to work until the bosses leave for the day, resulting in the very long "voluntary overtime" workdays for which Japan has become infamous.

In the 2010s, the postwar cement buildings in central Tokyo, Osaka, and elsewhere were replaced, one by one, with elegant high-rise office towers. Many companies have taken this opportunity to rethink their office layout and to break open the rigid structures, and they are creating new office spaces and work cultures. In some of these new, beautiful offices—inspired by Silicon Valley's bright collaborative offices and matched with sophisticated Japanese design—workers no longer have assigned desks. Rather, they have a locker in which they keep their work documents and belongings, and when they arrive at work each morning, they pick a space commensurate with the day's assignments: a large table for group meetings, a quiet space for deep work, or a sofa for conversation. In one IT company that occupies two floors in an office tower, an employee was charged with building highly detailed location software that would enable people to find their colleagues more easily. In addition to being able to attract new talent to the company, the purpose with this redesign is to pull people out of their old routines and to introduce more fluidity and individuality into the workplace.[14]

The task of office redesign itself has also opened up an opportunity to involve employees in the creative activity of imaging a new workspace. At one large machinery company, employees expressed a strong preference for assigned cubicles with high walls; upon further probing the design team found that employees really wanted options—for privacy, meeting, interacting, and collaborating—while also maintaining a small personal space where they could anchor their belonging to the company. Shared workspace rental companies, such as WeWork, have attracted attention in Japan thanks to this growing interest in experimenting with workspace as an agent of culture change. Before designing their main offices, some large companies have taken out medium- or long-term leases from such rental firms in order to identify best practices and observe office worker behavior and adaptation in terms of mindset. At one level, this may be just a means to compete for young talent in the tight labor market. But there is also a true curiosity about the relationship between workspace design and employee productivity, and Japan is now conducting interesting experiments in this area.

The new office design has also brought unexpected challenges. Perhaps the most telling has been a new anxiety among employees on how to prove to their bosses that they are working hard. Traditional performance metrics such as face time or effort exerted no longer work in the new office setting, because the boss can no longer constantly canvass the room. Employees need to find new ways of showing not only that they are following the rules and putting in their time, but that they are getting things done. As intended, this is beginning to shift employee incentives toward having to show results. Although uncomfortable, this anxiety signals that the new office spaces are injecting the intended turbulence into the stodgy processes of the old system. Employees also need to trust their bosses to be fair in making this transition toward new assessments. This, in turn, puts a new responsibility on the bosses that may require new training, as well as a redefinition of the roles and functions of the HR department so it can take over the tasks of performance evaluations.[15]

ADJUSTING THE ASSEMBLY LINE MENTALITY

For most employees, even those in support of change, the primary concern remains how their work will be assessed and the performance indicators that will be applied. Traditionally, face time and "doing as best as one could" were key, and given a preference for equality rather than equity, Japanese office work has long been based on an "assembly line mentality" that counted easily observable metrics, as if in car production.[16] For example, a typical assessment may be based on how many reports were written or presentations given, with the assumption that more is better, as opposed to the quality of their content. Efficiency, insofar as it was assessed at all, was also measured as a process, not an outcome: that is, in terms of how long it took, not what it produced. In daily office life, to this day there is often only one right way to do a certain menial task, such as filling out a form, and there are many forms that appear unnecessary. Some requirements or metrics bear no relation to the desired outcome, and some assignments are done simply for the sake of the assignment, wasting time and resources. One employee at a global subsidiary of a large Japanese company reflected on this difficulty: the Tokyo office requires activity reports from all global subsidiaries at regular intervals, and there is a prescribed form, including length and typeface used. A report that fails to conform will have to be redone. To make this even more demoralizing, the producers of such reports are often under the impression that, with the exception of checking on the properly sized font, nobody in the divisions for which their reports are intended ever reads them.

When breakthrough innovation and sensing and seizing new business opportunities are the goals, metrics such as number of pages written or reports produced are counterproductive. Creativity is associated with excitement and ideation, and outcomes cannot be easily assessed by standard benchmarks. Companies will need new ways of assessing employees that better reflect their goal of an alignment toward innovation. However, in many large Japanese companies, the assembly line mentality still runs deep, and simplistic metrics are still often considered a fair way to judge performance. How to shift this mentality and create a new culture of speed and agility in getting things done is one of the largest remaining challenges in Japan's business reinvention.

THE VALUE OF TIME

Last but not the least, efficiency is about using time better. Ultimately, a shift toward agility in global competition will require altering processes that prioritize standardization, and considering the opportunity cost of time. However, this is perceived by many Japanese not just as contradictory to due process, but as impolite. Aversion to assertive and quick decision making is often expressed as a concern over "safety," and safety tends to take precedence over all other goals. As anybody who has participated in a Japanese office meeting will attest, Japan's tight culture requires enormous patience. In traditional business meetings the order of speaking, what can be said, and how it may be said are narrowly prescribed. Often, the fear of coming across as "KY" (dense) is a formidable deterrent to saying anything at all. It is rare that younger employees speak without being asked, and everybody is incredibly polite, sometimes to the point of meaninglessness.

A root cause of these office habits is that an individual's time has traditionally not been valued, neither as important to employees nor as an opportunity cost to the company. Rather, time was seen as belonging to the employer, as the employee's price to pay for job security. Spending many hours, in meaningless meetings or at one's desk, was considered a strong signal of dedication and sacrificing one's personal agenda for the larger good. To this day, meetings often do not end on time. Even though it is utterly impolite to be late to a meeting, if only by one minute, there remains a strongly shared understanding that no one can leave the meeting before the convener ends it—and sometimes they do not. Rushing is seen as unkind. Making a proposal to speed up the agenda may be counterproductive.

This is in contrast to the Western office setting, where running meetings long would be seen as disrespectful of the participants' own agendas and needs. Nor do all employees always have to attend all meetings. Slowly but certainly, this view is also spreading in Japan. And as we will see in Chapter 9, the arrival of women in managerial positions, the advent of dual careers, and new rules on individual vacation time are beginning a shift to more fluid and efficient structures, and starting to address this largest and deepest remnant from the traditional lifetime employment era.

Leadership

Perhaps the biggest challenge in bringing about change in all these deeply entrenched ways of doing things is that the initiative has to come from decisive leadership at the top and be executed through a powerful top-down process. This, in and of itself, is a huge break with the past and has brought both supply and demand challenges. Change management—building new alignments and changing ingrained behavior—is a difficult and often uncomfortable and even frustrating endeavor. It requires a lot of work, new management skills, and employee acceptance of a new leadership style.

As of 2020, Japan's senior management cohort as well as most of the general managers are children of the bubble or immediate post-bubble periods. They were raised in and often continue to embody the *monozukuri* alignment. They were promoted through the ranks in an era when the role of the Japanese CEO was to be the benevolent leader who balanced all interests. It was considered normal for a CEO to be ambiguous about goals or fail to give the necessary level of detail when setting directions. Operations were delegated to the general managers, and suggestions for new businesses or strategic direction were typically generated at that mid-level and reported up the ladder from there. In the stereotypical CEO office of the postwar period, there was little strategy formulation, and senior executives were often neither expected nor trained to be decisive leaders.

But Japanese leaders can in fact be very impactful. The positive spin on Japan's corporate protocol is that while the preparation is slow, the execution is fast. Many people with experience doing business in Japan report that it can take forever for a Japanese company to make a decision: a proposal has to go to the top, where all need to sign off; then it is sent back to the mid-level, where it is rotated among a large number of general managers who, affected or not, also all need to agree before it can go back to the top. However, this long process also means that once the decision to turn the ship has been issued, everybody has already signed up and can charge full speed ahead. A powerful leader can use this cultural feature for highly effective change management.

Thus, the complication is not the system itself, but the supply of powerful CEOs. As we have already seen, most Japanese CEOs are "lifers" with the company, who have been promoted through the ranks based on their ability to conform. They were groomed in the traditional "middle-up, top-down" approach, and often don't see themselves as strategic thinkers. Instead, they ratify suggestions from their general managers—who are also not strategists but operations managers. The general managers often have a narrow view of their assignments and personal goals, and are rarely eager to suggest radical change.[17] They, too, were raised through the company, and promoted for setting and executing on operational goals. As a result, Japanese companies have cadres of excellent managers, trained in the legacy *monozukuri* tradition, but comparatively few leaders. The strategy difference between the two is captured by the old adage that "management is ensuring that the trains run on time; leadership is about ensuring that they are headed to the right destination."[18] In the early 21st century, a scarcity of leadership talent with the vision to chart a new course was one of the biggest reasons why some large Japanese companies fell behind in their corporate reinvention.

Because employees have long been trained in-house, universities have faced little demand to teach management skills. Even today, few MBA programs train students in leadership and organizational behavior, and traditionally these two disciplines are often not even represented in the faculties of university departments of commerce. Corporate managers learn their craft from their bosses, which leads to a continuation and ossification of corporate structures.[19] There is thus a dearth not only of professional CEOs but also of Japanese business schools and high-level executive education programs. Outstanding consulting services remain scarce, too, even as that industry is beginning to grow. And for Japanese senior managers who attended business schools in the West, transposing lessons learned from foreign case studies into the Japanese setting is often seen as difficult.

All this combines to make this moment in time critical for Japan's reinvention. Sensing a need to change and compete differently in the digital economy, several large companies have promoted new-style CEOs to the top, individuals who have a clear sense of direction and the skills it takes to turn their cargo ship onto a new course. In the Old Japan, they might have been viewed as rocking the boat, but now they are needed to do exactly that. Meanwhile, companies still run by traditional, salaryman-type CEO-administrators are struggling. This is dividing Japan's large companies into success and failure cases. The failure stories are all fairly similar, and revolve around missed opportunities. The success stories are much more interesting and variegated. Because the system is so ossified, it takes extraordinary creativity and energy to effect change and overcome resistance. The individuals who are currently managing the corporate renewal are outstanding leaders who know how to be responsive to the needs and expectations of the existing organization while launching a culture change toward future competitiveness.

Example: AGC, Inc.

Several of Japan's largest companies are making strides in managing the dual strategy in terms of adding to their existing core a new tasks-people-structure-culture nexus for exploration. One example is the company previously known as Asahi Glass. As of 2019, AGC is the largest glass and materials manufacturing company in the world, with revenues of more than $14 billion, and 54,000 employees located in more than 30 countries.[20] AGC is also the most diversified company of its ilk, operating four main businesses: flat glass (including building and industrial glass), automotive glass, chemicals, and electronics materials (including glass substrates for LCD screens). In each of these, it is exploring new technologies. For example, the flat glass business has developed a new window glass with built-in 5G antennas, the automotive business is exploring intelligent look-through touch-panel windshields, and the chemical business is extending its core competencies into the life sciences.

AGC was founded on September 8, 1907, as part of the Mitsubishi group.[21] It was the first Japanese company to produce glass, and at that time relied on imported raw materials from Europe. When World War I interrupted those supplies, AGC extended its business into chemicals so as to be able to make its own soda ash. Over time, the chemicals business turned AGC into a leading global provider of specialty chemicals. The construction boom after World War II allowed AGC to dominate Japan's flat glass market, and the company was quick to license, copy, and co-generate new global developments in glass manufacturing technologies. Consistent with the growth and diversification priorities of the time, AGC also aggressively entered new businesses, such as glass for TV screens, glass fiber, and lightweight and glass-reinforced cement.[22] After the two oil crises of the 1970s, in an effort to reduce its dependency on energy and looking for smarter, lighter, and less polluting businesses, it added electronics as a fourth business area. This allowed AGC to ride Japan's dominance in LCD screens in the 1980s and 1990s. To this day, AGC (together with the U.S. company Corning Inc.) leads the global market in glass substrates for smartphone screens.

The bubble economy of the 1980s brought even more diversification, and the subsequent bust, downsizing and losses. Newly emerging competition from South Korea and Taiwan became a huge competitive threat, and the rise of China brought further pressure to exit some of the commodity markets and focus on specialty glass, specialty chemicals, and new applications of ceramics and electronics. To compete and maintain its dominance, AGC needed to change how it innovates and how it designs and manages its new specialty segments, while remaining the largest glass company in the world.

At this critical juncture, in 2015, AGC appointed Takuya Shimamura as the new CEO, a career AGC manager with a background in the chemicals and electronics divisions. His performance gap analysis revealed that the company remained too dependent on its mature businesses, and there was strife at the general manager level about the direction of the company. In fiscal year (FY) 2018, with AGC's total sales at $14.5 billion, glass accounted for 48% of sales, and chemicals for 30%. This was concerning because the dependence on glass appeared to be rising just as Chinese competitors were making great inroads. The LCD panel business, which had earned high returns in the early 2000s, was struggling after the 2008 global financial crisis. Profits were generally low: in FY 2013, the operating margin was 6%, dropping to 4.2% in 2014. And, the return on equity had fallen to only 1.4%, far below the 8% threshold set forth by the government's Abenomics program and its shame index. This had made the company quite conservative and focused on chasing the stock price or ROE hurdle, and general managers had begun to put too much emphasis on short-term results.[23]

But above all, there was a culture issue. People were afraid of making mistakes, and they did not say much even when asked directly. Most general managers seemed to be afraid to take an initiative, and some looked as if they just wanted to wait out the time until they could retire and collect their final bonus. There was no energy, and employees looked tired. Turnover was rising among younger engineers, which was a critical problem given the looming labor shortage. Shimamura's predecessor had been an autocratic CEO and a micromanager, which had made employees anxious and dampened initiative. As a result, although new business segments were planned, the necessary innovation alignment had not been developed.[24]

To confront these challenges, Shimamura and his senior management team pulled five levers to refuel and shake up the tone and processes of AGC. Upon the announcement of his appointment as CEO in November 2014, Shimamura personally sent an email to all employees—a rare event, at least in Japanese companies. The message was that he saw his role as switching the lights back on. To send a not-too-subtle message, he also distributed a list of the 20 habits of a bad manager. This included items such as being too quick to say "no, but, or however," to make excuses, to withhold information, to pass the buck, to cling to the past, to not listen, or to fail to express gratitude. Next, he announced a new management policy, "AGC Plus," and unlike other such documents, it was not written by an external consulting company or a general manager, nor did it contain many glitzy slides with targets to reach. Rather, it was Shimamura's direction statement, summarized as: "Our goal is to create value for our stakeholders."

To follow up on this plan to return the company to long-term strategic thinking, Shimamura launched a series of dialogue sessions with mid-level managers (in their late 40s and just below the general manager level) at the Tokyo headquarters. For many of these mid-career employees, it was the first time they had attended a meeting with the CEO, and Shimamura came prepared with a list of questions that they were invited to answer. Out of this grew an initiative to get buy-in for change from this future generation by inviting ten high-potential managers to participate in the Vision 2025 planning process. Again, outside consultants were eschewed, and the internal staff was left to its own devices in drawing an outline of what the company should look like ten years onward. In February 2016, the proposals of two teams were merged and adopted as the company's Vision 2025. To underscore that these were not just exercises in paper shuffling, Vision 2025 included a strategic investment budget of ¥500 billion (almost $5 billion). This was to support any compelling new business plan suggested by any of the four business areas. Out of this grew the previously mentioned business explorations in the life sciences and automotive businesses.

Moreover, to retain the best and brightest among the younger engineers, AGC designed new processes to stoke their entrepreneurial spirit. The so-called Gong Show was launched, as a chemistry version of a hackathon, that is, an event where engineers and production staff could pitch new business ideas to senior management. There were no limits: ideas could range from speeding up a production process to developing a new product to compete in the digital transformation. Several of these ideas were adopted, including establishing a new mobility unit in the automotive business. Shimamura also set aside time for town hall meetings with younger employees, to stop the attrition among millennials, and after four years of regular events, the brain drain among the younger workers had slowed.

Lastly, Shimamura and his senior team turned to the general managers, some of whom, more or less quietly, continued to resist the expansion of business into specialized niches. Between 2016 and 2017, AGC held six rounds of off-site retreats, each lasting two days. The objective was to accelerate the culture change by working with these resistors. The weekend scheduling offered extended time for all managers to voice their concerns and make their reservations heard. They were grouped into structured breakout sessions and tasked with drawing their own proposals to bring AGC forward, which they presented to the senior management team. On the basis of these presentations, top management then made the hard choices and asked change opponents to assume different assignments, depriving them of any leadership function in the change process. This drastic measure came as a complete shock to the entire organization and marked the turn to a new AGC that would not tolerate old habits.

Research on the management of culture change has identified five primary ways in which culture can be changed: (1) *direction*: strong consistent signaling from top management, (2) *buy-in*: heavy involvement of employees in the change effort, (3) *examples*: the showcasing of exemplars of the new culture, (4) *social approval*: celebration and rewards for those who have changed, and (5) *reorientation*: careful alignment of the HR systems—including selection, training, and promotions—in support of the new culture. When leaders deploy these five levers, culture can be managed and changed.[25]

This is what AGC's senior leadership put into practice. The change agenda of AGC was a top-down program, but it pulled the levers of inclusion and worked by creating buy-in at the various levels of the company. At a measured pace, the company has begun to formulate new strategies and build new businesses, and reformers have been empowered. All told, Shimamura held more than 130 face-to-face meetings with employees at all levels of the organization and visited more than 50 global plants and sales offices. Commenting about initial resistance, he said: "I could tell from the employees' faces that they were doubting my message at first. They had heard it before, with no change."[26] After three years of relentless travel and communication, a new sense of urgency and innovation was running through all divisions of AGC. By FY 2019, operating profit had increased to 16%, and the company was developing various new specialty glass and chemical products to build out its own aggregate niche strategy.

The AGC example highlights the three main themes of this chapter.

Corporate culture can be managed; guiding culture change in a tight culture requires structured processes and organized events; and managing culture requires leadership from the top, which is rare in Japan but certainly exists. Some Japanese companies are sophisticated and creative about their approaches, from office redesign to innovation tours, workshops, and brainstorming events. And as we will see in the next chapter, they are also catching a tailwind in their change efforts from the looming labor shortage. Contributing to their successes is a palpable excitement among young employees about working for companies that are truly changing and building a New Japan work environment.

EMPLOYMENT AND INNOVATION

The Reinvention of the *Kaisha*

On May 13, 2019, the CEO of Toyota Motors, Akio Toyoda, said at a press conference: "Without new incentives for employers, it will be difficult to uphold the system of lifetime employment."[1] This was not at all a threat to lay off workers, but a warning of something much larger—a fear that Japan's structural labor shortage was beginning to affect the traditional balance between the rights and responsibilities of employers and those of employees in ways that will undermine the entire system. As employees demand more career individualization, companies are searching for new ways to design labor relations that make sense for the company, the employees, and the economy overall. And they are confronting these issues just as they are put under increased pressure to improve performance metrics and develop new processes for innovation and diversity.

In the same press conference, Toyoda also announced that Toyota is currently undergoing a "once-in-a-century transformation" equivalent to a "full model change," with the goal of steering the company toward a deep dive into AI and autonomous technologies, through new global alliances. The biggest hurdle, Mr. Toyoda said, was finding the talent to make this shift: "I don't care about what school they went to, their gender or their nationality. All that is irrelevant. All I want to know is what they want to do here in this company. This is the kind of culture I want to create."[2] How to adjust to the new labor shortage and rising job mobility, while continuing to provide job stability to those who want it, is currently the largest circles for Japanese companies to square.

The challenge is that lifetime employment is coming under a triple threat. The first threat is the labor shortage, which has greatly increased the bargaining power of employees and is affecting the rights and responsibilities tradeoff that used to form the core logic of the postwar system. The second is a shift in workstyle desires and expectations among millennials, reflected in their preferences regarding work content, skill formation, and individualized career paths. For example, in a 2019 survey of newly hired employees, 56% said they do not want or expect to work for the same company for their entire careers.[3] Government reforms have answered those demands, and the 2019 Workstyle Reform Law ushered in a new work environment with more meritocracy and work-life balance. And finally, global pressures to compete and innovate at the technology frontier demand new structures to spur innovation, as well as new HR policies to foster employee creativity. Ideally, companies, employees, and the government would all like to uphold the many benefits of lifetime employment, but the need for change is also real.

The ongoing reforms have already earned the tagline "the end of the Japanese *kaisha*."[4] Perhaps in no other area is Japan's reinvention thornier than in the matter of adjusting the employment system. Any change to this system, long celebrated as the anchor of not just the economy but the entire society, has tremendous consequences. For example, as we saw in Chapter 3, ending the *shūkatsu* hiring process has huge implications, not only for HR practices and promotions but also for university curricula, corporate training assignments and corporate culture, work-life choices, the welfare system, and family structures—as well as the entire social contract. Not surprisingly, labor reform has divided the country. Trade unions and labor activists are pitted against Keidanren, the large business association. Government itself is split, both along party lines and within the bureaucracy. Within ministries, conservatives are increasingly at odds with reformers, and across ministries, those tasked with social policy face a strong group of reformers in pro-business ministries like METI. Companies are caught between a need to abide by society's traditional expectations, and the need to satisfy the prime minister's call for higher profitability. Employees, too, are divided between the *anzen dai-ichi* (safety first) camp, and those who want faster career progress, performance pay, and greater work-life balance. As with the other conflicts we have seen between valuable tradition and desirable change, the solution has been to roll out reform cautiously, with careful consideration to limit the downsides for society at large. When all is said and done, it will have taken Japan a generation to modify and adapt the system, so as to allow people and companies to adjust while retaining the system's most valuable stabilizing aspects.

This chapter explains how workstyle changes are impacting Japan's business reinvention. Following an introduction to the costs and benefits of lifetime employment, the chapter analyzes the three threats to the system: the labor shortage and the new competition for talent, including women and foreigners; workstyle reforms and slowly emerging new work patterns and labor fluidity; and the new challenge of attracting and retaining talent for innovation. I zoom in on the new system of "dual jobs" that I perceive as a mechanism to square the circle, namely to reduce some of the costs of lifetime employment in order to maintain its core benefits. The example of Recruit, the top Japanese HR company, then highlights how the dual jobs system is already being spearheaded by some New Japan companies. Finally, the government has jumped in on this initiative and launched J-Startup, which may lead to the creation of a more balanced innovation ecosystem that eschews some of the dog-eat-dog harshness of Silicon Valley. With J-Startup, young entrepreneurs can launch new business ideas in an embedded system with large firms as supporters. Overall, Japan's attempts to adjust to the times while building mechanisms of stability into the new system offer an example of evolving labor relations that are strikingly different from those in the United States and Europe.

The Costs and Benefits of Lifetime Employment

Similar to the system centered on the organization man in the United States of the 1960s and 1970s, Japan's lifetime employment system entails both significant benefits and substantial costs for employers.[5] On the one hand, lifetime employment translates into employee loyalty and dedication. Employees identify with the company, and they embrace teamwork, comradery, and knowledge sharing. Due to perceived equality (thanks to wage parity), morale and motivation are high. Companies assume the full costs of employee education, and in return the payoffs from these investments in domestic training and even study abroad accrue fully to the company. The highly targeted on-the-job training contributes to organizational learning and to honing company-specific areas of expertise. Because older employees are not worried about being replaced, they are happy to acquire new skills and proud to transfer knowledge to younger workers. New business exploration and development is facilitated by the fact that people are less resistant to transfers into new assignments because their salary remains unchanged and they will not lose their jobs. The company has more control over intellectual property and fewer concerns about leakage. It is also much easier to groom in-house CEOs and thus avoid the huge costs of outside CEO friction and failure.

On the other hand, lifetime employment is very expensive for companies. It turns labor into a fixed cost and requires outlet valves, such as a flexible cadre of non-regular workers, so companies can adjust to cyclical downturns. The employee structure is also bound to become top-heavy as the workforce ages, which is expensive in terms of benefits and pensions. Another huge cost factor is the so-called hiring mistakes, people who turn out to be not a good fit or to lack the requisite skills, but who cannot be laid off. This explains why HR managers are typically risk averse during the *shūkatsu* interviews and prefer to hire applicants whose personality profile is a good match to their firm. Over time, however, hiring people who are all very similar in disposition will limit diversity. And because lifetime employment limits labor mobility, there is little cross-fertilization or influx of new ideas. As we saw in Chapter 8, while there is huge pressure to please the boss, lockstep promotion in the first ten years means there is little incentive to perform exceedingly well. In ill-managed companies, complacency and slacking may become an issue. In the worst-case scenario, over time the lack of options and mobility may begin to make the job feel like a straitjacket, and resentment rises. Even in great companies, ossification and a sense of accomplishment pose a large challenge: routines that lead to success may over time become obstacles to change.

In the 21st century, global competition and performance expectations have made the downsides more expensive, and the upsides more difficult to preserve. The reinvention and the need for new processes of innovation translate into a need for a different type of workforce: one with more independent thinkers rather than conscientious soldiers. The challenge before Japan, then, is how to reform the employment system in ways that keep as many of the benefits as possible while removing the costs, and do it in a way that matches the strong tight-culture preferences for security, predictability, and consideration of all interests. The approach that the U.S. chose in the 1980s was to open the flood-gates to the externalization of labor, coupled with an almost exclusive focus on money to motivate people.[6] This is not a path Japan would follow. Instead, the ongoing workstyle reforms attempt to address labor shortage dynamics and introduce a new fluidity into the system while upholding an employee's option to pursue a lifetime career. These dual goals are now addressed by couching the reforms in a larger innovation system agenda.

Structural Labor Shortage

Japan is the first OECD country to face the economic and societal challenges of a rapidly aging population. Due to rising life expectancies and declining fertility rates, no other country is aging or shrinking faster than Japan. This is bringing a host of policy challenges, from social welfare and pension funding to increasing urbanization. For companies, it necessitates a new era of HR management practices that can address the new fluidity, power, and interests of employees.

Assuming a continuation of current trends, Japan's workforce is predicted to shrink by at least 20% over the next two decades, from the current 65 million people in 2017 to 52 million by 2040.[7] This has already created an acute labor shortage. Exhibit 9.1 shows Japan's unemployment rate (the bars) as well as the ratio of available jobs to the number of job applicants (the line). Beginning in 2014, this line crossed the value of 1, indicating more job openings than job seekers. Since then, the ratio has topped 1.6 open jobs per applicant.

Given its structural causes, this situation did not come as a surprise. Labor reforms, which began in earnest with the first major postwar revision of the Labor Law in 2003, have pushed a transition away from the old system, in steady and piecemeal fashion. In the 16 years leading up to Prime Minister Abe's legal reforms in 2019, the country has been nudged toward a new mindset regarding "normal" conduct at work, by means ranging from Prime Minister Koizumi's Cool Biz campaign to the celebrating of companies that make progress on employee diversity. The government has also publicly shamed exploitative work situations, by highlighting *karōshi* (death by overwork) cases and blacklisting companies that demand excessive "service overtime" (unpaid extra work). This nudging reflected the already occurring changes in labor relations, and culminated in the 2019 reforms, as we will see later.

Meanwhile, facing this growing labor shortage, companies are exploring new ways to structure their operations. They are looking for a new balance between measures to retain their own employees while also increasing flexibilities and mid-career hiring. Lately, Japan has become known for its proactive embrace of automation and robots, but this is not a solution yet. To increase the labor pool, companies are hiring more elderly, female, and foreign workers.

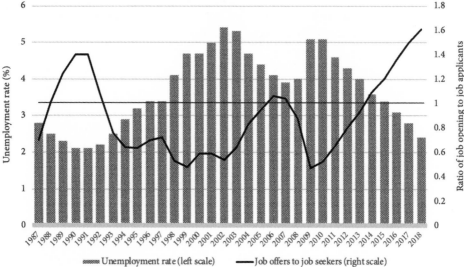

Figure 9.1. Unemployment and the Ratio of Job Openings to Job Seekers, 1987–2018.
Source: Japan Institute for Labour Policy and Training.

A stepwise increase in the retirement age, currently at 65 and envisioned to increase to 70 in a decade, will slow down the workforce shrinkage somewhat, but it comes with its own downsides, such as continuing the male-dominated orientation and more resistance to corporate culture changes.

WOMENOMICS

The most obvious way for Japan to increase diversity and the labor pool is to hire more women into the managerial tracks of the core workforce. Female work participation in Japan has long been fairly high, but most women have held (and still hold) non-regular jobs. In the late 1990s, it was exceedingly rare to see a woman in a management meeting. This led Kathy Matsui, a Goldman Sachs economist in Tokyo, to coin the term *Womenomics* to describe the great economic losses caused by not fully engaging women, or not alleviating career obstacles such as the so-called mommy trap (i.e., career segregation or truncation due to maternity leave).[8] Womenomics became an important part of the 2012 Abenomics policy program when the government issued an official goal for women to hold 15% of managerial positions in the private sector by 2020.

Given stepwise promotion patterns that apply to all lifetime employees, this process cannot easily be sped up. But given that as of 2019, more than 60% of women younger than 35 worked in regular career tracks, within a decade Japan's office scene will most certainly look different from the way it does today.[9]

Statistically, women's employment in Japan today no longer differs from the rates in other OECD countries. Japan's female labor participation rate—meaning women older than 15 years engaged in the workforce—has risen from 55% in 1999 to 71% in 2018. This is higher than the rates in the U.S. (66%) and the EU (62%).[10] Japan also looks quite similar to other countries in terms of pay differentials, with average female pay at a level of around 75% of male pay. This is the same as in the United States and Europe, and it is mostly due to differences in jobs, as women tend to hold more non-regular jobs. In Japan, as of 2018, 56.1% of employed women held non-regular jobs, which provide no job security or benefits and are less well paid, compared to only 22% of employed men who held such positions.[11]

That said, qualitative differences continue to loom large. Given the tight-culture norms regarding what it is appropriate to ask for, many female Japanese professionals report that proposing a change in tone or asking for more demanding assignments is difficult. The U.S. concept of "leaning in"—that is, of women proactively contributing to the reorientation of workplace rules and asking for change—is just as relevant for Japan, but it has to be done differently. And, to this day, subconscious biases as to what women can or should do remain strong. As long as men get the more important assignments, they will continue to be promoted faster. The path to diversity and inclusion is further frustrated by a particular type of conservative male manager—in the office vernacular referred to as an "uncle" (oji-san) boss—who gets away with repeated public displays of chauvinism and discrimination. Deeply ingrained gender biases continue, and the system itself is still often rigged in favor of men. A shocking example of this bias was the 2018 admissions scandal at Tokyo Medical University, where the university had systemically lowered the scores of female applicants on the grounds that female doctors do not pursue their careers as reliably as males.

Another obstacle is the HR system in most companies, where an employee's direct boss is solely in charge of promotions. It is said that this has made abusive power situations more common in Japan than in countries that use multiple feedback mechanisms for employee assessments. Of course, this is also a challenge for male employees, and it is no coincidence that the term "power harassment" was coined in Japan. Abusive work situations and hated bosses are the fodder of many movies and TV dramas on workplace dynamics. The situation gets worse when sexual harassment combines with power abuse. And because the Womenomics changes have been rolled out very quickly, many companies still lack structures through which employees can report abuse, and those that exist often remain unused because—as is the case globally—this could be seen as causing trouble and might trigger retribution. Women also still have comparatively fewer networks that can lend feedback and support, both internally and across companies. The lack of a sizable support network is known globally to be a big handicap for women compared to men when it comes to benefiting from encouragement, promotions, and patronage.[12]

Nonetheless, Womenomics is gaining traction. Compared to the situation of women in private companies and government in Japan 20 years ago, the progress is remarkable.[13] While Japanese women are going about this change quietly, they are entering the ranks of regular employment in increasing numbers. This change is also reflected in Mr. Toyoda's comment: the labor shortage means that companies can no longer afford to discriminate as they jockey to hire the best talent. Abenomics has helped with its nudging: creating benchmarks, celebrating companies that make progress, and shaming those that don't. As of 2018, about 20% of *kachō* (section chief) positions in the private sector were held by women, up from almost zero in the late 1990s.[14] This bodes well for a future increase in the ratio at senior levels, which in 2018 was only 5%. In a series of industries, from robotics (Yushin Precision Equipment) and mobile e-commerce (DeNA) to fashion retail (Uniqlo), asset management (Nomura), and investment banking (Daiwa Securities), women have assumed senior roles and CEO positions, and they are harbingers of a new era in Japanese management.

As companies and government agencies compete for workers, they are realizing a new need to offer flexible hours and a better work-life balance. Most large Japanese companies now offer maternity leave of up to a very generous three years, although in reality there continues to be a career penalty and many women do not make full use of the policy. In addition to adjusting office workflow by moving meetings earlier in the day, some companies—and even METI, the economics ministry—are opening in-house daycare centers or giving support to local childcare facilities. These initiatives are not just to attract women, but also reflect a growing interest among male millennials in adjusting their salaryman work life so they can play a more active family role. Dual career families are on the rise. And, while this is still uncommon, some fathers now take their children to their company's daycare center. This means that they, too, have to end their workday at a reasonable hour to take the children back home. This takes some of the weight off young working mothers, who are usually the ones chided for constantly pushing their colleagues to be more efficient and get things done at work before six o'clock. It also forces companies to accommodate employees in working from home after dinner, which further benefits dual careers. As stepwise adjustments percolate through the system and companies compete for workers, the definition of a "normal" workday is changing.

Foreign Workers and Immigration

Another solution to alleviate the pains of the labor shortage is to increase the number of foreign workers. By 2019, their number had already risen to 1.5 million, a 200% increase over 2015, marking six years of consecutive growth. Of these, about a quarter are from China and another quarter from Vietnam, and 11% from the Philippines. One third work in manufacturing and about 15% each in retail and restaurants.[15] We already saw in Chapter 5 that the number of foreign students has risen to over 270,000, and a further increase in foreign workforce participation is widely expected. While these figures may seem comparatively low, and insufficient to sustain the current size of the workforce, within Japan this a clear departure from the past.[16]

Almost by design, tight cultures, with their strong norms and low tolerance for deviants, are more controlling about the processes of immigration. There are strict assumptions about language acquisition and careful processes to initiate foreigners into the country's behavioral norms. This is just as true for Japan, as it is for Norway, South Korea, or Singapore. For example, Japan has very particular rules about what kind of garbage is collected on what days of the week, and how it is to be separated, cleaned, and even folded. This is totally understandable in a super-densely populated metropolis such as Tokyo, but quite bewildering to any newcomer to the city. But these rules are among the first things a foreigner is asked to learn and strictly obey upon arrival in Japan, and social sanctioning runs high for those who get it wrong.

Local and city governments are structuring a variety of events to guide the integration and education of immigrants, at school and at work, as well as opening new schools for language and skill acquisition. This is in line with U.S. research showing that the most significant predictor of successful assimilation is language acquisition.[17] Compulsory initiation programs also aim at upholding "safety first" norms that the Japanese deem indispensable in times of extreme events like earthquakes. These *anzen dai-ichi* exercises are taken very seriously, driven by a genuine concern to ensure that foreigners know how to stay out of harm's way. During the Tohoku earthquake and tsunami, a heart-warming story cycled through the news of a Japanese factory owner who risked his life to ensure that his twelve trainees from China were running uphill to escape the rising waters. All these activities of initiation and assimilation introduce a self-selection mechanism, whereby living in Japan is most attractive to people drawn to its structure and regularity. Although Japan's progress on immigration reform may appear slow and highly restrictive, it offers an interesting alternative to policies adopted elsewhere.

Reflecting the structured processes of integration, the government has also created specific visas and job categories for immigrants. One category allowed guest workers under the label of "trainees" on special time-limited visas. The positive connotation of learning and training reduced some of society's resistance to this new inflow of foreigners.[18] However, these temporary trainee positions were insufficient to meet the corporate demand for laborers, and immigration reform became part of the 2012 Abenomics program, which established new visa categories by skill levels, such as for "specified skilled workers" in various manufacturing businesses.

At many New Japan companies, change is occurring even faster. The startup company Mercari—a flea market app and one of Japan's two unicorn startups—has hired mostly foreign engineers for its IT and innovation team.[19] In 2010, Rakuten, Japan's largest e-commerce company, launched a campaign labeled "Englishnization," which made English the first language across the entire company. Initially ridiculed for forcing Japanese to work with each other in poor English, this policy greatly facilitated attracting foreign talent and managing foreign acquisitions. It also sent a strong signal to Japan's high school students: if you want to work for a New Japan company, you'd better put effort into your English skills.

Some large companies have even begun to proactively seek out foreign office staff as ambassadors of culture change. The aggregate niche strategy as well as active foreign M&A activities require new managerial skills for a global workforce. Even in business segments where Japanese companies dominate a niche with domestic manufacturing, products still must be sold in global business-to-business markets, a process that requires new global customer relations and negotiation skills. Likewise, the sharp increase in cross-border acquisitions and corporate venture capital demands a new type of global manager that can create synergies from these investments. Cutting-edge research and open innovation, too, thrive through international collaborations.

Companies are realizing that global management requires not just the ability to speak English, but rather a new mindset and the ability to be an effective professional in a variety of unfamiliar cultures. Some have now begun to actively hire young or mid-career foreign employees and, more or less explicitly, are encouraging them to be different and break the rules. This is seen as a lever for changing the company mindset and building these global skills. Upon arrival, the foreigners often encounter awkward behavior or even rejection for doing their job all wrong, or not quite following the behavioral code properly. Yet soon enough, some of their Japanese colleagues quietly welcome the opportunity to adjust certain aspects of the overly rigid rules of office workflow.

Workstyle Reform

On April 1, 2019, one of the most important laws in the midst of a series of labor reforms went into effect, under the title Reforms of Work Practices (*hataraki-kata kaikaku*).[20] These reforms reflected some of the already ongoing changes in large firms, but nevertheless brought substantial changes in wage structure and pay differentials, new rules on diversity and welfare, overtime prohibitions, and a new system that allows a lifetime contract employee to work for two employers simultaneously. Taken together, they meant a long overdue normalization of some of the most excessive outgrowths of the postwar employment system, such as excessive work hours, as well as a move toward the individualization of career paths. But they have also altered the economic logic of employment or, as Akio Toyoda suggested, challenged the very logic of lifetime employment itself.

Meritocracy Pay

A major game changer is that pay structures will now be determined not just by tenure but also by job category and personal knowledge and skills. This is major because meritocracy necessitates more performance transparency, which until now was often purposely kept ambiguous in an effort to be polite and considerate to all employees. HR departments must now replace wage parity with differentiated assignments and personal performance assessments, which requires building new skills in evaluations. They also need to restructure the traditional apprenticeship-like training program in the first few years of employment, when everybody is treated and promoted in the same way. The shift in the definition of *fair*—from equal to equitable—is likely to introduce a new type of intra-office competition, which may be encouraging to some but may also cause greed and resentment. The rise in labor mobility will further increase wage differentials by introducing horizontal benchmarking. The benchmark of company size for wages is slowly being replaced by market rates based on the skills of an individual employee.

What is more, the new law stipulates "equal pay for equal work," meaning that non-regular employees with assignments similar to lifetime employees will now have to be paid the same. This introduces more fairness into the two modes of employment, but it is a huge blow to the operations of HR departments in all Japanese companies, as it reduces the utility of the non-regular work category for adjusting payroll over the business cycle. One possible outcome is a muddling of the two categories, which would bring further adjustments going forward.

Work Hours and Diversity

The second area of workstyle reform reflects the millennial generation's shift in work expectations and the rights-responsibility tradeoff with their employer. Reform measures in the categories of welfare and diversity establish new employee rights, including medical leave, maternity leave, childcare or eldercare support leave, and protection against dismissals. Working hours, and in particular overtime, are now strictly regulated. While there are various categories, for most employees overtime is now limited to 100 hours per month and 720 hours annually, and companies that exceed these limits will be sanctioned.[21] This change is already taking hold, as people have begun to return home at more reasonable hours, and workstyles are becoming more flexible, including the ability to do telework and to adjust work hours to family constraints. In the long run, these new restrictions bring more challenges for the HR function in further shifting the emphasis in assessments from time served to output created.

Companies are now also required to force employees to take at least five consecutive days of paid vacation per year (out of a total vacation time of ten paid days).[22] This is a true shock to office practices, in particular the deeply ingrained notion that all employees have to attend all meetings. As we saw in Chapter 2, to this day, at many companies, taking a vacation is still considered causing a nuisance for those who must fill in during the colleague's absence. During the postwar period, the government had introduced many national holidays—for example, to celebrate young people, old people, the seasons, and previous and current emperors' birthdays—to ensure that workers got a modicum of time off. There is also a rule that if such a day falls on a weekend, the following Monday is a holiday, as well as a strong norm about such holidays being truly "off." But all that is still done in unison: everybody is vacationing at the same time. The new vacation rule, with at least five consecutive days, is too long for all to take at the same time. It will require companies to build new mechanisms to allow individuals to take off at their own time. Returning to the imagery of the baseball time-out in Chapter 2, companies need to develop a new mindset and allow for meetings without the outfielders. The very essence of decision making may have to be streamlined to reduce the need for all to be present and to agree.

Labor Mobility

The workstyle reforms were launched before the groundswell of increasing job mobility. That mobility has increased due, in part, to the ongoing corporate refocusing and pivoting, including mergers, carve-outs, and other organizational shifts that have changed employers' needs and job offerings. But it also reflects an attitude shift, especially among younger employees, who are no longer interested in dedicating their entire lives to one company. Nor is job changing any longer taboo among employees in their 40s, especially high performers in failing companies. This new mobility affects the core logic of the quid pro quo of the old system in terms of the rights and responsibilities of employers and employees.

In 2018, Japan's private sector employees totaled 56 million people, of whom 35 million (62%) held lifetime employment jobs.[23] At that time, reflecting the continued endurance of Japan's employment system, a survey of lifetime employees still indicated a very low level of job changers, of only 5.3%. Nevertheless, that represented a big increase from 3.7% in 2016. And, the numbers varied greatly by age group: 19% of millennials (respondents in their 20s and 30s) had already changed their jobs, and when asked what they were looking for, 40% wanted to earn a higher salary, and 60% wanted to find a more interesting job with a better work-life balance. Overall, 72% thought that job changing was a forward-looking and positive thing to do.[24] A 2019 survey of 1,260 young, new company hires confirmed this sentiment: 57% said they would be open to a job change, the highest number on record.[25]

Reflecting this new interest in finding not any job, but the right one, the number of newly hired university graduates who immediately register on a job-changing platform has skyrocketed by 30 times between 2017 and 2019.[26]

The declared purpose is to enter the "second *shūkatsu*" right away. As startup companies are sprouting up to cater to this new demand, HR departments are struggling to structure onboarding training programs for employees who are not committed to the firm for the long haul. Together with the changes in the *shūkatsu* system itself, this reflects a deep change in the employment zeitgeist.

Can Lifetime Employment be Saved? The Dual Jobs System

Perhaps the most drastic change made by the workstyle reforms is the official introduction of the dual jobs system. The logic of the traditional lifetime employment system is predicated on serving only one master, and matches employees' values of loyalty, dedication, and reciprocal obligations with employers' responsibilities of education and welfare provisions. The exclusivity restriction had long been included in each company's "business rules" (*shūgyō kisoku*), Japan's version of a combined employment contract and business code of conduct. The business rules form the basis of work relations and the overall give-and-take between the company and its workers. They cover all company regulations, from wages, working hours, and vocational training to retirement pay, and also limit employee rights regarding job rotations and work locations, as well as choice in attire and hairstyle. To help employers, especially smaller firms, draft this document, the government issues an annual template of the "model business rules."

The 2018 template revision removed a provision that employees could not have a second job, leaving it to each company whether to allow employees to take on a second or side job. Until that time, dual jobs were very limited in Japan: in 2018, of the total workforce, only 4% had a side job, slightly below the 5% in Germany and 7% in France. In Japan, most of those with dual jobs worked for small companies, and having dual jobs was practically unheard of among salarymen.[27] And even going forward, the relevance of this new dual job system will probably not be so much in how widely it is used, but rather in how it introduces new pressure valves, and how these may evolve into a new system of innovation.

Japan's largest companies are divided on the notion of dual jobs. In a 2019 survey, half of Japan's largest employers reported that they would not adopt the new system.[28] The single most cited reason is the administrative challenge, including which employer bears responsibility for pay and benefits. Many companies also fear a leak of intellectual property, and are worried about conflicts of interest. Reflecting their tight-culture setting, many CEOs are also concerned about the upheaval it will cause in the organizational structure and how they will integrate outsiders meaningfully into their work schedules. Akio Toyoda's comment at the beginning of this chapter hints at an even deeper concern, namely that without a counterbalance to the bargaining power that this system affords to employees, it may lead to a situation where the employers will be stuck with only those who have no outside opportunities, while the superstars take on dual jobs and freely take their knowledge elsewhere. In this view, the enhancement of employee rights has to be somehow matched by a reduction in employer obligations, and this may endanger the system of lifetime employment altogether.[29]

However, the new system can also be interpreted much more positively, as a means to help thaw the rigidities of the labor system while preserving its stabilizing features. This is why the other half of the largest firms are preparing to allow dual jobs. The first advantage is that the new system enables large companies to attract talent despite the labor shortage, by signaling to high performers that they will not be put into straitjackets with features of indentured slavery at equal, low pay. Rather, they will be allowed to pursue more individualized career and mobility options. Second, the dual jobs system may help to reduce the costs of hiring mistakes by reducing the risks in job changing: employees can now stay at one job while testing out another with a different firm. The value for companies of offering this insurance is to entice misfits or underperformers to leave, which is much easier than laying them off. If successful, this would greatly lubricate the system and reduce one of the biggest costs of the traditional system. This, in turn, would allow companies to hire more people and uphold the core concept of lifetime employment.

And finally, some companies hope that if a few employees experiment with this system—almost as if on a sabbatical—it would rejuvenate the organization, introduce new cross-fertilization, and increase energy and motivation among the workforce.[30] In fact, this concept of "entrepreneurialism with job safety" is already at the core of a new movement by innovative companies that seek to attract great talent and then offer employees the freedom to start their own company with the option to return. This is best seen by way of an example, and one of the companies at the forefront of this is Recruit, Japan's leading personnel and appointment booking agency.

Example: Recruit Holdings Co.

Recruit Holdings is, in its own words, a constantly self-cannibalizing, cutting-edge provider of information services, and is widely seen as one of Japan's top contenders to play in the global GAFA (Google, Amazon, Facebook, Apple) league. Thanks to the acquisitions of Indeed (2012) and Glassdoor (2018), Recruit is the world's largest online staffing agency, and it is also Japan's largest domestic staffing, internet-based reservations, matchmaking, and lifestyle arrangement needs company. It generates annual global revenues of about $20 billion, has 40,000 employees, and launches 988 new business applications annually.[31] Recruit is as much a beneficiary as it is an enabler of Japan's changing employment system, as it proactively shapes new processes of work and innovation in its HR practices.

Seasoned readers may recall this company from the bubble years of the 1980s, when a political bribery and insider trading scandal involving the stock of its real estate subsidiary, Recruit Cosmos, toppled Prime Minister Noboru Takeshita and put Recruit founder Hiromasa Ezoe's name in the headlines for many months. Ezoe founded the company in 1960, as a student at the prestigious University of Tokyo, with a recruiting magazine to connect fresh graduates with hiring companies. Since then, Recruit has owned, and shaped, the *shūkatsu* process (including, in the 1990s, bringing about the uniform dress code through ads for the discount suit company Aoki in its job magazines). The bursting of the bubble economy left Recruit with excess debt, and in 1992, the company was bought by Daiei Inc., the maverick discount retailer. When Daiei fell into distress at the turn of the century, Recruit was sold off to a PE fund. All the while, Recruit expanded its business, and continued to dominate Japan's staffing services and catalogue advertisement businesses. In 2012, Masumi Minegishi, who had joined the company in 1989, became CEO, and in 2014 Recruit Holdings went public. The proceeds from the IPO were then used for aggressive global investments, including the acquisition of Glassdoor for $1.2 billion in 2018, and the company embarked on a period of dramatic global sales growth.

Recruit began as a catalogue business, and from job information expanded to apartment rentals (with the magazine *Suumo*), bridal services (*Zexy*), and beauty salon and restaurant reservations (*Beauty*, *Hot Pepper*). In the 1990s, Recruit realized early that the Internet would eventually kill the magazines, and it was quick to adopt a dual approach. Out of the new internet business grew the "ribbon" business model, Recruit's word for its platform that connects clients and users for any and all services they might seek or offer. This platform allowed new extensions into reservations (e.g., restaurants, hairdressers, hotels, and hot springs), travel, and dating, all the while expanding the staffing options to include temp workers and mid-career job changers. All told, Recruit now runs over 200 online consumer lifestyle services.[32]

Today, Recruit Holdings has three main businesses: Staffing (the original domestic staffing business), Media & Solutions (the core business of advertising and matching), and HR Technology (global online HR businesses, including Indeed and Glassdoor). In 2013, Recruit added a series of services with names beginning with "Air." The first was called AirREGI (REGI being short for "register"), a point-of-sales application. This was based on a marketing push in which Recruit handed out iPads to participating small-scale business owners for more efficient payment processes. These iPads created a Recruit stronghold within Japan's small business service sector, and in 2014, the associated services were extended to AirWAIT (appointment scheduling), AirPAY (financial services), AirMATE (operations management), and AirSHIFT (HR management). While the initial AirREGI service is free, the small hair salons, restaurants, shops, and other businesses pay a monthly fee for the subsequent services.

All of these activities sit on the ribbon platform, and you can easily sense how this access to information on small businesses and their users, combined with staffing information, makes Recruit a global player in data drilling (i.e., data collection, of which more in Chapter 10). Recruit is now aggressively investing in developing AI engines to analyze these platform components. In 2016, the company opened the Recruit Institute of Technology, now known as Megagon Labs, in Silicon Valley. For a glimpse into the near future, consider this new application: Recruit has developed an AI methodology that can predict whether you are about to look for a new job, based on your recruitment data (including your personality profile and biographical and salary information) combined with changes in your recent performance assessments, marital status, leisure activities, financial situation, hairstyle, dining habits, and so forth. This forecast is for sale to corporate customers, who may use it as a means to retain high-performing talent.[33]

Of particular interest here is Recruit's HR approach. The company is a front-runner in encouraging its employees to be entrepreneurial, but in contrast to other large employers, it keeps these people in its orbit and may even invest in them. Any employee who quits Recruit to start their own company is still considered part of the Recruit family, and there is a website of Recruit alumni, their startups, and their new corporate positions.[34] This creates a double benefit. First, Recruit is better able to attract young talent with real skills, and reaps the benefits of their high energy and motivation for perhaps five years. Second, if the startups are successful, they may create future business opportunities as well as a valuable network of competence, consisting of companies that are all loyal to Recruit. And if they fail, the former employees have a human and business network to rely on, and Recruit may well rehire them. Other New Japan companies, such as DeNA, the successful mobile portal and e-commerce company, have followed suit, creating similar families of loyal startup firms and alumni employees.

Encouraging people to be entrepreneurial but keeping them in one's orbit is new in Japan. Traditionally, somebody who left an employer in mid-career was gone for good; sometimes, these quitters were seen as traitors and met with ostracism. While this reflected the keen sense of inside-outside that has long characterized Japanese thinking, it has also long been identified as wasteful. The dual jobs system now offers a new way for more established companies to structure transitions in and out of a lifetime employment job so as not to waste the loyalty and dedication of former employees. In the 2010s, Sony started a program of encouraging entrepreneurship whereby Sony invests in the startup and offers the employee the option to return, regardless of outcome. And in 2018, Panasonic introduced a new system of *fuku-shoku* (rejoin the company) into its business rules, whereby lifetime employees who leave the company may return to their previous position, under the same conditions as when they left, for a period of five years.[35]

In this sense, the dual jobs reform represents a mechanism for traditional firms to structure processes of open innovation for a few, while maintaining lifetime employment for most of their employees. Japan is the first country to be exposed to this drastic demographic aging and labor shortage. The mechanisms it is employing to cater to talent are necessarily trial-and-error and will be interesting to observe going forward.

J-Startup: An Alternative Approach to Building an Innovation Ecosystem

The movement to build networks of entrepreneurs through offering sabbaticals, or more or less explicit extensions of employment, is also connected to a new government policy aiming to build a new, Japan-style innovation ecosystem. Even though companies such as Recruit offer a rich soil and plant the seeds for entrepreneurial activity, overall, Japan's venture capital and startup scene has remained comparatively small, despite tremendous government policy efforts and funding budgets. In the 2010s, two systemic obstacles were identified as hindering the growth of a well-rounded innovation ecosystem: the lack of individual career risk-taking, and the lack of true involvement by Japan's largest companies in investing in or acquiring startup companies. The workstyle reforms played directly into this initiative to foster entrepreneurship, rolled out under the banner of J-Startup.[36]

Japan's rebuilding following World War II rested on an initial, huge wave of entrepreneurship that resulted in global brands like Toyota, Honda, Matsushita (Panasonic), and Sony. Unwittingly, the postwar industrial policies then created barriers to entry for new market participants, foreign and domestic alike, and the success of the postwar business model with its rigid industry hierarchies dominated by government-anointed winners obstructed market mechanisms and prevented later entrepreneurs from growing their companies into contenders. Smart engineers and young entrepreneurs were drawn into large firms, and the role of small firms was to become those large firms' trusted suppliers. The high status of large firms and their salaryman employees translated into the view that starting a company was an admission of failure, a negative career move that could be explained only by an inability to find a lifetime position.

To this day, most indicators of Japanese entrepreneurship and venture capital remain comparatively low. For example, on average for the years 2012–2014, total VC investment expressed as a percentage of GDP was only 0.03% in Japan, compared to 0.37% in the United States.[37] Japan's entry/exit rate, a measure commonly used as a yardstick for the dynamics of new firm creation and failure, currently hovers at around 5% (compared to 10% in the U.S.). As a side note, while this low entry/exit rate is often decried as yet another indicator in which Japan is lagging, it may be simply an expression of Japan's superior safety nets that help people to avoid the wasteful slash-and-burn failures of Silicon Valley. However, the low exit rate also underscores an important limitation of Japan's "market for ideas," namely fewer exit options. This discourages big bets by venture capitalists, and that in turn discourages new entries.

Japanese startups typically rely on going public and listing on the stock market for exits. For example, in 2014, Japan recorded 116 startup IPOs, but only 36 acquisitions by a large firm. While IPOs may be more glamorous, corporate acquisitions are the lifeblood of any innovation ecosystem, as they provide fast, often lucrative exits and encourage serial entrepreneurship. Selling a startup company to a large corporation is by far the main fuel for innovation in Silicon Valley; in 2014, the U.S. venture industry reported a total of 122 startup IPOs compared to 918 corporate acquisitions.[38] Thus, involving large firms is now seen as the key to solving Japan's entrepreneurship puzzle.

In 2016, Abenomics launched a novel approach to building a more robust, Japan-style innovation ecosystem, under the heading J-Startup.[39] This was different from innumerable previous government attempts in that, unlike the dizzying array of individual programs put forth by various ministries, it represented an effort by the Cabinet Office to combine and connect all programs into one unified initiative to build a new ecosystem. Moreover, it aimed specifically at mobilizing large companies to engage in true, open innovation with startup companies, and it became yet another instance of highly effective nudging and shaming. Also, through the dual jobs provision, J-Startup was directly linked to the workstyle reforms, and provided the banner of innovation as an impetus for change.

Similar to many legacy programs, J-Startup began by picking winners. In 2018, METI—the ministry eventually put in charge of implementing the program—assembled an expert committee of 66 people with experience in venture capital and tasked them with picking 92 startups as winners from an applicant pool of 10,000. These 92 winners then received government funding and, more importantly, access to a group of 122 supporters from large domestic and foreign companies and venture funds. These supporters were charged with building a network, granting access, and providing funding and mentoring.[40]

In the next step, the core intent is to trigger a more active involvement of large firms over the next decade. In addition to some hard benefits, like new tax breaks, the primary tool is nudging. The names of the startups as well as the large company supporters are listed on the J-Startup website. The program organizes regular "venture cafes" that mimic Silicon Valley events and are widely seen as hip and innovative. Their purpose is to engender social approval for participating in open innovation. The large firm supporters are also nudged to sign onto the dual jobs system and engage with entrepreneurial employees, similar to the approach Recruit has launched. These large firms are now widely celebrated, and by implication, seen as good employers. This nudging has worked. By 2018, Keidanren—the large employer lobbying association—had signed up to J-Startup and praised investing in startup firms as a new way of organizational renewal. It remains to be seen whether governments can build innovation ecosystems, but the engagement of the traditional Keidanren companies in new economy processes of innovation is a clear sign of a new direction.

The J-Startup initiative combines with the new HR approaches of Recruit, DeNA, Panasonic, and a growing number of large companies to drive Japan toward an alternative version of how to structure an innovation ecosystem. The harsh realities of Silicon Valley, with its high-flying excesses, repeated failures, and exorbitant losses do not work for Japan—it is not something that Japanese society would gladly suffer. Rather, in line with the country's tight-culture leanings, Japan's version of an innovation ecosystem demands a more structured approach, one where new company formation is embedded in existing networks that provide stability. Allowing lifetime employees to start their own companies while keeping them close, and offering the insurance of being able to return to salaried positions should they fail, is the type of balanced approach to entrepreneurship that may work in Japan. It may also allow Japan to build its own system of open innovation while maintaining its basic concepts of employment, and accordingly, social stability.

All of this is unfolding at the time of this writing. As of 2019, perhaps the biggest sign that change is happening is rising wages. The labor shortage has put pressure on pay, in particular for specialist positions, and new job mobility brings horizontal wage comparison and further contributes to a rise in salaries. In 2018, inflation-adjusted wages climbed by almost 3%, the highest jump since 1997. In July 2019, the traditional IT company NEC made headlines by offering to pay the best of its new hires in the R&D department a starting salary exceeding $90,000 and announced a new interest in hiring mid-career IT specialists. This was a complete break with the seniority pay system of the past. Concurrently, Sony raised its top salaries for AI researchers by 20%.[41] Meanwhile, in another reversal of previous pay structures, starting salaries at startup companies now exceed those in large firms. And by 2019 the salaries of mid-career salarymen who switched from a large firm into a domestic startup increased by 40%, which exceeded the pay jump they could get from switching to a listed company.[42] As working for smaller and newer companies is becoming more socially acceptable, the legacy companies face new pressures to revise their hiring and labor contracts.

Still, it appears unlikely that the underlying stability offered in Japan's labor system will be removed entirely. It also seems unlikely that Japan's companies will lose their role as social anchors, technology leaders, and safe havens, as it is not in anybody's interest to unravel the traditional structure completely. Many employees still much prefer job stability over multiple iterations of job hunting. Given the labor shortage and new competition for talent, companies also benefit from offering lifetime employment if they can find new mechanisms to strike a new balance between employers and employees.

(10)

JAPAN GOING FORWARD

Reinventing for the Digital Economy

A partner at a large global consulting firm in South Asia recently visited UC San Diego, and after hearing about this book project, he responded with a blanket dismissal: "No way Japan can compete in the digital economy. Middleware, maybe, but the U.S. and China will make all the money with their stronghold on data. Japan can pick up the breadcrumbs in the hardware—maybe." This is the standard response I am getting these days: many think that Japanese companies will not and cannot be big players in the digital economy. They say that Japanese software is not user-friendly, except for video games, and conclude that this means Japan cannot possibly be a player in AI. But we also know that Japanese engineers can make trains run on time like nobody else, and build the best industrial robots. And while we are focused on how the GAFA businesses will split the spoils of the personal data bonanza with Alibaba and its new Chinese AI startups, several Japanese companies have already positioned themselves to leverage their manufacturing and systems operations skills toward the digital economy. Rather than the business model innovation that the GAFA firms are pushing, Japanese companies are betting on digital manufacturing platforms as the basis on which to compete going forward. The question then is, can Japanese companies reinvent *monozukuri*—the art of making things—for the digital age?

Despite the widespread skepticism, Japanese companies have started to make headway. But in contrast to the U.S. and Chinese focus on platform businesses, e-commerce, social media, and the sharing economy, Japanese firms have started from the ground up, leveraging their expertise in manufacturing and influence in global supply chains. Changes may be slow to materialize, but as with the reinvention over the past 25 years, quiet does not mean stagnant. As we have seen in previous chapters, Japan's tight culture necessitates gradual change. This may disadvantage Japanese firms in the digital race. But it also allows them to study what works and what doesn't for the trailblazers, and focus on areas in which they have a competitive advantage. In some ways, Japan's future within the digital space may reflect the major economic and societal reforms outlined in this book—gradual by U.S. standards, but consequential and globally influential, nonetheless.

The digital transformation has burst onto the scene with countless acronyms and expressions. The *internet of things* (IoT) refers to a new system in which all things have a chip, are constantly connected, and can interact. *Industry 4.0* refers to a new IoT manufacturing paradigm characterized by machines and parts equipped with sensors and wireless connectivity to create an interconnected system that can visualize an entire production line and make decisions on its own. *Big data* is short for the large sets of information collected from all these parts and machines, and *AI* (artificial intelligence) is the means by which machines will eventually be able to learn and to teach themselves. *5G* is the technology base needed to accommodate this vast amount of data exchange, and the *cloud* is made up of the equipment that houses all the information. The new connectivity requires new hardware, from sensors to robots, and new smart grids to control the new flow of energy and autonomous systems in the future smart cities. The technology shift encompassed by these terms requires changes so dramatic that it is already seen as a disruption.

The aggregate niche strategy has put Japanese manufacturers in an excellent position to play in hardware, as we saw in Chapter 4. But is dominance in sensors and smart meters really all we can expect from Japan, as the pundits are predicting? The ongoing business reinvention suggests that Japanese companies would like to do more. This is why Hitachi is selling off its old crown jewels and buying new ones, Toyota wants a complete model change, FANUC is lifting its veil of secrecy, Recruit is creating a global HR orbit, and Panasonic and Sony are hustling to get their acts together. The digital transformation promises new opportunities in many areas where Japanese companies can compete.

The Future of Manufacturing:
The Digital Shopfloor

While Japan's reinvention story can also be told for the retail, logistics, and finance sectors, this book has focused on manufacturing, because it is critical to Japan's economy and lies at the heart of Asia's competitive dynamics. It is also Japan's first step into the digital economy. Japan's long-standing experience in making complicated things well has been key to its success. Within Japan, management strength in *monozukuri* is celebrated as "knowledge of the *gemba*," meaning the shopfloor. The word *gemba* entered the English language in the 1980s, with the rise of the Toyota Production System and lean manufacturing, where "doing the *gemba*" specifically refers to quality control and *kaizen* through careful management and monitoring of the shopfloor. The future of industry in the digital era will be discovering and defining what "doing the *gemba*" means in the digital age.

The Digital *Gemba*

The typical manufacturing shopfloor of today is already highly automated, of course, but its many processes are not yet unified into one central system. Rather, there are layers of manufacturing and software programs that run individual machines. Engineers and operations management people think about the current structure as a "production automation pyramid" that has been developed incrementally since the 1960s. The pyramid has five levels. At the bottom are the machines that make things and are equipped with sensors, actuators, and other devices that feed information into the control level where the minute details of production are governed. Levels 2 to 4, then, form a hierarchy of production and planning software, each level performing distinct parts of the manufacturing process, including making robots interact with one another and giving concrete production orders to machines. The top level is the ERP, or enterprise resource planning system, which schedules the entire production process weeks and months out, including what products will be built, in what quantity, and with what parts. Today, German and Japanese companies, from Siemens and SAP to FANUC, Yaskawa Electric, and Yokogawa Electric are strong competitors in this field. In the United States, Rockwell Automation, Honeywell, and GE operate in this space, and in 2016, the Chinese company Midea acquired the German robot manufacturer KUKA to fast-track its entry into the fray.

This complicated, layered system of multiple software programs is now awaiting its disruption, dubbed Industry 4.0. The idea behind digital manufacturing is that one integrated systems solution can speak to all parts and all levels of the shopfloor. The internet of things means that all parts are constantly online, through the 5G network, and are providing complete production information in real time. What is more, because the product remains constantly connected to the IoT world throughout its entire product life cycle, manufacturers own its "digital twin": a data file that contains complete information about the product's entire history, from manufacturing, application, and utility to functionality decline, timing of repairs, replacement, and defaults. Advances in big data enable real-time analysis of this information, and the existence of AI means that over time the robots that make the products will learn how to adjust to this information. And unlike people, these robots do not need to sleep or take lunch breaks or sick leaves; only a monthly checkup is needed to keep them going 24/7. In this system, the cloud then houses everything that is knowable, in real time, including which suppliers store how many parts and where parts and machines are located at any given time.

This is every engineer's dream: if all is known, all can be optimized. There is never any downtime or interruption due to everyday human error. In addition to speed and sheer output capacity, this disruption also obviates our thinking about economies of scale in manufacturing, which posits that the cost of production declines as the number of items produced increases, due to learning, speed, and capacity utilization. In a digital manufacturing world, it is expected that eventually robots will learn instantaneously and that changeover from one task to another will be done with a toggle switch. This will greatly reduce the cost of single piece production and allow high customization and buyer-specific single lot manufacturing.

What is holding up this manufacturing nirvana is that a complete 5G, IoT, and information-sharing network does not yet exist, and the integrated solutions and platforms are just now being built. Equally important, as of 2019, there is not yet a known use case that demonstrates the value added by such a hyper-unified and -optimized system, nor is it known what kinds of efficiencies this future complete information will create. Still, it is certain that global manufacturing is moving in this direction, and the competitive jockeying for position has begun, even as the goal line remains unclear.

VALUE CREATION IN THE DIGITAL MANUFACTURING

To help guide a conversation about the value creation potential of the various levels of production of the future, Figure 10.1 presents a graphical representation of the business layers associated with the new digital manufacturing. The bottom bar is the current production level at the shopfloor, divided into two business segments: machines and equipment, and software systems. This is where value creation is currently centered. The onset of the digital transformation and launching of 5G networks is introducing the new middle layer of advanced, integrated manufacturing systems. Think of these as much smarter machines with much more advanced sensors and software that constantly interact through connection on platforms. This is the current hotbed of competition.

As indicated by the dotted arrow, the upper layer is still in the future: it takes the data produced in the manufacturing of parts and their subsequent deployment and performance, scrapes it for relevance and patterns, and offers forecasts of future needs and solutions to persistent challenges. A common vision is that this upper layer—the cloud, the new connectivity software applications (the "middleware"), and of course big data analytics and AI—will create value by providing feedback loops into the shopfloor. It is widely assumed that this is where the money will be. Famously, Alibaba's founder, Jack Ma, has referred to data as the "new oil." Most people are aware of the marketing value of personal data gathered through places such as Amazon and Google, but we should also think about how data will drive and, eventually, optimize manufacturing.

The question in regard to Figure 10.1 is, where are Japanese companies likely to compete in this value creation? The main players in this competition are based in the United States, Germany, Japan, and China. In the bottom and middle layers, the three global electric machinery giants compete in all areas, led by Germany's Siemens (seen as the 800-pound gorilla) and followed, to a lesser extent, by GE and Hitachi, which is now doubling down on building strong competencies in this realm. But reflecting the *monozukuri* strengths of Germany and Japan, the real technology push at the bottom layer is provided by several smaller companies based in those two countries. Industry leaders in machinery, sensors, and robots in Japan include Keyence, FANUC, Mitsubishi Electric, Omron, Okuma, Yaskawa, and Fuji Electric. In software systems, Japanese competitors are led by Mitsubishi Electric and Yokogawa Electric, and several smaller firms. Competitors on the equipment side include Trumpf, Bosch, and Dürr of Germany and Rockwell Automation and Honeywell of the

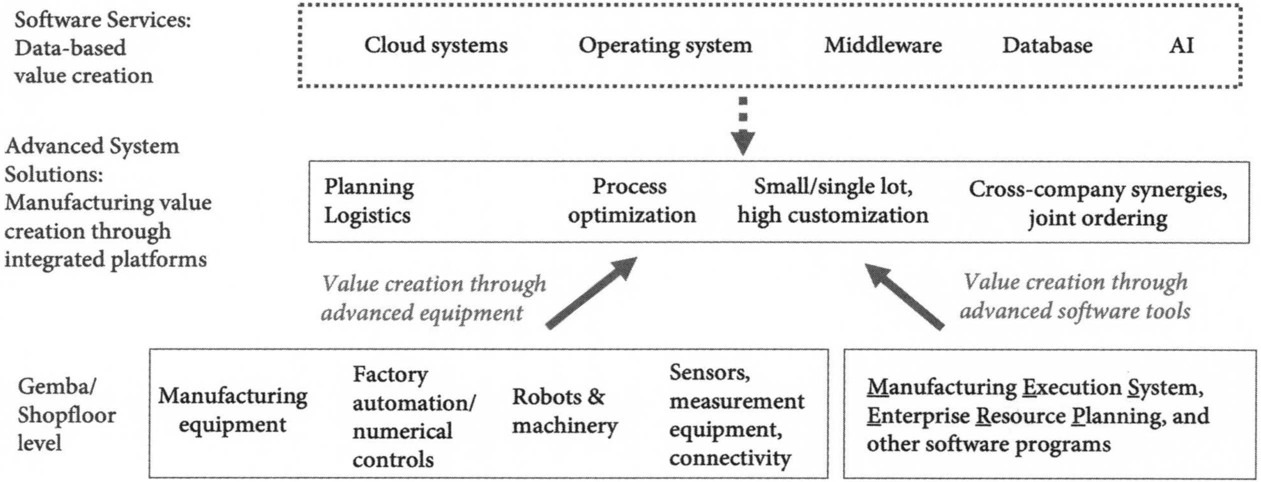

Figure 10.1. Business Value Creation in the Digital Manufacturing Age. Source: Based on chart in Ministry of Economy, Trade and Industry (2018b).

United States, and on the software side, SAP, ABB, and Schneider Electric in Europe, and Autodesk in the U.S.

The second level—value creation through advanced system solutions—is currently up for grabs, and it is widely expected that this competition will also be led by Japanese and German companies. The main players in Japan are Mitsubishi Electric, FANUC, DMG Mori, Hitachi, and Denso, with NEC and Fujitsu also in the mix. The magic words are *edge computing* and *digital manufacturing platform*, and one possible future outcome is that these tools may supersede the cloud in relevance.

EDGE COMPUTING

Edge computing refers to computation, data storage, and security (encryption) that is not in the cloud but closer to the device where it is needed. For example, in autonomous driving, edge computing means that the information from the car's sensors is controlled and reacted to in real time, within the car; only broader information, such as traffic conditions, is shared with the cloud. The same approach applies to buildings (e.g., security systems in hotels) and factories, each with its own, specialized edge computing technology. The advantages of edge computing include reducing the bandwidth needs of the data centers in the cloud, enhancing data privacy, and improving security systems. Edge computing requires a "box" in the actual location (the car, hotel, or factory) that serves as the main computing device. The winners in this business area will be companies that can produce the most cost-effective boxes with the fastest real-time control responses and best cipher algorithms for security. A leading global competitor has emerged in Mitsubishi Electric, which is building out an aggregate niche strategy, beginning with its e-F@ctory edge computing business, and extending into buildings and the automotive sector.[1]

For factory automation, an additional business opportunity is to combine edge computing with digital manufacturing platforms, where the manufacturer's data can be uploaded, stored, shared, and traded. The billion-dollar strategy question is whether this is a winner-take-all industry, akin to Facebook's social media platform, where network effects are such that eventually everyone will connect in only one place to store, access, and share their shopfloor information about parts, logistics, and so forth. In 2016, the erstwhile secretive and closed FANUC prepared for this possibility by launching its open global manufacturing platform, FIELD, which allows manufacturers to connect all their automation equipment with applications that help to improve operational efficiency and product quality. Because it is open, users can add their own systems (such as their current ERP and MES software), interlink globally with other cloud-based manufacturing platforms such as Siemens's MindSphere, and of course, use FANUC's FIELD apps and associated equipment.

FIELD is only one of many digital manufacturing platforms competing to gain traction. Hitachi, Denso, GE, Siemens, Bosch, and ABB are all also building platforms, some proprietary and in-house and others semi-open, such as Siemens's MindSphere and GE's Predix. For example, Hitachi's Lumada is an attempt at collecting all data from all Hitachi businesses and customers, thus creating knowledge through connectivity that is semi-proprietary and therefore perhaps more trustworthy. Which of these platforms will win, and how many there will be, remains to be seen.

In addition, there are also several new initiatives to set up platforms through consortia to build larger network effects (the more users, the higher the utility). In 2017, six Japanese companies, led by Mitsubishi Electric, launched the Edgecross Consortium, with the goal of competing for the dominant design for IoT connectivity. The consortium's purpose is to extend connections beyond the current framework of companies and industries by offering an open software platform to align factory automation with IT. In Germany, Adamos and Software AG's Cumulocity IoT are examples of similar explorations. As of 2019, it appears that the digital manufacturing platform battle will be fought predominantly between Japan and Germany.

The Cloud

While Japan is positioned well on the shopfloor and in integrated systems, the top level—the cloud—is currently occupied squarely by companies in the United States and China. Amazon Web Services (AWS), Alphabet (Google), Microsoft, IBM, Oracle, Cisco, and Intel are among the U.S. companies that are exerting tremendous effort in building out operating systems and AI applications. China's effort is led by Alibaba and Huawei. The general tenor, at least as of 2019, was that Japan and Germany would not be strong competitors here, as this level is disconnected from the actual shopfloor and requires vastly different core competencies. Moreover, the U.S. and Chinese companies are already involved in many aspects of people's day-to-day lives and have thus built dominant footholds in gaining access to and collecting data. To continue with Jack Ma's imagery, they have already installed the tools to drill for oil.

This is precisely why global factory automation leaders such as FANUC and the Edgecross Consortium have launched their free and open platforms: to be data drillers. And because U.S. and Chinese firms are less strongly represented at the shopfloor level, Japan and Germany can dominate global manufacturing and supply-chain data. What remains to be seen is whether a company like FANUC, which can lay claim to a significant portion of global automobile manufacturing data, can derive enough value out of this information to compete in the upper layer.

Another strategy variable in this upper level is whether latecomers to the cloud may be able to piggyback or leapfrog the significant R&D efforts currently being carried out in the United States and China. Since the ultimate nature of the upper-layer businesses remains unclear, it is possible that whoever develops the first real use case can grab an important part of the market. As e-commerce companies are experimenting with drones, car companies with autonomous systems, and manufacturers with robots, any first mover in the technologies of data analytics could be left hat in hand by a latecomer who, by strategy or sheer luck, strikes oil first with its data drilling in applications. In other words, it may be the manufacturing platforms, not the business model platforms, that hold the key to the future, because the users will invent the utility of the emerging technologies.

Reinventing for the Digital Economy: Enter SoftBank and Toyota

Japan's SoftBank has long been jockeying to become a preeminent data driller. Since the late 1990s, the company has made aggressive investments on both sides of the equation, that is, in both the lower levels of connectivity and the upper level of data-based value creation. SoftBank is guided by its corporate motto, "Information Revolution—Happiness for Everyone," and its unflappable founder, Masayoshi Son, famous for his knack of seeing where the train is going before it has even departed the station. SoftBank's bread-and-butter business is IT—it is one of Japan's top telecommunications providers, and in 2013, SoftBank became the majority owner of the U.S. telecommunications company Sprint, which has a large corporate client base. There was also a plan to merge Sprint with T-Mobile, to become one of the top three mobile phone providers in the U.S. with synergies in installing a 5G network.

From its origin, SoftBank has been a venture capital investor. Its global rise began in 1996 with a majority investment in Yahoo! Today, SoftBank owns Yahoo!Japan, Japan's largest internet portal and one of the largest e-commerce and consumer-to-consumer sales platforms. Yahoo!'s founder, Jerry Yang, was close friends with Jack Ma, and SoftBank bought a large stake in Alibaba, which stood at 29% in 2019.[2] Repeatedly, founder Masayoshi Son has placed audacious bets, won big, and then used the returns to further expand SoftBank's footprint. He has also repeatedly lost enormous amounts of money, such as during the first "dot-com bubble," which burst in 2000, with a wide range of investments that almost bankrupted the company. In 2016, SoftBank launched the $100 billion Vision Fund, followed by a second fund of comparable size in 2019, so that it can pool others' investments to amplify Son's investment approach. If only through sheer size, SoftBank has already disrupted Silicon Valley's VC industry. As of 2019, the Vision Fund's investments included stakes in real estate and mortgage services (e.g., WeWork, Compass, Sofi), in mobility and logistics (Uber, Grab, Didi Chuxing, GM Cruise, Manbang), in commerce (Flipkart, Alibaba, Coupang), and in future industry bets (ARM, Nvidia, Slack). The WeWork investment—and perhaps several more—turned into a huge debacle and required a write-off of at least $5 billion. Once again, critics thought that Son might be done in.[3] However, there was also an underlying method to the apparent madness. The common denominator of these portfolio companies is that each plays in at least one of the three layers of value creation in the digital economy, as shown in Figure 10.1, namely through their role in building capacity for data drilling.

Separately from the Vision Fund, SoftBank is also making its own investments. For example, in 2016, SoftBank sold a large stake in Alibaba in order to pay $31 billion to acquire ARM Holdings, a UK company with sales of $1.5 billion at that time. ARM's low-power and efficient chip design can be found in almost all cell phones and tablets in the world. In 2018, ARM acquired Treasure Data, a Silicon Valley startup firm that specializes in technology for processing and analyzing big data. Treasure Data was founded in 2011 by a team of Japanese engineers, and is related to Preferred Networks, a Japanese AI startup, of which more soon. Treasure Data's data-processing technology will allow ARM to enter the connected car market and collect driver data. This, in turn, would boost SoftBank's investments in Uber and Didi Chuxing (China's Uber), among others.[4]

SoftBank is now also making moves to position itself in the top layer, data-based value creation, through software services. In 2018, SoftBank launched a joint venture with Toyota called Monet, short for "mobility network." In Chapter 9, I cited Akio Toyoda's announcement of a "complete model change"–type of transformation for Toyota. This refers to changing the company from a car manufacturer into a transportation service provider. This shift will likely include an entry into MaaS (mobility as a service), and possibly even autonomous flying cars (basically, drones for people), or perhaps something else entirely. Already supplying more than half of Japan's taxi fleet, Toyota has equipped recent taxis with data collectors, audio and visual sensors, and AI processing capabilities. When you take a ride in such a taxi, it will know what language you are speaking (and what you are saying), what food you like, where you are going, how you are paying, and a host of other things about you. Of course, the taxis can also map the city. Then, after a few years of use in Japan, they will be sold as used taxis in Southeast Asia, further extending Toyota's data-drilling reach.[5] Monet also connects Toyota's data with SoftBank's cell phone user data, which adds more information on identity, location, payment, contacts, addresses, and the like—meaning that together the two companies have access to a trove of automotive, consumer, and personal data. One of Monet's first projects was to roll out just-in-time vehicle dispatch services and on-demand transportation through regional partnerships and corporate shuttles in Japan. Effectively, Monet is entering the Uber business (as of 2019, Uber is quite limited in its services in Japan), but without drivers.[6] Self-driving buses and automated door-to-door transportation are already being tested in Japan. Soon after Monet's launch in 2019, Honda Motors and Hino (the largest Japanese maker of light delivery trucks) bought into the venture, extending Monet's reach into logistics and deliveries.

Toyota is also a large investor in Preferred Networks (PFN), Japan's most prominent technology unicorn (a startup company valued at over $1 billion). Founded in 2014 by two Japanese engineers, PFN is building out world-class technological capabilities in natural language processing and machine learning, with applications in manufacturing, transportation, and the life sciences. Other than Toyota, PFN has also received venture capital from FANUC, Hitachi, and the trading house Mitsui & Co.[7] With PFN, Toyota and SoftBank are joining China and the United States in the digital data and AI services level of the new economy.

Perhaps even more importantly, through these explorations, Toyota and other Japanese manufacturing companies are moving quickly to create use cases for digital manufacturing. For example, just combining the Industry 4.0

advances of Toyota, Honda, and Hino and adding MaaS will open opportunities to define more clearly the future of "doing the *gemba*." In addition, Monet can connect with other Japanese companies that have already invested in use cases, like Komatsu, the main competitor of Caterpillar in construction and mining equipment and an early adopter of using GPS locators to reduce equipment theft. Komatsu is now leading an aggressive push to enhance fleet management and equipment technologies through digital manufacturing. And as we saw in Chapter 5, Japan is making large-scale inroads into Southeast Asia with its 650 million people, not just with AI taxis but also in banking, infrastructure installations and consumer products. This opens up a trough of opportunities to develop use cases and mine more terrain in the data-drilling mission.

The traditional Japanese companies tended to stymie entrepreneurial spirit rather than encourage it. But as we saw in Chapter 9, this too is changing. Recruit—the HR services and media solutions company that now owns Glassdoor and all kinds of reservation networks and business directories—is spearheading a new type of innovation system that encourages employees to start their own business yet remain in their employer's orbit. This model further helps Japan's push into the digital economy. For example, Keyence, the world's preeminent designer of sensors, has emerged with innovative approaches for fostering the new supply of talented, creative entrepreneurs critical for Japan to compete in the digital era. For almost two decades, Keyence has been Japan's most profitable company (just ahead of FANUC), with its highly advanced sensors capturing a global dominant market share. Keyence is widely seen as a "crazy" company within Japan, as it is secretive, super-demanding, and super high-paying. The industry insider joke is that Keyence engineers earn so much money that they can afford to buy their own gravestones at age 40. In reality, most Keyence engineers do quit at that age but then either begin or join a startup company. Other companies are setting up similar systems of entrepreneurship in networks. A new type of social organization of startup companies is emerging that replaces the slash-and-burn, rise-fast-and-fall-deep approaches of Silicon Valley with a more balanced, organized setup for new company creation. This shift in the organization of entrepreneurism, in turn, is enabling large firms to further push their reinvention for the digital economy.

Thus, Japan is approaching the digital transformation from the bottom up: it is creating use cases from the shopfloor and in edge computing while building networks for a play in the data and cloud spheres. While U.S. and Chinese IT firms are investing heavily in AI technologies and data mining capacities,

Japanese companies are leveraging their competitive advantage in manufacturing and approaching the disruption from the business demand side, with their pivot foot planted steadily on the shopfloor. They may not make headlines or be as ubiquitous as the GAFA companies, but in the long run they may be just as influential, including in the cloud. While it is still too early to tell how this will all shake out, it appears that many outside observers may find they were too quick to dismiss Japanese companies in the digital economy. In a pattern that has become a theme in this book, many Japanese companies may be moving quietly and methodically, but they are definitely in the competitive mix.

Takeaways from this Book: Why the New Japan Matters

Japan once again matters. Japanese companies anchor global supply chains in hundreds of products without which the world cannot make semiconductors, computer screens, cars, or airplanes. This has made it the most important player in the Asian economy. Domestically, Japan's business reinvention is not only invigorating financial markets and business opportunities, but producing new companies that are emerging as important contenders in the digital economy. This reinvention begins with social stability as an important goal, and seeks to balance the need for corporate performance and profit with stakeholder and shareholder interests in long-term value creation. The processes of change are anchored in the social norms of being polite and appropriate and avoiding turbulence, which has made the process slow and steady. As companies are trying to find a new balance between their responsibilities and employee rights, and as CEOs are trying to balance the new discipline from the markets with mechanisms to thwart self-interested investors, HR practices are shifting to accommodate more diversity, and society is looking for a new work-life balance. In all of these aspects, Japan's choices and tradeoffs are governed by strongly shared societal preferences for stability, order, and predictability, and thus the results are very different from those seen in the U.S. Therefore, Japan's reinvention matters in more than just a business sense, as it can also inform a discussion on how capitalism can be kind and considerate.

The chapters of this book have revealed how Japanese industry has leveraged its strong base in manufacturing into a new aggregate niche strategy that has made Japanese inputs important anchors of the global supply chains. "Japan Inside" means that the role of Japanese business in our national economies and daily lives is mostly invisible: even if you know what you are looking for, it's impossible to tell who made the polarizer film in your cell phone screen or the sensors and microcontrollers in your car. Japan is more important than most realize. Japan's role in the world economy has also become much more multifaceted, as Japanese companies are now critical investors, financiers, and market participants in the United States, Asia, and Europe. This process began more than two decades ago, and now it is not uncommon for young Europeans or Americans to think of Honda or Sony as domestic brands.

Within Japan, large companies are unraveling their diversified conglomerates by carving out even central pieces of their former business portfolios. But they are doing so without sacrificing their preferences for stability and while remaining considerate of all interests. When this slimming down is done through a sale to private equity, the deal is specifically structured to sustain business units' long-term value creation, integrity, and employment. Nevertheless, with this unraveling, the power of market discipline has arrived. Corporate governance reforms have opened boardrooms to outsider directors, and senior management in the C-suite to interactions with shareholders. The increase in shareholder rights has attracted new investments and new types of deals, and the fast-growing M&A market is encouraging and enabling further refocusing and strategic change.

Inside companies, management processes are changing to introduce more diversity and creativity. To accommodate societal preferences for structure and due process, these changes are being rolled out methodically, through highly organized events, group excursions such as innovation tourism, and a slow but steady redesign of office space and workflow. Employment practices are adjusting to the times, with new freedom for employees to pursue individualized careers and more opportunities for dual careers, even as there is a widely shared interest in finding ways to allow the basic tenets of lifetime employment to remain intact.

All this is done with a goal not so much of replacing the old and bringing in the modern, but of creating something entirely new to combine the best of both. The goal is to reinvent the *kaisha* such that it can benefit from the legacy strengths of *monozukuri*, with its incremental improvement, built-in quality, and conscientious, methodical, dedicated work, and at the same time build a new structure and culture conducive to being a creative, agile disruptor in the deep technologies that will allow Japan to compete in the digital economy. This is where, as of 2019, many Japanese companies are struggling to make progress.

This is a Herculean task that will take more time to accomplish, and not all will succeed. Some initiatives will stall, others may backfire, and perhaps in the end lifetime employment will not be saved. But as more and more companies begin to experiment with these new designs, we learn more about the choices and tradeoffs necessary to uphold the balance between the need to succeed and the obligation to care about all parts of society.

The aggregate niche strategy may not afford competitive advantage forever, but it is critically important at this moment of transition for Japanese industry. It allows companies to win through the upgrading of *monozukuri* and to stretch and leverage these manufacturing skills into launching pads for a new role in digital manufacturing and advanced, integrated system solutions. Clearly FANUC, Toyota, and SoftBank and other, lesser known but equally important, Japanese companies will emerge as big players in the digital economy. And as they structure new ways of employment to allow people to start new businesses under a large firm's umbrella, a new design for a less disruptive, more embedded system of innovation may also be emerging.

Japan's reinvention is real. Its slow pace may have put some observers to sleep, but if we compare Japanese business today to what it was in the late 1990s, the changes are enormous. Women have entered the regular workforce and are promoted, like everyone else, in lockstep—which means that in about ten years they will occupy more than 20% of managerial positions. While hierarchies still matter, meritocracy has entered the equation in important ways, and as employment structures open up, the pace of this change may increase exponentially. Japanese CEOs, except for the founder firms, change out in six-year rotations, which means that the next cohort, entering around now, will be "Abenomics CEOs." They were groomed as senior managers under the new normal of seeking increases in performance, not just sales. And less quietly, an aggressive group of companies—from SoftBank, Uniqlo, Nidec, Recruit, and Rakuten to the seemingly more traditional Mitsubishi Electric, Hitachi, Panasonic, Toyota, Bridgestone, and AGC—are proactively building new business areas that will make them influential players in the future in Japan and in the global economy.

Even as all this change is happening, some things are certain to remain the same. Japan will always be a tight culture—with a widespread consensus on strongly held norms. Some of the content of these behavioral norms of Japanese business is slowly being nudged toward a new normal, as companies modify what it means to be considerate, appropriate, or disruptive at the workplace. And how this new normal is defined is key to the reinvention. We already see more individualized fashion at work, more dual career families, shorter working hours, and even different styles, tones, and procedures in meetings. That said, stability and safety first—*anzen dai-ichi*—are bound to remain a core value. In a country with 1,500 earthquakes per year, there is just no other way. As a result, decision making will probably always remain *slow*—a word that, in Japan, often carries the positive connotation of careful and thorough. Due process is important, and uncertainty creates anxiety. By necessity, slow means that Japanese companies may miss out on windows of opportunity, but many in Japan prefer losing out over losing big. The slow approach reflects a societal preference, and in many ways, it is also proving economical in terms of preserving the country's social fabric, education, infrastructure, and global status in times of crisis. And, slow does not mean stagnant. As the business reinvention is progressing, Japan is emerging as a model for other countries in the region. As Asia's most affluent nation, for many young Asians, Japan is increasingly the place to look up to.

Japan's reinvention is happening at an important moment in time for U.S. businesses. Reflecting the lingering pains from the 2008 global financial crisis, calls are becoming louder for increased corporate social responsibility. In August 2019, the U.S. Business Roundtable—an association of the country's leading CEOs—issued a position paper stating that the "new purpose of the corporation" should be more than just managing toward a higher stock price.[8] Since these same people earn their salaries based on their company's stock price, many doubted how sincere they really were. Nevertheless, this movement gives additional relevance to Japan's management practices and the Japanese understanding of the role, rights, and responsibilities of the company. Perhaps Japan's biggest lesson from the bubble economy—when the Nikkei Index hit 39,000 in December 1989, only to plunge to 8,000 in 2003—was that neither the high nor the low value contained any information regarding the quality of Japanese companies or their managers. The stock price is important for Japanese companies, of course—for corporate finance, investor relations, and a host of other management matters—but many in Japan remain cautious about relying on it for making decisions, setting salaries, or evaluating performance. Japan's experience reminds us that companies can pursue profit while caring for people.

Still, all kinds of things could derail Japan from the trajectory I have described in this book. It is unclear how the trade war between the United States and China will affect Asia in general, and Japan in particular. There is always the possibility of a large earthquake that knocks Japan off course. As things change, companies may make the wrong choices and give up their strengths while retaining their weaknesses. Some may end up adopting the worst global practices, and others may succumb to the powers of the vultures or the lure of money. For the economy overall, the simmering challenges of debt, demographics, and regional stability may affect this trajectory as well. Regardless of these various scenarios, following Japan's evolution will be informative for our own future. Given its economic and global impact, its sophistication in societal structures and behaviors, and its stability as an anchor in Asia, Japan will surely continue to be a pivotal player in the global economy.

NOTES

PREFACE

1. "Washington: Mondale's Tough Line," *New York Times*, October 13, 1982.

2. Calculated from World Bank, *GDP (current US$)—Japan*, https://data.worldbank.org/indicator/NY.GDP.MKTP.CD?locations=JP.

3. BBC, "China Overtakes Japan as World's Second-biggest Economy," February 14, 2011, https://www.bbc.com/news/business-12427321.

4. The U.S. rate was 5.35 homicides per 100,000 inhabitants. See Wikipedia, "List of Countries by Intentional Homicide Rate," https://en.wikipedia.org/wiki/List_of_countries_by_intentional_homicide_rate. For homeless people in Japan, official estimates were at 25,000 at the peak in 2003, down to 6,000 people in 2017. See Nippon.com, "Zenkoku no hōmuresu wa 5534 jin: Kōsei rōdōshō no 2017 chōsa" [5,534 Homeless people nationwide: 2017 Survey by the Ministry of Health, Labor and Welfare], https://www.nippon.com/ja/features/h00221.

5. Cited in Pilling (2014).

CHAPTER 1

1. Ando (2018); "Japan Inc. sitting on ¥506.4 trillion mountain of cash," *Japan Times*, September 3, 2019.

2. Morgan Stanley Research (2018).

3. "'Fukugyō kaikin' de kowareru Nihon no 'kaisha': Shain no 'honrai gyōmu' no meikakuka ga fukaketsu ni" [The introduction of "dual jobs" means the end of the Japanese "kaisha": The necessity to lay out future expectations for employees], *Nikkei Business*, April 27, 2018.

4. Kent Calder (2017) labeled this the "liberalize slowly, compensate generously" approach; see also Schaede and Grimes (2003) on Japan's "managed globalization."

5. Calculated from NEDO (2018); see Chapter 4 for more details on these data, and Chapter 5 on Japan's global production networks and economic impact.

6. Schaede (2008).

7. O'Reilly and Tushman (2016).

8. Throughout, all dollar amounts refer to U.S. dollars. The exchange rate used for approximate conversions is US$1 = ¥100, and the end-of-calendar-year exchange rate for precise conversions and exhibits.

9. Calculated from Japanese Cabinet Office data, updated October–December 2018, https://www.esri.cao.go.jp/en/sna/data/sokuhou/files/2018/qe184_2/gdemenuea.html. Koo (2011) calculates that the loss of national wealth in stocks and real estate alone equaled three years of 1989 GDP, compared to the U.S. having lost national wealth equivalent to one year of 1929 GDP during the Great Depression.

10. Schaede (2008).

11. See *Japan Revitalization Strategy*, June 14, 2013, https://www.kantei.go.jp/jp/singi/keizaisaisei/pdf/en_saikou_jpn_hon.pdf, a government document revised almost annually under the Abe administration.

12. Gelfand et al. (2011); Gelfand (2018). Gelfand (2018) refers to tight cultures as nations of "rule makers" as opposed to "rule breakers."

13. Chatman and O'Reilly (2016).

14. Capgemini (2018). For these comparisons, HNWI were defined as people with investable assets exceeding $10 million, not counting their primary residence, collectibles, consumables, and consumer durables. Note that exchange rate fluctuations influence these data in year-on-year comparisons.

15. Lazonick (2014). This work is seen as the foundation for the 2018 Accountable Capitalism Act, proposed by Senator Elizabeth Warren; see Matthew Yglesias, "Elizabeth Warren Has a Plan to Save Capitalism," *Vox*, August 15, 2018, https://www.vox.com/2018/8/15/17683022/elizabeth-warren-accountable-capitalism-corporations. See Lazonick and Shin (2019), and Pilling (2018) for the larger picture on the "growth delusion."

16. Kitao and Yamada (2019).

17. Koo (2011).

18. See, e.g., Paul Krugman, "Apologizing to Japan," *New York Times*, October 30, 2014.

19. See Pilling (2018) on the focus on GDP and economic growth, and the problems that has caused.

20. Lazonick (2009a; 2009b).

21. Davis (2009); Lemann (2019).

22. Abegglen and Stalk (1985); Dore (1987); Aoki and Dore (1994).

CHAPTER 2

1. Anzen Dai-ichi Kyōkai (the Safety First Association) was founded in 1917, and the green cross flag was designed for Japan's first "Safety Week," in 1919. See Ryoichi Horiguchi, *History of the Green Cross*, https://sites.google.com/site/ryoichihoriguchi/home/greencrosslogos, accessed February 2019.

2. Seen in Kyōbashi, Tokyo, September 2017. The sign was in both English and Japanese (*Anzen wa chūshin to naru kachi de aru*).

3. This was in front of the Oazo Building, Tokyo Station.

4. See Ahmadjian and Schaede (2015) for an overview of the literature; and also Dore (1973, 1983, 1987); Sako (1992); Ouchi (1981); Clark (1979); Ballon (1970); Abegglen (1984); and Abegglen and Stalk (1985).

5. E.g., Benedict (1946).

6. North (1990) defines institutions as "humanly devised constraints that structure political, economic and social interactions." For extensions in adjacent disciplines, see Powell and DiMaggio (1991); Kahneman (2001); Pinker (2002); Thaler and Sunstein (2008); and Levitsky and Ziblatt (2018). The fields of cognitive, social, organizational, and cultural psychology have long provided depth and nuance to our understanding of how cultures shape attitudes and behavior.

7. E.g., Loewenstein and Chater (2017).

8. Kahneman (2001); Thaler and Sunstein (2008).

9. E.g., Pelto (1968); Hofstede (2001); Meyer (2014).

10. Hofstede (1983, 2001).

11. Gelfand et al. (2011); Gelfand (2018).

12. Chatman and O'Reilly (2016).

13. Gelfand et al. (2011).

14. Henrich (2015); Wilson and Wilson (2009).

15. Gelfand (2018, 39).

16. These three behavioral norms map with moral and business ethics theories of consequentialism, deontology, and virtue; see, e.g., MacIntosh (2017); Whetstone (2001); and *The Stanford Encyclopedia of Philosophy*, s.v. "consequentialism," "deontological ethics," and "virtue," https://plato.stanford.edu. In the tight-loose setting, Uz (2015) lays out three levels of behavior: *psychology* (e.g., feeling uncomfortable, uneasy, frightened, etc., in an interpersonal situation); subjective states and *attitudes* (e.g., how severely an appearance is judged as inappropriate); and *behavioral inhibitions* (e.g., what kind of choices and decisions one dares to make).

17. O'Reilly and Chatman (1996).

18. Kato et al. (2020).

19. Kato et al. (2010).

20. O'Reilly (1989); O'Reilly and Chatman (1996); O'Reilly and Tushman (2016).

21. Zielenziger (2006); Kitanaka (2012); Tam and Taki (2007); Yoneyama and Naito (2003).

CHAPTER 3

1. *Shūkatsu* is an abbreviation of *shūshoku katsudō* (job search activities). Also see Yoshiko Uehara, "Shūkatsu: How Japanese Students Hunt for Jobs," nippon.com, March 30, 2016; "Tight Labor Market in Japan Forces Companies to Revamp Recruitment," *Japan Times*, April 22, 2019; "Keidanren to Scrap Long-held Japan Recruitment Guidelines in 2021," *Japan Times*, October 9, 2018.

2. Abegglen and Stalk (1985); Vogel (1979); Dore (1987); Clark (1979); Ballon and Tomita (1988); Schaede (2008).

3. In the 1970s, the average debt-equity ratio exceeded 6. See also Patrick and Rosovsky (1976); Johnson (1982); Yamamura and Yasuba (1987); Calder (1988); Hoshi-Kashyap (2001); Schaede (2008); and Murphy (2014).

4. Schaede (2000b; 2008).

5. Womack et al. (1990) coined the term *lean production*. See also Monden (1983); Liker (2004); Cole (1994, 1998); Smitka (1991); Ahmadjian and Lincoln (2001); Lincoln et al. (1996); and Lincoln and Gerlach (2004).

6. Pascale and Rohlen (1983).

7. Aoki (1988).

8. Drucker (1981); Dore (2000).

9. The list of industries is only a snapshot, based on company website commentary on remarkable innovations. See Hitachi, "History (1910–1960)," http://www.hitachi.com/corporate/about/history/1910.html, and Toshiba, "Chronology of History," https://www.toshiba.co.jp/worldwide/about/history_chronology.html.

10. E.g., Rohlen (1979); Clark (1979); Abegglen and Stalk (1985; Lincoln and Kalleberg (1990).

11. See Ballon and Tomita (1988) for double-counting shipments to inflate sales; and Schaede (2000a) on cartels.

12. Waldenberger (2016).

13. There was a lot of friction in this system, with domestic issues ranging from alcoholism, domestic violence, seclusion-seeking (*hikikomori*), extramarital affairs and cheating, to depression; see, e.g., Kitanaka (2012); Borovoy (2005, 2008).

14. Ministry of Internal Affairs and Communications (2019).

15. Schaede (2008).

16. Lemann (2019).

17. Schaede (2008), ch. 9.

18. E.g., McMillan (1990); Ahmadjian and Lincoln (2001); Lincoln and Gerlach (2004).

19. Kent Calder (2017); Schaede and Grimes (2003); Schaede (2008).

20. Patrick and Rohlen (1987).

21. Vogel (1979); Hamada et al. (2011); Hoshi and Kashyap (2001).

22. New financial instruments were introduced with deregulated rates. The resulting competition for new clients caused distortions between low borrowing and high savings rates and encouraged Ponzi schemes. The following summary of the bubble economy events is based on Schaede (1990, 2008); Hoshi and Kashyap (2001).

23. "Back from the Grave: It Has Taken 16 Years for Commercial-property Inflation in Japan to Turn Positive," *Economist*, October 11, 2007; "Japan's Land Boom Spilling across the Sea," *Chicago Tribune*, November 19, 1989.

24. For details, see Schaede (2008).

25. Koo (2011).

26. Nithin Coca, "She bilked Japan's banks in the run-up to the lost decade," OZY, August 27, 2019,

https://www.ozy.com/flashback/she-bilked-japans-banks-in-the-run-up-to-the-lost-decade/95409.

27. I thank Grayson Sakos for this suggestion.

28. Schaede (2008).

29. Schaede (2008; 2013b).

30. Author's calculations based on data from the Nikkei Economic Electronic Databank System (NEEDS).

31. Schaede (2000b); Esty and Kanno 2016; "Corporate Bankruptcies in Japan at 10-Year Low," nippon.com, January 25, 2019, https://www.nippon.com/en/japan-data/h00374/corporate-bankruptcies-in-japan-at-10-year-low.html.

32. Gill (2001); Kitanaka (2012); Borovoy (2005); Schaede (2013b).

CHAPTER 4

1. In 2016, Japan contributed 10% to global manufacturing output, compared to China (20%), the U.S. (18%), Germany (7%), and South Korea (4%). See West and Lansang (2018).

2. Figures from *Nikkei Shinbun*; see "Buhin kyōkyū teishi, seisan ni dageki" [Part supplies interrupted: A big blow to production], *Nikkei Shinbun*, March 19, 2011; "Buhin fusoku: sekai in eikyō" [A lack of part supplies: Impact on global economy], *Nikkei Shinbun*, April 6, 2011.

3. Dr. Seiuemon Inaba, founder of FANUC, interview with the author, May 2015.

4. Kurishita (2012); "A Japanese Plant Struggles to Produce a Critical Auto Part," *New York Times*, April 27, 2011.

5. See more on this dispute in Chapter 5. After extensive and complicated negotiations, the restrictions on photoresists were removed on December 20, 2019. "As Japan and South Korea Clash at WTO over Trade, Rest of World Reluctant to Get Involved," Reuters, July 25, 2019; "Seoul Eyes Crash Program to Shield Chip Industry from Japan Ban: Subsidies and Deregulation Planned, but Tech Prowess Hard to Match," *Nikkei Asian Weekly*, July 18, 2019.

6. Porter (1985).

7. See Schaede (2008) for context and further citations.

8. Komori (2015).

9. O'Reilly and Tushman (2016).

10. Bradley et al. (2006); Kushida (2011).

11. Xing and Detert (2010).

12. "Anatomy of Huawei's Latest Model," *Nikkei Asian Review*, June 26, 2019.

13. Ministry of Economics, Trade and Industry (2004).

14. Calculations based on data from NEDO (2018).

15. Nikkan Kōgyō Shinbun-sha (2014).

16. Yamaguchi (2009); JSR Corporation, "Business Results and Financial Highlights," http://www.jsr.co.jp/jsr_e/ir/financial_highlights.shtml.

17. Japan Products, "Top 10 Japan's Chemical Companies List in 2017," http://japan-product.com/top10-japan-chemical-companies-2017.

18. "Mitsubishi's Long-Lived Success Points to Weakness in Japan's Economy," *Wall Street Journal*, April 15, 2016.

19. Schaede (2008).

20. Many of the smaller banks fell behind and are troubled to this day. The larger banks have merged into large financial holding companies, led by MUFG, SMBC, and Mizuho, and by 2018, had once again risen into the ranks of the global top ten financial institutions by assets. Their declining role as main banks has been confirmed in several studies, e.g., Hoshi et al. (2018).

21. "Japanese Companies Act Changes to Encourage Investment," *Daily Journal*, October 22, 2014. The law was revised in 2015 to include new provisions regarding governance, takeovers, and financial levers for mergers and acquisitions, such as stock conversions.

22. Vogel (2006); Schaede (2008).

23. Kahneman (2001); Thaler and Sunstein (2008).

24. Government of Japan (2019).

25. Goshal and Bartlett (1988).

26. Yoshino and Endo (2005).

27. Yoshino and Endo (2005).

28. Yoshino and Endo (2005).

29. E.g., Hirakawa (2016); Sato (2017); Iwase (2015).

30. "Panasonic to Have No Board Members from Founding Family," *Nippon News*, March 1, 2019, https://www.nippon.com/en/news/yjj2019030100842/panasonic-to-have-no-board-member-from-founding-family.html; "Panasonic to End LCD Panel Production amid Tough Competition," *Japan Times*, November 21, 2019; "Panasonic Exits Chipmaking with Sale to Taiwan Player," *Nikkei Asian Review*, November 28, 2019.

31. The following discussion draws on Sony's corporate website, "Corporate Info," https://www.sony.net/SonyInfo/CorporateInfo/business, and "Investor Relations," https://www.sony.net/SonyInfo/IR.

32. Goshal and Bartlett (1988).

33. Jake Adelstein and Nathalie-Kyoko Stucky, "How Sony Is Turning into a Ghost in Japan and around the World," Kotaku, November 14, 2012.

34. Mana Nakazora, "Sony at Sea: Gap with Matsushita Electric Refuses to Close," JP Morgan Japan Credit Today, October 27, 2005.

35. E.g., Sato (2017).

36. Douglas A. McIntyre, "Howard Stringer, Who Ruined Sony, Retires," 24/7 Wall St., March 11, 2013, https://247wallst.com/investing/2013/03/11/howard-stringer-who-ruined-sony-retires.

CHAPTER 5

Grayson Sakos coauthored this chapter, and Benjamin Irvine made important contributions.

1. "What Will Japan Buy Next," *Newsweek*, November 10, 1991.

2. "Japan's Big 3 Automakers Built More Cars in U.S. Than Detroit 3 Last Year," *Co-
lumbus Business First*, June 1, 2016.

3. "Japanese Companies Have Created 840,000 American Jobs," *Quartz*, March 29,
2017, https://qz.com/942619/japanese-companies-have-created-80000-american-jobs.

4. U.S. Bureau of Economic Analysis, "2018 Trade Gap is $621.0 Billion," https://
www.bea.gov/news/blog/2019-03-06/2018-trade-gap-6210-billion. The following discussion focuses on the trade deficit in goods only, and ignores services.

5. UN Comtrade Database, 2019, https://comtrade.un.org/data.

6. The 1994 North America Free Trade Agreement (NAFTA) extended the definition of "local content" to include Canada and Mexico.

7. Schaede (2019); calculations based on data from Japan External Trade Organization (JETRO), Japanese Trade and Investment Statistics, https://www.jetro.go.jp/en/
reports/statistics.html.

8. "Sony Launches AI Joint Venture with US, Japanese Partners," *Nikkei Asian Review*, November 22, 2017; "Jointly Developed U.S.-Japan Interceptor Knocks Down
Medium-Range Missile in Test," *Japan Times*, October 27, 2018.

9. Office of the United States Trade Representative, "United States Wins WTO Semiconductor Case," https://ustr.gov/archive/Document_Library/Press_Releases/2005/
June/United_States_Wins_WTO_Semiconductor_Case.html.

10. Author interviews with industry observers, Tokyo, 1995.

11. Haggard et al. (1997).

12. "Inside the Lose-Lose Trade Fight between Japan and South Korea," *Nikkei Asian
Review*, July 31, 2019; "Korea's Dispute with Japan Spills into National Security," *The
Diplomat*, August 27, 2019; "Japan Partially Reverses Curbs on Tech Materials Exports
to South Korea," *Nikkei Asian Review*, December 20, 2019; "Moon and Abe Try to Break
Ice but Relations Still Frozen," *Nikkei Asian Review*, December 25, 2019.

13. Calculated from Japan Customs, Trade Statistics of Japan, http://www.customs.
go.jp/toukei/suii/html/time_e.htm.

14. UN Comtrade Database, 2019, https://comtrade.un.org/data.

15. "How Samsung Dominates South Korea's Economy," *CNN Business*, February
17, 2017.

16. "Inside the Lose-Lose Trade Fight between Japan and South Korea," *Nikkei Asian
Review*, July 31, 2019.

17. "South Korea's Manufacturing Hub Braces for Japan Export Controls," *Nikkei
Asian Weekly*, August 27, 2019.

18. In 2018, almost 20% of China's exports were shipped to the U.S., followed
by 6% to Japan. Statistics treat Hong Kong separately, but it is China's largest port

for Asian trade, and should be considered jointly; OEC (Observatory of Economic Complexity), China, https://atlas.media.mit.edu/en/profile/country/chn; Naughton (2018).

19. Ministry of Foreign Affairs of Japan (2017).

20. Naughton (2018).

21. McBride and Chatzky (2019).

22. "Japan Inc. to Speed Up China Exit in Response to More Tariffs," *Nikkei Asian Weekly*, August 5, 2019; "Japan's Manufacturers Grow Cautious about Production in China," *Nikkei Asian Weekly,* May 20, 2019.

23. "Xi Touts 'New Era' of China-Japan Ties in Shadow of Trump," *Nikkei Asian Weekly*, December 23, 2019.

24. Calculated from World Bank data, "Population, Total," https://data.worldbank.org/indicator/SP.POP.TOTL. PPP stands for "purchasing power parity."

25. ASEAN (2017), p. 41.

26. "Japan's MUFG Bank to Take Over Indonesian Peer: Bank Danamon to Merge with a Local Group Lender as First Step," *Nikkei Asian Review*, January 23, 2019.

27. "MUFG Leads Japan Megabanks' Charge into SE Asia: Focus Shifts to Non-Japanese Businesses, Consumer," *Nikkei Asian Review*, July 7, 2017.

28. See Thomson Reuters, *Global Project Finance Review: Managing Underwriters*, 2018, http://www.pfie.com/Journals/2018/04/25/e/v/u/PFI-Financial-League-Tables-Q1-2018.pdf.

29. Ministry of Foreign Affairs of Japan, information by country, such as https://www.mofa.go.jp/region/asia-paci/vietnam/index.html; ASEAN (2017); and JETRO, Japanese Trade and Investment Statistics, https://www.jetro.go.jp/en/reports/statistics.html.

30. "Japanese Investment in Myanmar Soars to All Time High," *Japan Times*, May 28, 2018; "Japan Insurers Enter Myanmar in Joint-Venture Frenzy," *Nikkei Asian Review*, April 26, 2019.

31. Fallows and Fallows (2018).

32. I am grateful to Michael J. Alfant, Chairman and CEO of Fusion Systems Co., for this observation.

33. "Anime a \$21bn Market—in China," *Nikkei Asian Review*, May 2, 2017.

34. Japan Student Services Organization (JASSO), International Students in Japan 2018, https://www.jasso.go.jp/en/about/statistics/intl_student/data2018.html.

35. Genron NPO, *The 7th Japan–South Korea Joint Public Opinion Poll (2019)*, http://www.genron-npo.net/en/7th-Japan-South%20KoreaJointOpinionPoll.pdf.

36. Japan National Tourism Organization, Tourism Statistics by Country of Origin, 2018, https://www.jnto.go.jp/jpn/statistics/visitor_trends/index.html.

37. Eleanor Warnock, "Towards a Beautiful Country: Japan's Cosmetics Exports," *Tokyo Review*, January 9, 2019; author's conversation with Ashley Dutta at the National Bureau for Asian Research.

38. Japan Info, "Japanese Dramas vs Korean Dramas," https://jpninfo.com/13167.

39. Calculated from data from Biz/Zine, "The current situation of M & A by Japanese companies" [in Japanese], August 30, 2018, https://bizzine.jp/article/detail/2963; and MARR Online, "M & A Review in 2018," https://www.marr.jp/marr/category/MAkaiko/entry/13030.

40. "Japan Inc Signed Record 777 Overseas M&A Deals in 2018," *Nikkei Asian Review*, February 28, 2019.

41. "Japan Firms Have $890 Billion in Cash. Here's Where They Might Spend It: Japan Inc. Dominates M&A in Asia," Bloomberg, January 6, 2019.

42. "Boom in Japanese M&A Deals: Abenomics Is Incentivizing Japanese Companies to Look for Opportunities Abroad," *Global Finance*, October 18, 2018; "Asahi to Buy AB InBev's Australian Unit in $11.3bn Deal," *Nikkei Asian Review*, July 19, 2019.

43. "Why Japan Is Gambling on M&A Growth," *Financial Times*, April 29, 2018.

44. See "Jidō unten ya IOT, shin-gijutsu ga hiraku M&A dai-ekkyō jidai" [The great new era of M&A: Unsealing new technologies such as in autonomous cars and IoT], *Nikkei Business*, January 18, 2019.

45. "Why Japan Is Gambling on M&A Growth," *Financial Times*, April 29, 2018.

46. "TomTom Sells Telematics Unit to Bridgestone for $1 Billion," Bloomberg, January 21, 2019; Jidō unten ya IOT, shin-gijutsu ga hiraku M&A dai-ekkyō jidai" [The great new era of M&A: Unsealing new technologies such as in autonomous cars and IoT], *Nikkei Business*, January 18, 2019.

CHAPTER 6

1. "Secretive Robot Maker FANUC Targeted by Activist Investor Loeb," *Japan Times*, February 19, 2015; see also Esty and Kanno (2016); "Drivers of Change: FANUC," *Financial Times*, March 17, 2016.

2. "George Clooney Rebuts Loeb's Critique of Sony," *New York Times*, August 2, 2013.

3. "Japan Toys with Shareholder Capitalism Just as the West Balks," *Economist*, May 28, 2019; Hill (2017); Lemann (2019); Elizabeth Warren, "Accountable Capitalism Act," https://www.warren.senate.gov/newsroom/press-releases/warren-introduces-accountable-capitalism-act.

4. See the Preamble to the 2014 *Ito Review of Competitiveness and Incentives for Sustainable Growth: Building Favorable Relationships between Companies and Investors* by Ito (2014); Aronson (2015).

5. Williamson (1993).

6. Lazonick and O'Sullivan (2000); Lazonick (2009a; 2009b); Lazonick and Shin (2019); O'Reilly and Main (2010); Kreps (2018).

7. For a good summary of the scandal, see Wikipedia, "Olympus Scandal," https://en.wikipedia.org/wiki/Olympus_scandal.

8. "String of Scandals Puts Japanese Investors on Edge," *Financial Times*, May 29, 2016.

9. Aida and Sakakibara (2017); author interviews with Japanese fund managers, Tokyo, 2019.

10. "Pension 'Whale' Blows Past Japanese Equity Investment Target: GPIF to Focus Next on Supporting Sustainable Companies," *Nikkei Asian Review*, July 7, 2018; "The Giant of Tokyo's Stock Market Reveals Its Investment Secrets," Bloomberg, August 22, 2016.

11. "BOJ Is Top-10 Shareholder in 40% of Japan's Listed Companies," *Nikkei Asian Review*, June 27, 2018.

12. Ito (2014); Milhaupt (2018).

13. See the *JPX-Nikkei 400: Factsheet*, https://www.jpx.co.jp/english/markets/indices/jpx-nikkei400/tvdivq00000031dd-att/e_fac_1_jpx400.pdf.

14. Author interviews with JPX400 committee members, Tokyo, 2014.

15. Ito (2014); Ministry of Economy, Trade and Industry (2017c).

16. Chattopadhyay et al. (2017).

17. JPX/TSE (2018); Goto (2014); Killeen and Prentice (2015).

18. E.g., Vogel (2019); Milhaupt (2018); Benes (2019); Hokugo and Ogawa (2017); Nakamura (2018).

19. Ministry of Economy, Trade and Industry (2018a; 2018b).

20. Goto et al. (2017).

21. Author interviews with industry executives, Tokyo, 2015–2019. A 2018 revision of the corporate governance code brought an increase in the rights and assignments of the board of directors, emphasis on the quality rather than the quantity of outsiders, truly independent directors, more board diversity, and more transparency. See Ministry of Economy, Trade and Industry (2018a; 2018b). For background, see also Eguchi and Shishido (2015); Waldenberger (2017); Nakamura (2018).

22. Saito (2015); Yeh (2014).

23. Milhaupt (2018); Johnson (1982).

24. "A Revolution in the Making: Corporate Governance in Japan," *Economist*, May 3, 2014.

25. Financial Services Agency (2017); Hokugo and Ogawa (2017).

26. Goto (2018); Hill (2017).

27. Goto (2018) cites METI Minister Amari to define the goal of the code as creating a "desirable market economy system" and building safeguards against "U.S.-style governance" through restrictions on stock-based compensation and share repurchases.

28. For the FSA list, see *List of Institutional Investors Signing Up to "Principles for Responsible Institutional Investors,"* https://www.fsa.go.jp/en/refer/councils/stewardship/20181214/en_list_02.pdf.

29. "The Rise and Fall of Carlos Ghosn," *New York Times*, December 30, 2018; "The Hardest Fall," *Business Week*, December 16, 2019.

30. "Chief of Japan's State-backed JIC Resigns amid Pay Dispute," Reuters, December 10, 2018; "All Top JIC Execs from Private Sector Quit in Fight with METI," *Asahi Shimbun*, December 10, 2018.

31. O'Reilly and Main (2010); Lazonick and Shin (2019).

32. Waldenberger (2013); Eguchi and Waldenberger (2017).

33. Waldenberger (2013).

34. "Kōgaku yakuhin hōshū ranking" [Highest executive pay ranking], *News-Post Sebun*, December 3, 2018, https://www.news-postseven.com/archives/20181203_815650.html; calculated from Social Security Administration, Wage Statistics for 2017, https://www.ssa.gov/cgi-bin/netcomp.cgi?year=2017.

35. Waldenberger (2013).

36. "The New Pay Gap: What Firms Report Paying CEOs versus What They Take Home," *Wall Street Journal*, August 25, 2019.

37. Equilar, "New York Times 200 Highest-Paid CEOs," https://www.equilar.com/reports/table-equilar-200-new-york-times-highest-paid-ceos-2019.html.

38. Calculated from "Kōgaku yakuhin hōshū ranking" [Highest executive pay ranking], *News-Post Sebun*, December 3, 2018, https://www.news-postseven.com/archives/20181203_815650.html.

39. Ibid.

40. Iwai and Ueki (2017).

41. Waldenberger (2013); author interviews with several CEOs, Tokyo, 2018.

42. Sakawa et al. (2012).

CHAPTER 7

1. In 2019, Hitachi had $85 billion in revenues, half of which was generated abroad. Its largest businesses were IT Systems (20% of revenues), Social Infrastructure (23%), Electronic Systems (11%), Construction Machinery (9%), High Functional Components (16%), and Automotive Systems (10%). Even with the ongoing exits, it still counted 803 subsidiaries and 418 equity-method associates and joint ventures. See Hitachi Ltd., Consolidated Financial Results for Fiscal 2018, https://www.hitachi.com/IR-e/library/fr/backnumber/2018.html.

2. "*Scoop*: Hitachi, Kyū-Hitachi Medico baikyaku kentō, sentaku to shūchū kasoku e" [Scoop: Hitachi is looking into selling the medical company; choose-and-focus is speeding up], *Nikkei Business*, August 9, 2019. "Japan Posts Record Number of M&A Deals as Restructuring Booms," *Financial Times*, December 22, 2019; "Hitachi to Sell Chemical and Medical Equipment Units for $6bn," *Nikkei Asian Review*, December 18, 2019; "Hitachi Pursues 10% Profit Margin by Trimming Fat," *Nikkei Asian Review*, December 19, 2019.

3. In the Kokusai Electric deal, KKR kept the chip-making equipment unit and sold a 40 percent stake in the video solutions business back to Hitachi and Japan Industrial Partners, Inc (JIP). See "KKR to Buy Hitachi Unit Valued at $2.3 Billion," Reuters, April 26, 2017.

4. "Hitachi Considers Selling Hitachi Chemical," *Japan Times*, April 25, 2019.

5. Swenson and Rubin (2017). On short-termism and value destruction, see Lazonick (2009a; 2009b; 2014); Lazonick and O'Sullivan (2000); Appelbaum and Batt (2014).

6. Author interviews with Japanese CEOs and foreign fund investors, Tokyo, 2018–2019.

7. Appelbaum and Batt (2014).

8. Advantage Partners, "Private Equity in Japan," 2019, https://www.advantagepart-ners.com/en/descripion/description2.

9. Ministry of Economy, Trade and Industry (2017a).

10. MARR (2019); Ng (2018).

11. Burroughs and Helyar (1989).

12. Hammoud et al. (2017); Ministry of Economy, Trade and Industry (2017a).

13. Author interviews with industry executives, Tokyo, February 2019. Also see MARR Online, "M&A trends" [in Japanese], https://www.marr.jp/genre/graphdemiru; and MARR Online, "M&A review in 2018" [in Japanese], https://www.marr.jp/genre/market/MAkaiko/entry/13030.

14. "Why Japan Is Entering a Golden Era for PE," PEI Media, April 9, 2018; "Why Private Equity Giant KKR Finds Japan More Attractive Than China," *DealStreet Asia*, April 18, 2019.

15. Schaede (2008), ch. 6.

16. Sekine (2018).

17. Sekine (2018); "Japanese Wavers on Foreign Private Equity 'Vultures,'" *Financial Times*, October 21, 2018.

18. "Japan-Based Investors in Alternative Assets," 2016, https://docs.preqin.com/reports/Preqin-Japan-Based-Investors-November-2016.pdf; Ministry of Economy, Trade and Industry (2017a).

19. "Japan Inc.'s Vast Pool of Cash Is Growing Stagnant," *Nikkei Asian Review*, July 10, 2017; "Cash-hoarding Japanese Firms Please Investors as Share Buybacks Hit Record High," Reuters, February 17, 2019.

20. Jonathan Rogers, "Japan Post Bank to Establish Hedge Fund in Hunt for Yield," *Global Finance*, June 1, 2018. The JIC was engulfed in a huge scandal in late 2018 regarding its mission, organizational structure, and executive pay. The private sector leadership team was forced to resign over allegations of excessive pay, which was the façade reason for the deeper issues of mutual distrust regarding government control over the fund's investments. See, e.g., "CEO and 8 Other Execs of Japan's Innovation Fund Resign," *Nikkei Asian Review*, December 10, 2018.

21. Tokyo Metropolitan Government (2017); Capgemini (2018).

22. "Profits and Pitfalls—Taking Over a Japanese Company," *Nikkei Asian Weekly*, June 11, 2018; "Global Firms Seek a Piece of Japan Carve-out Action," *PEI Media*, November 5, 2018; "KKR Founders Set Sights on Japan Conglomerates," *Financial Times*, April 14, 2019.

23. Tokyo Metropolitan Government (2017). Many of the Japanese funds had less than $300 million in assets under management and focused on the small and middle markets. For a detailed list of PE funds in Japan as of 2019, see the website Investment in Japan, https://investmentinjapan.com/iij/wp-content/uploads/2019/10/E1909_JP-PE-PD_2Map.pdf.

24. Author interviews with PE fund investors and managers, Tokyo, 2019.

25. Author interviews with PE fund managers, Tokyo, 2019.

26. Author interviews with PE fund managers, Tokyo, 2019; "Profits and Pitfalls—Taking Over a Japanese Company," *Nikkei Asian Weekly*, June 11, 2018.

27. Author interviews with PE fund managers, Tokyo, 2019; Longreach Group, "Japan Carve-outs: Chips off the Block," https://www.longreachgroup.com/en/newsarticles.php#acticle1, June 14, 2017.

28. "Western Digital's Battle for Toshiba: A Tale of Threats and Culture Clashes," *Japan Times*, October 2, 2017; Mike Wheatley, "Toshiba and Western Digital Battle over Flash Memory Sale," SiliconANGLE, December 13, 2017, siliconangle.com.

29. Author interviews with PE fund managers, Tokyo, 2019.

30. Sekine (2018).

31. Author interviews with PE fund managers and Japanese corporate executives, Tokyo, 2019.

32. "Japanese Wavers on Foreign Private Equity 'Vultures,'" *Financial Times*, October 21, 2018.

33. Takafumi Horie was a startup founder in the IT sector who consistently violated all Japanese business norms, being noisy, direct, and altogether inappropriate. His attempt to launch a hostile takeover of a TV station was just too much for the establishment. See, e.g., "Ex-Livedoor Chief Gets 2.5-Year Jail Term," *Financial Times*, March 16, 2007. Also see "Yoshiaki Murakami, Once the Scourge of Japan's Boardrooms, Turns Peacemaker with Big Idemitsu-Showa Shell Sekiyu Win," *Japan Times*, July 7, 2018.

34. "Japanese Companies Cannot Ignore Advance of Activist Shareholders," *Nikkei Asian Weekly*, April 18, 2018; "Activist Funds Take Aim at Asia Inc's Complacent Boardrooms," *Nikkei Asian Weekly*, April 3, 2019; "Foreign Activist Funds Set Their Sights on Japan's Smaller Companies," *Nikkei Asian Weekly*, February 7, 2019.

35. "Yoshiaki Murakami, Once The Scourge of Japan's Boardrooms, Turns Peacemaker with Big Idemitsu-Showa Shell Sekiyu Win," *Japan Times*, July 7, 2018; "A Successful Strategy for Activist Investors in Japan: Ask, Don't Tell," *Wall Street Journal*, April 17, 2019.

36. Gow et al. (2017).

37. Ibid.; Nakagami (2016); Author interviews with senior managers at Misaki Capital, 2018 and 2019.

38. Yasunori Nakagami, in interview with author, Tokyo, February 2019.

39. "Jidō unten ya IOT, shin-gijutsu ga hiraku M&A dai-ekkyō jidai" [The great new era of M&A: Unsealing new technologies such as in autonomous cars and IoT], *Nikkei Business*, January 18, 2019; Also see "The current situation of M&A in Japanese companies" [in Japanese], Biz/Zine, August 30, 2018, https://bizzine.jp/article/detail/2963.

40. Author interview with M&A specialist, Tokyo, February 19, 2019.

41. Author interviews with Japanese bank executives, Tokyo, September 2018.

42. "Chinese Group to Get Control of Japan Display after $2.1 Billion Bailout," Reuters, April 12, 2019.

CHAPTER 8

1. Larry Golkin, "20 Tanker Tips," https://www.usps.org/ventura/art-03-3-tanker-tips.html.

2. March (1991); O'Reilly and Tushman (2016).

3. The following is an application to the Japanese situation of the model developed in O'Reilly and Tushman (2016); and Tushman and O'Reilly (1997).

4. For details on Japan's postwar shopfloor management, see Cole (1994).

5. See O'Reilly and Tushman (2016) for examples of how U.S. companies are managing the ambidexterity process.

6. Hitachi Ltd., *Mid-term Management Plan 2021*, https://www.hitachi.com/New/cnews/month/2019/05/190510/f_190510pre.pdf.

7. See Chesbrough (2005) for the original concept.

8. Ministry of Economy, Trade and Industry (2017b).

9. Ministry of Economy, Trade and Industry (2019a).

10. Data derived from a database constructed by Sasaki and Schaede (2019) for the years 1996–2012.

11. Author interviews with Japanese managers, Tokyo, 2018, and Silicon Valley, 2017–2019.

12. Ibid.

13. Cool Biz was also credited with saving energy and emissions. For the 2016 summer, it was estimated to have brought about a 1.14 million–ton reduction in CO_2 emissions, equivalent to the CO_2 emissions of about 2.5 million households for one month. See Wikipedia, "Cool Biz Campaign," https://en.wikipedia.org/wiki/Cool_Biz_campaign.

14. Based on author interviews with senior managers and employees, and multiple office visits, Tokyo, March 2018. See also Masumi Koizumi, "Office Makeovers Focus on Comfort and Productivity as Activity-based Working Takes Hold in Japan," *Japan Times*, May 2, 2019.

15. Author interview with innovation lab consultants of a large Japanese company, 2019.

16. Author interviews with managers at several large manufacturing firms, spring 2019.

17. Karube et al. (2009); Kato et al. (2010)

18. O'Reilly and Tushman (2016), 26.

19. Waldenberger (2016); Eguchi and Waldenberger (2017).

20. Data from the AGC company website, and Wikipedia, "AGC Inc.," https://en.wikipedia.org/wiki/AGC_Inc.

21. Noda and Collis (1995).

22. Ibid.; Kato et al. (2020).

23. Kato et al. (2020).

24. Ibid.

25. O'Reilly and Chatman (1996).

26. Ibid.

CHAPTER 9

1. "Shūshin koyō, 'kigyō insentibu hitsuyō,' Jikōkai kaichō" [JAMA Chairman Says Incentives Needed for Employers to Keep Lifetime Employment], *Nikkei Shinbun*, May 13, 2019; "'Shūshi kōyō muzukashii' Toyota shachō hatsugen de Pandora no hako aku ka?" ("Lifetime Employment Is Difficult: Has Toyota's CEO just Opened a Pandora's box?) *Nikkei Business*, May 14, 2019.

2. "In search of Akio Toyoda's successor: Toyoda wants a new culture," *Automotive News*, April 15, 2019.

3. Tenshoku, kahan ga teikō nashi" [Majority not opposed to job-changing], *Nikkei Shinbun*, May 27, 2019.

4. "'Fukugyō kaikin' de kowareru Nihon no 'kaisha': Shain no 'honrai gyōmu' no meikakuka ga fukaketsu ni" [The introduction of "dual jobs" means the end of the Japanese "kaisha": The necessity to lay out future expectations for employees], *Nikkei Business*, April 27, 2018.

5. Pfeffer and Baron (1988); Schaede (2008), ch. 9.

6. Pfeffer and Baron (1988); Lazonick (2009b); Lemann (2019).

7. "Japanese Workforce Projected to Be 20% Smaller by 2040," *Japan Times*, January 15, 2019. The workforce is defined as people aged between 15 and 65 years old.

8. For a detailed analysis, see Matsui et al. (2019).

9. Statistics Bureau of Japan, 2019 Labor Force Survey, www.stat.go.jp/english/data/roudou/lngindex.html.

10. Matsui et al. (2019).

11. Ibid.

12. Author interviews with professional women in Tokyo, 2017–2019.

13. "Womenomics: Cracks Are Beginning to Show in Japan's Glass Ceiling," *Financial Times*, July 17, 2019.

14. Gender Equality Bureau, Cabinet Office, Government of Japan (2018).

15. "Foreign workers in Japan Double in 5 Years, Hitting Record," *Nikkei Asian Review*, January 25, 2019.

16. Okada (2018).

17. Lazear (1999).

18. Roberts (2017).

19. "More Japanese Companies Hire Talent from Overseas Universities," *Nikkei Asian Review*, January 30, 2019.

20. Japan Institute for Labor Policy and Training (2018); Vogel (2018).

21. The "white-collar exemption" exempts professionals in law, consulting, or accounting with an income exceeding roughly $100,000 from the overtime rules.

22. In 2017, workers took an average of 51% of their paid vacation time; the goal is to raise this to 70% by 2020. "First Overtime Caps for Big Japanese Firms and Mandatory Use of Paid Leave to Come into Force April 1," *Japan Times*, March 27, 2019.

23. Ministry of Internal Affairs and Communication (2019).

24. "Mainabi chōsa, tenshokuritsu 5% no jōshō: 20dai no sonzaikan takamaru"

[Mainabi survey: Job-changing rate has topped 5%, the presence of millennials is becoming more important], *Nikkei Shinbun*, April 23, 2019.

25. "Tenshoku, kahan ga teikō nashi" [Majority not opposed to job-changing], *Nikkei Shinbun*, May 27, 2019.

26. "Nyūshago sugu sai-shūkatsu kyūzō: jōken awazu, rizoku ishiki mo usuku" [Rapid increase in second shūkatsu immediately after the job start: Conditions are not met and sense of belonging is weak], *Nikkei Shinbun*, August 7, 2018.

27. Ibid.

28. "Fukugyō kaikin, shūyō kigyō no 5-wari" [50% of largest firmest allow dual jobs], *Nikkei Shinbun*, May 20, 2019.

29. Author interviews with business and government executives, Tokyo, 2018 and 2019.

30. "'Fukugyō kaikin' de kowareru Nihon no 'kaisha'" [The introduction of "dual jobs" means the end of the Japanese "kaisha"].

31. Recruit, Annual Report 2018, https://recruit-holdings.com/who/reports/highlight.html.

32. Buche et al. (2016); Megagon corporate website, https://www.megagon.ai.

33. "Japan's Recruit Employs AI to Stop Workers from Quitting," *Nikkei Asian Review*, September 10, 2018. In 2019, Recruit was involved in a scandal regarding its unauthorized sale of job-seeker information, which the company claimed was an unintended data glitch; see "Japan's Recruit Sold Job-seeker Data to Honda in Privacy Scandal," *Nikkei Asian Review*, August 10, 2019.

34. Rikurūto shusshin no kigyōka/keieisha/yūmeijin no matome [Overview: Famous people, managers and entrepreneurs that have graduated from Recruit], website, https://matome.naver.jp/odai/2134855976914479801.

35. Author interviews with company executives, Tokyo, 2018 and 2019.

36. This section has greatly benefited from discussions with Ryosuke Fujioka and his term paper (2019). For a history of VC policy in Japan, see Schaede (2008), ch. 10.

37. Ministry of Economy, Trade and Industry (2017b).

38. Ministry of Economy, Trade and Industry (2019a).

39. The original program name was Venture Challenge 2020. Japan Economic Revitalization Office, 2016.

40. J-Startup, J-Startup Summary, www.j-startup.go.jp/en/about; Ministry of Economy, Trade and Industry (2019b).

41. "NEC, shinsotsu ni nenshū 1000man enchō: IT jinzai kakuho ni kikenkan" [NEC hikes starting salaries to $90,000: Concerns over retention of IT talent], *Nikkei Shinbun*, July 9, 2019.

42. "Sutātoappu tenshoku, nenshū 720man en chō, jōjōkigyō koe" [Job-changer salaries at startups exceed $70,000, more than at listed firms], *Nikkei Shinbun*, March 20, 2019.

CHAPTER 10

1. Mitsubishi Electric, e-F@ctory Overview, https://www.mitsubishielectric.com/fa/sols/efactory/index.html.

2. For background on the emergence of SoftBank as a telecommunications company, see Schaede (2008).

3. "The Most Powerful Person in Silicon Valley," *Fast Company*, February 2019. On the WeWork debacle, see "WeWork Mess Leaves SoftBank's Masa Son $6 Billion Poorer," *Bloomberg*, November 5, 2019; "Rajeev Misra Built SoftBank's Huge Tech Fund. Now He Has to Save It," *Wall Street Journal*, October 30, 2019; "SoftBank Founder Calls His Judgment 'Really Bad' after $4.7 Billion WeWork Hit," *The Wall Street Journal,* November 6, 2019.

4. "SoftBank Builds Data Empire to Challenge US Tech Giants," *Nikkei Asian Review*, July 31, 2018.

5. "Guuguru & Uber tsubushi no Toyota takushi" [The Toyota taxi that will squash Google and Uber], *IT Media Business Online*, October 30, 2017, https://www.itmedia.co.jp/business/articles/1710/30/news019.html.

6. SoftBank, "Toyota and SoftBank Agreed on Strategic Partnership to Establish Joint Venture for New Mobility Services," Press release, October 4, 2018, https://www.softbank.jp/en/corp/news/press/sbkk/2018/20181004_01.

7. Preferred Networks, "Preferred Networks Raises a Total of over 2 Billion Yen from FANUC, Hakuhodo DYHD, Hitachi, Mizuho Bank, and Mitsui & Co," Press release, December 11, 2017, https://preferred.jp/en/news/pr20171211.

8. Alan Murray, "America's CEOs Seek a New Purpose for the Corporation," *Fortune*, August 19, 2019, https://fortune.com/longform/business-roundtable-ceos-corporations-purpose.

REFERENCES

Abegglen, James C. 1984. *The Strategy of Japanese Business*. Cambridge, MA: Ballinger.

Abegglen, James and George Stalk Jr. 1985. *Kaisha: The Japanese Corporation*. New York: Basic Books.

Ahmadjian, Christina L. and James R. Lincoln. 2001. "Keiretsu, Governance, and Learning: Case Studies in Change from the Japanese Automotive Industry." *Organization Science* 12(6):683–701.

Ahmadjian, Christina L. and Ulrike Schaede. 2015. "The Impact of Japan on Western Management: Theory and Practice." Pp. 49–57 in *The Routledge Companion to Cross-Cultural Management*, edited by N. Holden, S. Michailova and S. Tietze. New York: Routledge.

Aida, Takuji and Yoshito Sakakibara. 2017. *Nihon keizai no atarashii mikata* [A New Interpretation of the Japanese Economy]. Tokyo: Kinyū zaisei jijō kenkyūkai.

Ando, Yoichiro. 2018. "Japan—a Thriving, Highly Versatile Chip Manufacturing Region." *SEMI News*, October 3. https://blog.semi.org/semi-news/japan-a-thriving-highly-versatile-chip-manufacturing-region.

Aoki, Masahiko. 1988. *Information, Incentives, and Bargaining in the Japanese Economy*. Cambridge: Cambridge University Press.

Aoki, Masahiko and Ronald Dore, eds. 1994. *The Japanese Firm: The Sources of Competitive Strength*. Oxford: Oxford University Press.

Appelbaum, Eileen and Rosemary Batt. 2014. *Private Equity at Work: When Wall Street Manages Main Street*. New York: Russell Sage Foundation.

Aronson, Bruce E. 2015. "Japanese Corporate Governance Reform: A Comparative Perspective." *Hastings Business Law Journal* 11(1):85–118.

ASEAN (Association of Southeast Asian Nations). 2017. *Asean 50: A Historic Milestone for FDI and MNEs in ASEAN*. Jakarta: ASEAN Secretariat. https://asean.org/?static_post=historic-milestone-fdi-mnes-asean.

Ballon, Robert L. 1970. "Understanding the Japanese." *Business Horizons* 13(3):21–30.

Ballon, Robert L. and Iwao Tomita. 1988. *The Financial Behavior of Japanese Corporations*. Tokyo: Kodansha.

Benedict, Ruth. 1946. *The Chrysanthemum and the Sword: Patterns of Japanese Culture.* New York: Houghton Mifflin Harcourt.

Benes, Nicholas. 2019. "Japan's Shareholder Revolution—at Last." *Ethical Boardroom.* https://ethicalboardroom.com/japans-shareholder-revolution-at-last.

Borovoy, Amy. 2005. *The Too-Good Wife: Alcoholism, Codependency, and the Politics of Nurturance in Postwar Japan.* Berkeley: University of California Press.

Borovoy, Amy. 2008. "Japan's Hidden Youths: Mainstreaming the Emotionally Distressed in Japan." *Culture, Medicine, and Psychiatry* 32(4):552–76. https://doi.org/10.1007/s11013-008-9106-2.

Bradley, Stephen P., Thomas R. Eisenmann, Masako Egawa and Akiko Kanno. 2006. "NTT Docomo, Inc.: Mobile Felica." Harvard Business School Case Study 9-805-124. Boston: Harvard Business School Publishing.

Buche, Ivy, Howard Yu and Thomas Malnight. 2016. "Recruit Japan: Harnessing Data to Create Value." Case Study IMD824.

Burrough, Bryan and John Helyar. 1989. *Barbarians at the Gate: The Fall of RJR Nabisco.* New York: Harper & Row.

Calder, Kent E. 1988. *Crisis and Compensation: Public Policy and Political Stability in Japan, 1949–1986.* Princeton: Princeton University Press.

Calder, Kent E. 2017. *Circles of Compensation: Economic Growth and the Globalization of Japan.* Stanford: Stanford University Press.

Capgemini. 2018. *World Wealth Report 2018.* https://worldwealthreport.com.

Chatman, Jennifer A. and Charles A. O'Reilly III. 2016. "Paradigm Lost: Reinvigorating the Study of Organizational Culture." *Research in Organizational Behavior* 36:199–224.

Chattopadhyay, Akash, Matthew D. Shaffer and Charles C. Y. Wang. 2017. "Governance through Shame and Aspiration: Index Creation and Corporate Behavior." Harvard Business School Working Paper 18-010. https://papers.ssrn.com/sol3/papers.cfm?abstract_id=3010188.

Chesbrough, Henry. 2005. *Open Innovation: The New Imperative for Creating and Profiting from Technology.* Boston: Harvard Business Review Press.

Clark, Rodney. 1979. *The Japanese Company.* New Haven: Yale University Press.

Cole, Robert E. 1994. "Different Quality Paradigms and Their Implications for Organizational Learning." Pp. 66–83 in *The Japanese Firm: The Sources of Competitive Strength*, edited by M. Aoki and R. Dore. Oxford: Oxford University Press.

Cole, Robert E. 1998. "Learning from the Quality Movement: What Did and Didn't Happen and Why?" *California Management Review* 41(1):43–73.

Davis, Gerald F. 2009. *Managed by the Markets: How Finance Re-Shaped America.* Oxford: Oxford University Press.

Dore, Ronald. 1973. *British Factory–Japanese Factory: The Origins of National Diversity in Industrial Relations.* Berkeley: University of California Press.

Dore, Ronald. 1983. "Goodwill and the Spirit of Market Capitalism." *British Journal of Sociology* 34(4):459–82. Doi: 10.2307/590932.

Dore, Ronald. 1987. *Taking Japan Seriously: A Confucian Perspective on Leading Economic Issues.* Stanford: Stanford University Press.

Dore, Ronald. 2000. *Stock Market Capitalism: Welfare Capitalism: Japan and Germany Versus the Anglo-Saxons.* Oxford: Oxford University Press.

Drucker, Peter F. 1981. "Behind Japan's Success." *Harvard Business Review,* January.

Eguchi, Takaaki and Zenichi Shishido. 2015. "The Future of Japanese Corporate Governance: Japan's Internal Governance and Development of Japanese-Style External Governance through Engagement." In *Research Handbook on Shareholder Power,* edited by J. G. Hill and R. S. Thomas. Elgar Online.

Eguchi, Takaaki and Franz Waldenberger. 2017. "Management Careers, Internal Control and Corporate Governance: Where Japan and Germany Differ." Working Paper 17/2. DIJ, German Institute for Japan Studies, Tokyo.

Esty, Benjamin C. and Akiko Kanno. 2016. "Fanuc Corporation: Reassessing the Firm's Governance and Financial Policies." Harvard Business School Case Study 9-216-042. Boston: Harvard Business School Publishing.

Fallows, James and Deborah Fallows. 2018. *Our Towns: A 100,000-Mile Journey into the Heart of America.* New York: Pantheon.

Financial Services Agency. 2017. *Principles for Responsible Institutional Investors: Japan's Stewardship Code—to Promote Sustainable Growth for Companies through Investment and Dialogue.* https://www.fsa.go.jp/en/refer/councils/stewardship/20170529/01.pdf.

Fujioka, Ryosuke. 2019. "Establishing Startup Ecosystem with Entrepreneurship: Japan's New Journey under Abenomics." Term paper, UC San Diego.

Gelfand, Michele J. 2018. *Rule Makers, Rule Breakers: How Tight and Loose Cultures Wire Our World.* New York: Scribner.

Gelfand, Michele J. and 42 coauthors. 2011. "Differences between Tight and Loose Cultures: A 33-Nation Study." *Science* 332:1100–04. doi: 10.1126/science.1197754.

Gender Equality Bureau, Cabinet Office, Government of Japan. 2018. *Women and Men in Japan 2018.* Tokyo: Cabinet Office, Government of Japan. www.gender.go.jp/english_contents/pr_act/pub/pamphlet/women-and-men18/index.html.

Gill, Tom. 2001. *Men of Uncertainty: The Social Organization of Day Laborers in Contemporary Japan.* Albany: State University of New York Press.

Goshal, Sumantra and Christopher A. Bartlett. 1988. "Matsushita Electric Industrial (MEI) in 1987." Harvard Business School Case Study 9-388-144. Boston: Harvard Business School Publishing.

Goto, Gen. 2014. "Legally 'Strong' Shareholders of Japan." *Michigan Journal of Private Equity and Venture Capital Law* 3:125–64.

Goto, Gen. 2018. "The Logic and Limits of Stewardship Codes: The Case of Japan." *Berkeley Business Law Journal* 15(2):365–408.

Goto, Gen, Manabu Matsunaka and Sōichirō Kozuka. 2017. "Japan's Gradual Reception of Independent Directors." Pp. 135–75 in *Independent Directors in Asia: A Historical, Contextual and Comparative Approach*, edited by D. W. Puchniak, H. Baum and L. Nottage. Cambridge: Cambridge University Press.

Government of Japan. (2019). *Abenomics: For Future Growth, for Future Generations, and for a Future Japan*. Tokyo: Government of Japan. https://www.japan.go.jp/abenomics.

Gow, Ian, Charles C. Y. Wang, Naoko Jinjo and Nobuo Sato. 2017. "Misaki Capital and Sangetsu Corporation." Harvard Business School Case Study 9-117-007. Boston: Harvard Business School Publishing.

Haggard, Stephan, David Kang and Chung-In Moon. 1997. "Japanese Colonialism and Korean Development: A Critique." *World Development* 25(6):867–81.

Hamada, Koichi, Anil Kashyap and David E. Weinstein, eds. 2011. *Japan's Bubble, Deflation, and Long-Term Stagnation*. Cambridge, MA: MIT Press.

Hammoud, Tawfik, Michael Brigl, John Öberg, David Bronstein and Christy Carter. 2017. "Capitalizing on the New Golden Age in Private Equity." *BCG Perspectives*. https://www.bcg.com/en-us/publications/2017/value-creation-strategy-capitalizing-on-new-golden-age-private-equity.aspx.

Henrich, Joseph. 2015. *The Secret of Our Success: How Culture Is Driving Human Evolution, Domesticating Our Species, and Making Us Smarter*. Princeton: Princeton University Press.

Hill, Jennifer G. 2017. "Good Activist/Bad Activist: The Rise of International Stewardship Codes." Sydney Law School Research Paper 17/80. https://papers.ssrn.com/sol3/papers.cfm?abstract_id=3036357.

Hirakawa, Noriyoshi. 2016. *Panasoniku V-Ji kaifuku no jijitsu* [The real story of Panasonic's V-shaped recovery]. Tokyo: Kadokawa.

Hofstede, Geert. 1983. "The Cultural Relativity of Organizational Practices and Theories." *Journal of International Business Studies* 14:75–89.

Hofstede, Geert. 2001. *Culture's Consequences: Comparing Values, Behaviors, Institutions and Organizations across Nations*. 2nd ed. Thousand Oaks: Sage.

Hokugo, Ken and Alicia Ogawa. 2017. "The Unfinished Business of Japan's Stewardship Code." Center on Japanese Economy and Business Working Paper. www.gsb.columbia.edu/cjeb/research.

Hoshi, Takeo and Anil Kashyap. 2001. *Corporate Financing and Corporate Governance in Japan: The Road to the Future*. Boston: MIT Press.

Hoshi, Takeo, Satoshi Koibuchi and Ulrike Schaede. 2018. "The Decline in Bank-Led Corporate Restructuring in Japan: 1981–2010." *Journal of the Japanese and International Economies* 47:81–90. https://doi.org/10.1016/j.jjie.2017.11.004.

Ito, Kunio. 2014. *Ito Review of Competitiveness and Incentives for Sustainable Growth—Building Favorable Relationships between Companies and Investors*. Ministry of Economy, Trade and Industry. https://www.meti.go.jp/english/press/2014/pdf/0806_04b.pdf.

Iwai, Katsuhiro and Hideo Ueki. 2017. *Japan's Corporate-Governance Reforms: A Progress Report*. London: Wellington Management. https://www.wellington.com/en/insights/japans-corporate-governance-reforms-progress-report/?_c=qipgt3h.

Iwase, Tatsuya. 2015. *Panansoniku no jinji kōsōshi* [An account of Panasonic's HR wars]. Tokyo: Kodansha.

Japan Economic Revitalization Office, Cabinet Office. 2016. "'Benchā charenji 2000' ni kakaru seifu-kankei kikan konsōshium oyobi adbaisarī bōdo (dai-ikkai) Jimukyoku setsumei shiryō" [Background information materials for the first meeting of the Intra-Government Consortium and Advisory Board related to "Venture Challenge 2020"]. Tokyo: Cabinet Office, Government of Japan.

Japan Institute for Labor Policy and Training. 2018. "Work Style Reform Bill Enacted." *Japan Labor Issues* 2(10):2–7. https://www.jil.go.jp/english/jli/documents/2018/010-01.pdf.

Johnson, Chalmers. 1982. *MITI and the Japanese Miracle: The Growth of Industrial Policy, 1925–1975*. Stanford: Stanford University Press.

JPX: Tokyo Stock Exchange. 2018. *Japan's Corporate Governance Code: Seeking Sustainable Corporate Growth and Increased Corporate Value over the Mid- to Long-Term*. https://www.jpx.co.jp/english/news/1020/b5b4pj000000jvxr-att/20180602_en.pdf.

Kahneman, Daniel. 2001. *Thinking, Fast and Slow*. New York: Farrar, Straus and Giroux.

Karube, Masaru, Tsuyoshi Numagami and Toshihiko Kato. 2009. "Exploring Organisational Deterioration: 'Organisational Deadweight' as a Cause of Malfunction of Strategic Initiatives in Japanese Firms." *Long Range Planning* 42(4):518–44.

Kato, Masanori, Ulrike Schaede and Charles A. O'Reilly III. 2020. "AGC Inc. in 2019: 'Your Dreams, Our Challenge.'" Stanford Graduate School of Business Case Study 103.

Kato, Toshihiko, Masaru Karube and Tsuyoshi Numagami. 2010. "Organizational Deadweight and the Internal Functioning of Japanese Firms: An Explorative Analysis of Organizational Dysfunction." Pp. 125–63 in *Dynamics of Knowledge, Corporate Systems and Innovation*, edited by H. Itami, K. Kusunoki, T. Numagami and A. Takeishi. Berlin: Springer.

Killeen, William and Mark Prentice. 2015. "Japan's Shareholder Revolution." *IQ Magazine—State Street Global Advisors* 1(Q3). https://www.ssga.com/publications/investment-quarterly/2015/japans-shareholder-revolution.pdf.

Kitanaka, Junko. 2012. *Depression in Japan: Psychiatric Cures for a Society in Distress*. Princeton: Princeton University Press.

Kitao, Sagiri and Tomoaki Yamada. 2019. "Dimensions of Inequality in Japan: Distributions of Earnings, Income and Wealth between 1984 and 2014," CAMA Working Paper 36/2019, Centre for Applied Macroeconomic Analysis, Australian National University.

Komori, Shigetaka. 2015. *Innovating Out of Crisis: How Fujifilm Survived (and Thrived) as Its Core Business Was Vanishing*. Berkeley: Stone Bridge Press.

Koo, Richard. 2011. "The World in Balance Sheet Recession: Causes, Cure, and Politics." *Real-World Economic Review*, no. 58. http://www.paecon.net/PAEReview/issue58/Koo58.pdf.

Kreps, David. 2018. *The Motivation Toolkit*. New York: Norton.

Kurishita, Naoya. 2012. *Renesasu Erekutoronikusu—Hitome de wakaru* [Renesas Electronics: A brief introduction]. Tokyo: Nikkan Kōgyō Shinbun-sha.

Kushida, Kenji E. 2011. "Leading without Followers: How Politics and Market Dynamics Trapped Innovations in Japan's Domestic 'Galapagos' Telecommunications Sector." *Journal of Industry, Competition and Trade* 11(3):279–307. doi: 10.1007/s10842-011-0104-7.

Lazear, Edward P. 1999. "Culture and Language." *Journal of Political Economy* 107(S6): S95–S126. doi: 10.1086/250105.

Lazonick, William. 2009a. "The New Economy Business Model and the Crisis of U.S. Capitalism." *Capitalism and Society* 4(2). doi: https://doi.org/10.2202/1932-0213.1054.

Lazonick, William. 2009b. *Sustainable Prosperity in the New Economy? Business Organization and High-Tech Employment in the United States*. Kalamazoo: W. E. Upjohn Institute for Employment Research.

Lazonick, William. 2014. "Profits without Prosperity." *Harvard Business Review* (September), 46–55.

Lazonick, William and Mary O'Sullivan. 2000. "Maximizing Shareholder Value: A New Ideology for Corporate Governance." *Economy and Society* 29(1):13–35.

Lazonick, William and Jung-Sup Shin. 2019. *Predatory Value Extraction: How the Looting of the Business Corporation Became the U.S. Norm and How Sustainable Prosperity Can Be Restored*. New York: Oxford University Press.

Lemann, Nicholas. 2019. *Transaction Man: The Rise of the Deal and the Decline of the American Dream*. New York: Macmillan.

Levitsky, Steven and Daniel Ziblatt. 2018. *How Democracies Die*. New York: Crown.

Liker, Jeffrey K. 2004. *The Toyota Way: 14 Management Principles from the World's Greatest Manufacturer*. New York: McGraw Hill.

Lincoln, James R. and Michael L. Gerlach. 2004. *Japan's Network Economy: Structure, Persistence, and Change*. Cambridge: Cambridge University Press.

Lincoln, James R., Michael Gerlach and Christina Ahmadjian. 1996. "Keiretsu Networks and Corporate Performance in Japan." *American Sociological Review* 61(1):67–88.

Lincoln, James R. and Arne Kalleberg. 1990. *Culture, Commitment and Control: A Study of Work Organization and Work Attitudes in the United States and Japan.* New York: Cambridge University Press.

Loewenstein, George and Nick Chater. 2017. "Putting Nudges in Perspective." *Behavioural Public Policy* 1(1):26–53. doi: 10.1017/bpp.2016.7.

MacIntosh, Eric. 2017. "Ethical Theories Summarized & Explained: Consequentialism, Deontology, Virtue Ethics, and Objectivist Ethical Egoism." *Objectivsm in Depth* (blog). https://objectivismindepth.com/2017/04/23/ethical-theories-summarized-explained-consequentialism-deontology-virtue-ethics-and-objectivist-ethical-egoism.

March, James 1991. "Exploration and Exploitation in Organizational Learning." *Organization Science* 2(1):71–87.

MARR. 2019. "Chūshō-kigyō no jigyō shūkei/saisei shien to PE fando no yakuwari" [The role of PE funds in facilitating small firm succession and restructuring projects]. *Senmonshi-MARR* [MARR Special Magazine], no. 294. https://www.marr.jp/marr/marr201904/entry/14102.

Matsui, Kathy, Hiromi Suzuki and Kazunori Tatebe. 2019. *Womenomics 5.0, 20 Years On.* New York: Goldman Sachs Portfolio Strategy Research.

McBride, James and Andrew Chatzky. 2019. *Is "Made in China 2025" a Threat to Global Trade?* Washington, DC: Council on Foreign Relations. https://www.cfr.org/backgrounder/made-china-2025-threat-global-trade.

McMillan, John. 1990. "Managing Suppliers: Incentive Systems in Japanese and United States Industry." *California Management Review* 32(4):38–55.

Meyer, Erin. 2014. *The Culture Map: Breaking through the Invisible Boundaries of Global Business.* New York: Public Affairs.

Milhaupt, Curtis J. 2018. "Evaluating Abe's Third Arrow: How Significant Are Japan's Recent Corporate Governance Reforms?" *Zeitschrift für Japanisches Recht*, Sonderheft 12:65–81.

Ministry of Economics, Trade and Industry, Ministry of Health, Labor and Welfare, and Ministry of Education, Culture, Sports, Science and Technology (Eds.). 2004. *Seizō kiban hakusho: "Monozukuri Hakusho" Heisei 15 nendo* [The 2003 manufacturing base white paper: *Monozukuri* white paper]. Tokyo: Government Publication.

Ministry of Economy, Trade and Industry. 2017a. *Dai-yonji sangyō-kakumei ni muketa risuku manē kyōkyū ni kan suru kenkyūkai: Puraibēto Ekuitei no sara naru katsuyō ni mukete* [Study Group for Risk Capital Supply for the 4th Industrial Revolution: Toward strengthening private equity activities]. https://www.meti.go.jp/report/whitepaper/data/pdf/20180629001_3.pdf.

Ministry of Economy, Trade and Industry. 2017b. *Inobēshion/benchā seisaku ni tsuite* [Report on innovation and venture policies]. https://www.kantei.go.jp/jp/singi/keizaisaisei/miraitoshikaigi/innovation_dai3/siryou4.pdf.

Ministry of Economy, Trade and Industry. 2017c. *METI Reference Materials for Ito Review 2.0*. https://www.meti.go.jp/english/press/2017/pdf/1026_003a.pdf.

Ministry of Economy, Trade and Industry. 2018a. *Practical Guidelines for Corporate Governance Systems (CGS Guidelines)*. https://www.meti.go.jp/english/press/2018/pdf/0928_005a.pdf.

Ministry of Economy, Trade and Industry. 2018b. *Seizōgyō o meguru genjō to seisaku kadai: Connected Industries no shinka* [The current status of manufacturing and policy tasks: The progress of connected industries]. https://www.meti.go.jp/shingikai/mono_info_service/air_mobility/pdf/001_s01_00.pdf.

Ministry of Economy, Trade and Industry. 2019a. *Dai yon-kai sangyō kaikaku ni muketa sangyō kōzō no genjō to kadai ni tsuite* [Report on the current situation and future tasks associated with the industrial structure for the 4th industrial revolution]. https://www.meti.go.jp/shingikai/sankoshin/2050_keizai/pdf/005_02_00.pdf.

Ministry of Economy, Trade and Industry. 2019b. *Sutāto-appu shien ni kan suru Keizai-sangyō-shō no torikumi ni tsuite* [METI policies regarding startup support measures]. www.kantei.go.jp/jp/singi/tougou-innovation/dai4/siryo3-4.pdf.

Ministry of Foreign Affairs of Japan. 2017. *Kaigai zairyū hōjin chōsa tōkei* [Annual report of statistics on Japanese nationals overseas]. shttps://www.mofa.go.jp/mofaj/files/000368753.pdf.

Ministry of Internal Affairs and Communication. 2019. *Rōdōryoku chōsa (shōsai shūkei) Heisei 30nen (2018nen) heikin (sokuhō)* [Digest of the 2018 (Heisei 30) Labor Force Survey, aggregated data]. https://www.stat.go.jp/data/roudou/sokuhou/nen/dt/pdf/index1.pdf.

Monden, Yasuhiro. 1983. *Toyota Production System: Practical Approach to Production Management*. Norcross: Industrial Engineering and Management Press.

Morgan Stanley Research. 2018. *Japan's Journey from Laggard to Leader*. Tokyo: Morgan Stanley.

Murphy, R. Taggart. 2014. *Japan and the Shackles of the Past*. Oxford: Oxford University Press.

Nakagami, Yasunori. 2016. *Tōshi sareru keiei, urikai sareru keiei* [Manage to find investors, manage to be traded]. Tokyo: Nihon Keizai Shinbun Shuppan-sha.

Nakamura, Tatsuya. 2018. "Nihon no kōporēto gabanansu kaikaku ni okeru tokushō" [Characteristics of corporate governance reform in Japan]. *Keiei keiri kenkyū* 111 (February): 213–49.

Naughton, Barry. 2018. *The Chinese Economy: Adaptation and Growth*. Cambridge, MA: MIT Press.

NEDO (New Energy and Industrial Technology Development Organization). 2018. "Heisei 29 nendo Nihon kigyō no mono to sābisu sofutobea no kokusai kyōsō pojishion ni kan suru jōhō shūshū" [Data collection regarding the global competitive position of Japanese manufacturing and software firms in 2017]. Tokyo: NEDO/ METI. https://www.nedo.go.jp/koubo/NA2_100050.html.

Ng, Ying. 2018. "SME Succession Crisis in Japan." *Preqin*, August 21, 2018. https://www. preqin.com/insights/blogs/sme-succession-crisis-in-japan/23463.

Nikkan Kōgyō Shinbun-sha, ed. 2014. *Jidai ni chōsen suru yūryō chūken/chūsho seizōgyō* [Outstanding small and medium enterprises that challenge the times]. Tokyo: Nikkan Kōgyō Shinbun-sha.

Noda, Tomo and David J. Collis. 1995. "Asahi Glass Company: Diversification Strategy." Harvard Business School Case Study 9-794-113. Boston: Harvard Business School Publishing.

North, Douglass C. 1990. *Institutions, Institutional Change and Economic Performance.* Cambridge: Cambridge University Press.

Okada, Yutaka. 2018. *Japan's Foreign Population Hitting a Record High.* Mizuho Economic Outlook and Analysis, Mizuho Research Institute. https://www.mizuho-ri. co.jp/publication/research/pdf/eo/MEA180913.pdf.

O'Reilly III, Charles A. 1989. "Corporations, Culture, and Commitment: Motivation and Social Control in Organizations." *California Management Review* 31(4):9–25.

O'Reilly III, Charles A. and Jennifer A. Chatman. 1996. "Culture as Social Control: Corporations, Cults, and Commitment." *Research in Organizational Behavior* 18:157– 200.

O'Reilly III, Charles A. and Brian G. Main. 2010. "Economic and Psychological Perspectives on CEO Compensation: A Review and Synthesis." *Industrial and Corporate Change* 19(3):675–712.

O'Reilly III, Charles A. and Michael L. Tushman. 2016. *Lead and Disrupt: How to Solve the Innovator's Dilemma.* Stanford: Stanford University Press.

Ouchi, William. 1981. *Theory Z: How American Business Can Meet the Japanese Challenge.* Reading: Addison-Wesley.

Pascale, Richard and Thomas P. Rohlen. 1983. "The Mazda Turnaround." *Journal of Japanese Studies* 9(2):219–63.

Patrick, Hugh T. and Thomas P. Rohlen. 1987. "Small-Scale Family Enterprises." Pp. 331–84 in *The Political Economy of Japan*, Part 1: *The Domestic Transformation*, edited by K. Yamamura and Y. Yasuba. Stanford: Stanford University Press.

Patrick, Hugh and Henry Rosovsky, eds. 1976. *Asia's New Giant: How the Japanese Economy Works.* Washington, DC: Brookings Institution.

Pelto, P. J. 1968. "The Difference between 'Tight' and 'Loose' Societies." *Trans-Action* 5:37–40.

Pfeffer, Jeffrey and James N. Baron. 1988. "Taking the Workers Back Out: Recent Trends in the Structuring of Employment." *Research in Organizational Behavior* 10:257– 303.

Pilling, David. 2014. *Bending Adversity: Japan and the Art of Survival.* New York: Penguin Books.

Pilling, David. 2018. *The Growth Delusion: Wealth, Poverty, and the Well-Being of Nations*. London: Bloomsbury.

Pinker, Steven. 2002. *The Blank Slate: The Modern Denial of Human Nature*. New York: Penguin Books.

Porter, Michael E. 1985. *Competitive Advantage: Creating and Sustaining Superior Performance*. New York: Free Press.

Powell, Walter W. and Paul J. DiMaggio, eds. 1991. *The New Institutionalism in Organizational Analysis*. Chicago: University of Chicago Press.

Roberts, Glenda S. 2017. "An Immigration Policy by Any Other Name: Semantics of Immigration to Japan." *Social Science Japan Journal* 21(1):89–102. doi: 10.1093/ssjj/jyx033.

Rohlen, Thomas P. 1979. *For Harmony and Strength: Japanese White-Collar Organization in Anthropological Perspective*. Berkeley: University of California Press.

Saito, Takuji. 2015. "Determinants of Director Board and Auditor Board Composition: Evidence from Japan." *Public Policy Review* 11(3):395–410. Policy Research Institute, Ministry of Finance, Japan.

Sakawa, Hideaki, Keisuke Moriyama and Naoki Watanabe. 2012. "Relation between Top Executive Compensation Structure and Corporate Governance: Evidence from Japanese Public Disclosed Data." *Corporate Governance: An International Review* 20(5):593–608.

Sako, Mari. 1992. *Prices, Quality and Trust: Interfirm Relations in Britain and Japan*. New York: Cambridge University Press.

Sasaki, Masato and Ulrike Schaede. 2019. "Japanese CVC and Open Innovation in Silicon Valley." Working Paper, UC San Diego, La Jolla.

Sato, Fumiaki. 2017. *Nihon no denki sangyō: shippai no kyōkun* [Japan's electronics industry: what we can learn from the failures]. Tokyo: Dai Nihon Insatsu.

Schaede, Ulrike. 1990. "The Introduction of Commercial Paper—A Case Study in the Liberalisation of the Japanese Financial Markets." *Japan Forum* 2(2):215–34.

Schaede, Ulrike. 2000a. *Cooperative Capitalism: Self-Regulation, Trade Associations, and the Antimonopoly Law in Japan*. Oxford: Oxford University Press.

Schaede, Ulrike. 2000b. "The Japanese Financial System: From Postwar to the New Millennium." Harvard Business School Case Study 9-700-049. Boston: Harvard Business School Publishing.

Schaede, Ulrike. 2008. *Choose and Focus: Japanese Business Strategies for the 21st Century*. Ithaca: Cornell University Press.

Schaede, Ulrike. 2013a. *Show Me the Money: Japan's Most Profitable Companies in the 2000s*. DBJ Discussion Paper Series (1211). https://www.dbj.jp/ricf/pdf/research/DBJ_DP_1211.pdf.

Schaede, Ulrike. 2013b. "Sunshine and Suicides in Japan: Revisiting the Relevance of Economic Determinants of Suicide." *Contemporary Japan* 25(2):105–26.

Schaede, Ulrike. 2019. "U.S.-Japan Business Relations and the Trade War with Asia." Pp. 11–27 in *Charting a Path for a Stronger U.S.-Japan Economic Partnership*, Saori N. Katada, Junji Nakagawa and Ulrike Schaede. NBR Special Report, no. 75. Washington, DC: National Bureau of Asian Research.

Schaede, Ulrike and William W. Grimes, eds. 2003. *Japan's Managed Globalization: Adapting to the 21st Century*. Armonk: M. E. Sharpe.

Sekine, Satoshi. 2018. "Nihon ni okeru Puraibēto-Ekuitei: Māketo no dōkō to Nihon kigyō no katsudō ni kan suru teigen" [Private equity in Japan: Market developments and proposals for Japanese firms]. *PwC Japan*, https://www.pwc.com/jp/ja/knowledge/thoughtleadership/2018/assets/pdf/private-equity.pdf.

Smitka, Michael J. 1991. *Competitive Ties: Subcontracting in the Japanese Automotive Industry*. New York: Columbia University Press.

Swenson, David and Robert Rubin. 2017. "A Conversation with David Swenson." Stephen C. Friedheim Symposium on Global Economics. https://www.cfr.org/event/conversation-david-swensen.

Tam, Frank Wai-Ming and Mitsuru Taki. 2007. "Bullying among Girls in Japan and Hong Kong: An Examination of the Frustration-Aggression Model." *Educational Research and Evaluation* 13(4):373–99. doi: 10.1080/13803610701702894.

Thaler, Richard H. and Cass R. Sunstein. 2008. *Nudge: Improving Decisions about Health, Wealth, and Happiness*. New Haven: Yale University Press.

Tokyo Metropolitan Government. 2017. "Guidance to the Asset Management Industry in Japan." http://www.senryaku.metro.tokyo.jp/bdc_tokyo/english/english-guidebook.

Tushman, Michael L. and Charles A. O'Reilly. 1997. *Winning through Innovation: A Practical Guide to Leading Organizational Change and Renewal*. Boston: Harvard Business School Press.

Ushijima, Tatsuo. 2010. "Understanding Partial Mergers in Japan." *Journal of Banking & Finance* 34(12):2941–53. https://doi.org/10.1016/j.jbankfin.2010.06.008.

Ushijima, Tatsuo and Ulrike Schaede. 2014. "The Market for Corporate Subsidiaries in Japan: An Empirical Study of Trades among Listed Firms." *Journal of the Japanese and International Economies* 31:36–52. doi: https://doi.org/10.1016/j.jjie.2013.12.001.

Uz, Irem. 2015. "The Index of Cultural Tightness and Looseness among 68 Countries." *Journal of Cross-Cultural Psychology* 46(3):319–35. doi: 10.1177/0022022114563611.

Vogel, Ezra F. 1979. *Japan as Number One: Lessons for America*. New York: Harper & Row.

Vogel, Steven K. 2006. *Japan Remodeled: How Government and Industry Are Reforming Japanese Capitalism*. Ithaca: Cornell University Press.

Vogel, Steven K. 2018. "Japan's Labor Regime in Transition: Rethinking Work for a Shrinking Nation." *Journal of Japanese Studies* 44(2):257–92.

Vogel, Steven K. 2019. "Japan's Ambivalent Pursuit of Shareholder Capitalism." *Politics & Society* 47(1):117–44.

Waldenberger, Franz. 2013. "'Company Heroes' versus 'Superstars': Executive Pay in Japan in Comparative Perspective." *Contemporary Japan* 25(2):189–213.

Waldenberger, Franz. 2016. "In-house Careers: A Core Institution for the Japanese Firm in Need of Reform." *Journal of Strategic Management Studies* 8(1):23–32.

Waldenberger, Franz. 2017. "'Growth Oriented' Corporate Governance Reform—Can It Solve Japan's Performance Puzzle?" *Japan Forum* 29(3):354–74. doi:10.1080/09555 803.2017.1284144.

West, Darrell M. and Christian Lansang. 2018. *Global Manufacturing Scorecard: How the US Compares to 18 Other Nations.* Washington, DC: Brookings Institution. https://www.brookings.edu/research/global-manufacturing-scorecard-how-the-us-compares-to-18-other-nations.

Whetstone, J. Thomas. 2001. "How Virtue Fits within Business Ethics." *Journal of Business Ethics* 33:101. https://doi.org/10.1023/A:1017554318867.

Williamson, Oliver E. 1993. "Opportunism and Its Critics." *Managerial and Decision Economics* 14(2):97–107. doi: 10.1002/mde.4090140203.

Wilson, David Sloan and Edward O. Wilson. 2007. "Rethinking the Theoretical Foundation of Sociobiology." *Quarterly Review of Biology* 82:327–48.

Womack, James P., Daniel T. Jones and Daniel Roos. 1990. *The Machine That Changed the World.* New York: Macmillan.

World Inequality Lab. World Inequality Database. https://wid.world/data.

Xing, Yuqing and Neal Detert. 2010. *How the iPhone Widens the United States Trade Deficit with the People's Republic of China.* ADBI Working Paper Series, no. 257. https://www.adb.org/sites/default/files/publication/156112/adbi-wp257.pdf.

Yamaguchi, Tsutomu. 2009. *With Chemistry We Can: The First 50 Years of JSR.* Tokyo: JSR Corporation.

Yamamura, Kozo and Yasukichi Yasuba, eds. 1987. *The Political Economy of Japan*, Vol.1: *The Domestic Transformation.* Stanford: Stanford University Press.

Yeh, Tsung-ming. 2014. "Large Shareholders, Shareholder Proposals, and Firm Performance: Evidence from Japan." *Corporate Governance: An International Review* 22(4):312–29. doi: http://dx.doi.org/10.1111/corg.12052.

Yoneyama, Shoko and Asao Naito. 2003. "Problems with the Paradigm: The School as a Factor in Understanding Bullying (with Special Reference to Japan)." *British Journal of Sociology of Education* 24(3):315–30. doi: 10.1080/01425690301894.

Yoshino, M. Y. and Yukihiko Endo. 2005. "Transformation of Matsushita Electric Industrial Co., Ltd. 2005 (A), (B), (C)." Harvard Business School Case Study 9-905-412/413/414. Boston: Harvard Business School Publishing.

Zielenziger, Michael. 2006. *Shutting Out the Sun: How Japan Created Its Own Lost Generation.* New York: Nan A. Talese/Doubleday.

INDEX

Note: page numbers in italics refer to figures or tables.